BIRD
WATCHER'S
BIBLE

BIRD WATCHER'S BIBLE

A COMPLETE TREASURY
SCIENCE · KNOW-HOW · BEAUTY · LORE

EDITED BY JONATHAN ALDERFER

NATIONAL GEOGRAPHIC

WASHINGTON, D.C.

CONTENTS

Preceding pages: Black-and-white Warbler (pages 2-3).
Birds fly over land and water in the company of a Simurgh, a mythical flying creature of medieval Persia,
in this painting in the British Library.

The Birds
in Your World

Scott Weidensaul

Thirty thousand years ago, someone stretched out a finger and, in the soft mud on the wall of the cave of Chauvet-Pont-d'Arc in southern France, traced an unmistakable outline: the round head, plump body, ear tufts, and face of an owl. Here, deep belowground, humans made the oldest paintings ever discovered—and one of the first objects our species chose to depict was a bird.

That doesn't surprise me at all. In the 30 millennia since that day, birds have lost none of their hold over humanity—and no wonder. They are beautiful, colorful, melodic, graceful, aerobatic, and swift; they are incredibly diverse, with nearly 10,000 species, and they are ubiquitous, found on every square foot of the planet except for the center of the Antarctic Plateau.

They are also breathtaking. Anyone would pause, slack jawed, at the spectacle of 600,000 Sandhill Cranes in cacophonous voice along the Platte River in Nebraska, rising in a hurricane of wings each dawn, or at the sight of a single, whirling flock of 40,000 Swainson's Hawks migrating through the muggy skies of eastern Mexico. Anyone, no matter how self-absorbed and disconnected from the natural world, would stand amazed at the display of a Marvelous Spatuletail Hummingbird, its curved, springy tail plumes bouncing like cancan dancers. And let's not even get into the more than 40 species of birds of paradise, so strange and otherworldly that any one of them could stop traffic single-handedly.

But every bird is astonishing—not just the flamboyant or bizarre, the garishly colored or extravagantly plumaged. Consider a House Sparrow filching crumbs beneath a sidewalk hot dog stand. Within that drab brown body lies an aerodynamic machine of incredible sophistication: hollow bones to pare down weight, massive pectoral muscles to power its wings, and a system of air sacs that squeeze every possible molecule of oxygen from each breath the sparrow takes.

Covering it all are thousands of feathers ranging from stiff wing primaries that generate thrust and lift, to light-as-air down for insulation, to hairlike bristles that function like eyelashes, and specialized feathers known as filoplumes that are scattered throughout its plumage and connected to nerve clusters, allowing the sparrow to instantly sense subtle changes in pressure across its whole body.

So yes, even that sparrow is astonishing—in fact, maybe especially that sparrow, which makes a fine living in the most humanized of environments, where it must watch not only for pedestrians, house cats, glass windows, and vehicles, but also for the increasing number of urban raptors like Cooper's Hawks, American Kestrels, and Peregrine Falcons that might prey upon it.

Lord and lady falconers accompanied by hounds hunt waterbirds in this miniature from the 1459 "Treatise on Falconry and Hunting."

This photo of a peacock in full display highlights the bird's fanciful appearance.

THE BIRD-WATCHING LIFE

I started birding as a kid in the mountains of eastern Pennsylvania, where I still live. It was a great place to learn about birds. Whip-poor-wills flew out of the woods and called at dusk from the stone wall behind the house, while on summer mornings, as the orioles sang, my mother brushed out her long, blond hair for the Chipping Sparrows, which used it to line the nests they built in the rose arbor beside our porch.

In autumn, we would visit Hawk Mountain Sanctuary and climb to North Lookout, a high, windy promontory of the Kittatinny Ridge along which tens of thousands of hawks, eagles, and falcons migrate each year. It was a vivid demonstration of the reach and drama of migration—Peregrine Falcons from Greenland passed us on their way to Argentina, Broad-winged Hawks from Quebec or Vermont headed for Costa Rica or Bolivia, and Golden Eagles from the subarctic tundra of Labrador were headed to the Appalachian hills, where they would spend the winter.

And as I grew up and began to travel, there were always birds to draw me to new places here and abroad. Decades later, I still remember my first spring in the Rockies, the trees alive with Western Tanagers and Townsend's Warblers, Calliope Hummingbirds in the alpine meadows, and squadrons of White Pelicans, their tangerine bills reflected in prairie lakes. Macaws and cotingas drew me to the Peruvian Amazon, Wedge-tailed Eagles and cockatoos to Tasmania, White Storks nesting on ruined castles to Spain. During the long dusk of a subarctic twilight, I watched millions of auklets whirling in a Möbius strip of flight above the steam-wisped cone of an active volcano in the Aleutians. Birds are always the icing on each new place I visit.

Birding is the most portable hobby imaginable. Whether you're traveling to a European capital or the Australian outback, the middle of the Pacific or the middle of Manhattan, around the corner or across the globe, there are always birds—usually new and exciting ones—to see. Binoculars and a field guide help, of course, but they're not required.

THE WORLD OUT YOUR WINDOW

And even if you're a determined homebody, unwilling to budge an inch, the global waves of migration will bring birds to you. Twice each year, the ebb and flow of migrants carries to my own yard birds born in Alaska and Nunavut, Siberia and Newfoundland. Tundra Swans on their way to the Northwest Territories fly high overhead, their bugling cries mingling with those of Snow Geese heading to Bylot Island in the Canadian Arctic.

Swainson's Thrushes that spent the winter in company with jaguars and howler monkeys in South America, and which will serenade wolves and caribou along Canada's Hudson Bay in a few weeks, feed beside Palm Warblers that hunted the shrubbery of Florida condominiums, but which will nest on the shores of Great Bear Lake with grizzlies and musk oxen. Cape May Warblers, which drank the nectar of mango flowers in Cuba all winter, and Baltimore Orioles, which did the same with jungle blossoms in Belize, hunt insects in my treetops. Flocks of shorebirds that spent the winter in Tierra del Fuego

Birds fly over sheep in this contemporary winter scene titled "Winter Woolies," by Lisa Graa Jensen.

or the coast of Brazil whiz overhead, bound beyond the northern horizon.

We humans have woven birds into the fabric of every culture on Earth—sometimes literally into the fabric, like the stunning feather cloaks of the old Hawaiian nobility, the dance regalia of competitors at Native American powwows across the West, or the battle adornments of New Guinean highlanders. Birds occupy potent niches within our religious and mythical lives: the dove of peace, the raven as trickster, the wise old owl, and many more.

A Greek auspex—which is related to the words auspices and auspicious—observed the flight of

birds to divine the future, a study the Romans called augury. Even today, birds straddle the real and the unreal: The hoot of an owl on a dark night can still raise hackles, and the sight of a bird flying in and out of a building, or tapping at a window, may awaken old superstitions about portents of death. (A bird at a window is, of course, usually just attacking its reflection, trying to drive what it thinks is an intruder from its territory.)

FOR THE LOVE OF BIRDS

Fortunately, for most people birds are simply a source of pure and unalloyed pleasure. Birding has never been more popular in the United States, with some estimates putting the number of bird-watchers—active birders, those who tend backyard feeders, bird photographers—at variously 46 million, 69 million, or 83 million, depending on who's counting and how. In Great Britain, up to three-quarters of all households put out food for the birds.

Whatever the precise number, a lot of people love birds—as many as one American in three. And why not? Birds bring life and movement, color and song into any day—sometimes at the most unexpected moments. The warm glow of a Varied Thrush at the feeder can transform a dull, snowy day into one of brilliant life; the flash and whir of a hummingbird hanging inches from your face, its gorget flashing in the sun, turns the drudgery of an afternoon's weeding into high adventure.

Birds are everywhere—always dazzling, always fascinating, always capable of lifting us out of our lives. All we have to do is look up.

John James Audubon painted Snowy Owls for The Birds of America, *which was published between 1827 and 1838.*

CHAPTER ONE

THE ANATOMY OF A BIRD

Kimball Garrett

A 1945 painting by Walter A. Weber depicts a Blue Bird of paradise in courtship display in New Guinea.

BUILDING A BIRD

VERTEBRATES ON THE WING

In his classic bird identification guides, Roger Tory Peterson often included endpapers showing silhouettes of perched and flying birds. He recognized that bird-watchers early on gain an appreciation of the vastly varying shapes, sizes, and structures of different birds. Of course it's true that variation among birds is almost trivial when compared to the extremes of body forms in mammals. (Think baleen whale, bat, weasel, and giraffe.) Nevertheless, we bird enthusiasts remain fascinated by the diversity found among birds. We think less about the characteristics birds share and the commonalities between them and other vertebrates—those animals with backbones.

THE BASIC VERTEBRATE BODY PLAN

Step back 400 million years. In the early Devonian period, vertebrates made the first tentative steps toward a terrestrial life; evolutionary modifications of the limbs, jaws, and breathing apparatus made possible the transition of vertebrate life onto land and

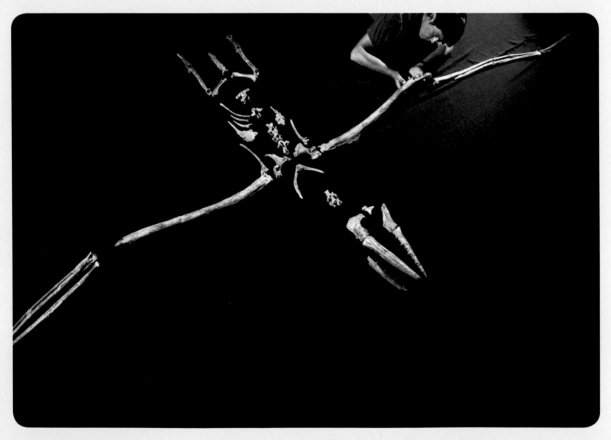

A giant seabird fossil helps modern scientists study the anatomy of flight. The seabird had a wingspread of nearly 17 feet and held slippery ocean prey with bony protrusions like teeth. These remains of Pelagornis chilensis *are seven million years old.*

American Tree Sparrow

into the myriad ecological niches that had developed with the earlier explosion of terrestrial invertebrates and land plants, and further diversified in co-evolution with the vertebrate newcomers. The explosion of vertebrate diversity that the ensuing epochs witnessed has been astounding, as amphibians, various reptile groups, birds, and mammals took to land, to the trees, and in some cases back to sea. And they took to the air, with flight as the key driver of avian evolution. The subsequent diversification of birds over the past 150 million years was tied in part to this mastery of the air and unfolded in concert with the booming success and diversification of flowering plants.

The body plans of vertebrates underwent radical transformations when ancient fishlike creatures left the water; the development of limbs was a key evolutionary innovation. But all modern vertebrates have, as Neil Shubin writes, an "inner fish." These limbs—as magnificent and accomplished as an albatross's wing, cheetah's legs, or primate's grasping arms—are built on a bone pattern traceable to the supporting bones of the pectoral and pelvic fins of fish. Even jaws and middle ear bones show a derivation from the structures supporting the gills of primitive fishlike creatures. It can be difficult to grasp that such different creatures as whales, kangaroos, hummingbirds, snakes, and toads share a number of important anatomical features that unite them as terrestrial vertebrates, or tetrapods. We see today only the end points of a long history of evolution and rely on the hard work of paleontologists, evolutionary biologists,

One of a pair of European Bee-eaters tosses its prey before removing the bee's stinger and eating the insect.

fossil collectors and preparators, and anatomists to guide us through a fascinating history.

And this brings us back to the 10,000 or so species of modern birds, along with their extinct brethren—from a two-gram hummingbird to a flightless Australian mihirung that might have weighed half a ton, from supreme aerialist swifts and frigatebirds to runners, divers, creepers, and even burrowers.

Bird Brain

In 1886, Frank Chapman surveyed 700 women's hats in New York City and found 542 decorated with feathers or whole birds of 40 species. That same year, Audubon Society pioneer Charles Warner coined the saying: "A dead bird does not help the appearance of an ugly woman, and a pretty woman needs no such adornment."

BUILT FOR FLIGHT

Birds are nature's most accomplished flying machines, and the essence of "birdness" is all about flight. Even modern flightless birds are largely shaped by the long evolutionary legacy of their flying ancestors. Getting airborne and staying there (and safely landing) are not trivial feats for a vertebrate animal, although true flight has evolved independently three times in vertebrates—in birds, bats, and extinct pterosaurs. Much of what we observe externally and internally in birds is part of the suite of characteristics that simultaneously enable them to fly and constrain their overall anatomical diversity.

Nature's airlines charge dearly for baggage, so birds travel light. Bird adaptations for flight include features that lighten and center their load and facilitate aerodynamic movement. Equally important is the power and efficiency of their muscles, and respiratory and circulatory systems, along with a brain

Bird Brain

The tiniest living bird is the Bee Hummingbird, found only in Cuba and nearby Isle of Youth. This two-and-a-half-inch sprite weighs less that a U.S. penny and slightly more than a paper clip. It can live up to seven years in the wild, even though its peak heart rate can top out at an incredible 1,200 beats a minute.

Sandhill Cranes come in for a landing at Bosque del Apache National Wildlife Refuge in New Mexico. Thousands of the big birds winter at the refuge, feeding in local fields by day, prompting the annual Festival of the Cranes in November.

ANATOMY OF A SUPREME FLYING BIRD

....

Covering huge expanses of the world's oceans through a mastery of the wind,
the albatross shows in spectacular form many of the key anatomical adaptations that allow birds to take to the air.

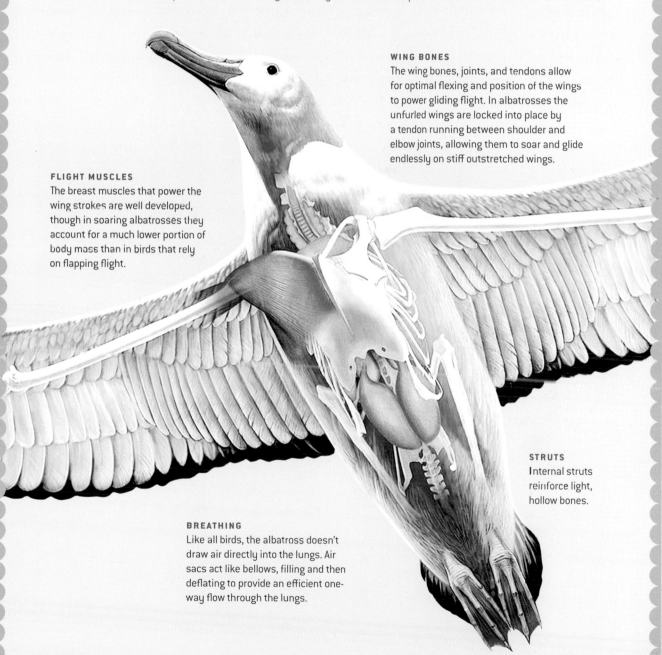

WING BONES
The wing bones, joints, and tendons allow for optimal flexing and position of the wings to power gliding flight. In albatrosses the unfurled wings are locked into place by a tendon running between shoulder and elbow joints, allowing them to soar and glide endlessly on stiff outstretched wings.

FLIGHT MUSCLES
The breast muscles that power the wing strokes are well developed, though in soaring albatrosses they account for a much lower portion of body mass than in birds that rely on flapping flight.

STRUTS
Internal struts reinforce light, hollow bones.

BREATHING
Like all birds, the albatross doesn't draw air directly into the lungs. Air sacs act like bellows, filling and then deflating to provide an efficient one-way flow through the lungs.

Western Tanager

and sensory system that regulate balance and reactions. Much of what adapts a bird to flight is visible externally: flight feathers tailored to unique flight styles, a fuselage contoured by dense body feathering, and a relatively lightweight bill. (There's no need for heavy jaws to house teeth in any modern bird.) The tail? Just feathers attached to the end of an abbreviated, internal set of tail vertebrae. The stick-like legs are powered mainly by muscles internal to the body.

Most of us have looked into the inner workings of a bird—if not the Thanksgiving turkey, then a fast-food specimen at local eateries. Internally, adaptations for flight abound. The wings are braced by a strong structural girdle including the well-developed coracoids (braces between the wings and the breastbone or sternum) and the furcula or "wishbone" (actually fused clavicles or "collar bones"). A variable "keel," an extension of the ventral midline of the breastbone, serves as a centralized attachment point for the massive musculature that powers the wings.

The rib cage is strengthened by overlapping processes, and the vertebral column shows a great degree of fusion in the thoracic region (where the ribs attach) and pelvic area. The long bony tail of reptilian ancestors and the earliest birds has been reduced to the pygostyle (so-called Pope's nose), fused caudal vertebrae to which the tail feathers are attached. The "hand" is a marvel of fusion in which the three remaining digits are greatly reduced, serving as attachment points for the flight feathers of the outer part of the wing. Importantly, most bones are hollow and thin-walled—some even invaded by air sacs from the respiratory system. Over and over, the mantra of the bird skeleton is reduction, fusion, lightening, and rigidity.

TASTY OR NOT?

Humans have long savored bird flesh as food. (Certainly no other predator ever invented the turducken, deboned chicken stuffed into a duck.) But some birds taste better than others. A tasting panel convened in Africa back in the 1960s compared the tastiness of representatives of 57 families of African birds, understandably giving a thumbs-up to such delectables as sandgrouse, Water Dikkops, and certain ducks. The least palatable were kingfishers, cuckoos, honeyguides, and wood-hoopoes. Perhaps not surprisingly, there was a general negative correlation between palatability and a bird's conspicuousness.

Bird Brain
In 1957, Don Featherstone created a kitsch icon—the pink plastic lawn flamingo—for Union Products of Leominster, Massachusetts. Working in clay, he sculpted the prototype while looking at photos of the real thing in *National Geographic* magazine. The lawn flamingo is prospering, but the real American Flamingo is a rarity in the United States.

The largest birds in the world, a group of Ostriches feeds at early morning light in Marakele National Park in South Africa. Flightless Ostriches have keen sight, which allows them to spot predators and flee at more than 40 miles an hour.

A bird's organs are only as big as they need to be. That male House Sparrow love machine with testes nearly half an inch in diameter at the height of the breeding season is practically a eunuch for much of the year, with gonads a tenth that size. The female's single ovary is similarly minimized outside the breeding season. The gizzard? At the bird's center of gravity, it beats heavy jaws for grinding food. Birds lack a urinary bladder, but their frequent urges are a small price to pay for the reduced weight.

Finally, birds can fly because they are small, relatively speaking, for vertebrates. The behemoths of the bird world—ostriches, elephant birds, mihirungs, and the like—are (or were) flightless. Few flying birds weigh more than 20 pounds, and the vast majority of agile flyers weigh less than a single pound.

◆ **MALLARD** ◆

ANAS PLATYRYNCHOS: The term "mallard," by the 1300s, referred to any wild male duck and derives from the Latin *masculus* for "male." *Anas* is from the Latin for "duck" and related to nature ("swim"); *platyrynchos,* "flat-beaked," is from the Greek *platys* for "flat" and *rhynchos* for "beak."

THE POWER TRAIN

Lightweight, feathered, well muscled, streamlined—these essential attributes of bird anatomy are coupled with an efficient high-octane motor to drive birds' mastery of the air. The huge muscles that power the up- and downstrokes of the wings surround the keeled breastbone, occupying an area near the bird's center of gravity. These muscles may account for more than a quarter of a bird's entire weight. The bulk of the leg muscles is also centralized, attaching to the pelvis and surrounding the thigh and upper part of the tibiotarsus bone, sometimes identified as the "drumstick."

Bird muscle runs the gamut from that with little blood supply and little oxygen use, which is best for rapid bursts of energy but less sustained action, to that with myoglobin, which allows greater oxygenation and is thus best for sustained action. The former is recognized as light meat; the latter, colored by the myoglobin, as dark meat. Powered flight calls for an efficient system to get oxygen to these muscles and to the organs, hence the superbly developed respiratory and circulatory systems of birds. Bird lungs are a model of efficiency, operating with a constant one-way flow through the microscopic tissues for efficient gas exchange and the reduction of "stale" air.

A bird's heart performs yeoman duties. A resting

Crimson Topaz hummingbirds frolic in Amazonian Brazil in this illustration by John Gould (1804–1881).

hummingbird's heart can beat more than 1,200 times a minute. A hummer's heart accounts for nearly 3 percent of an adult's body weight, though the hearts of larger birds are relatively smaller. Heart weight also varies with the environment: Birds adapted to high altitudes and highly migratory birds have hearts that are relatively larger than their low-altitude relatives.

Birds have a higher resting rate of metabolism than most mammals—mainly because they are small. This basal metabolic rate scales inversely with size so that small birds, with a greater surface area relative to their volume, have the highest rates. A House Sparrow at

Bird Brain
In 1942, design and construction began on Howard Hughes's massive H-4 Hercules military transport plane. Because of wartime metal shortages, this largest aircraft was built out of plywood. Dubbed the Spruce Goose, it flew only once, in 1947, for one mile at an altitude of 70 feet. It currently resides at an aviation museum in Oregon.

Ruff

rest under benign conditions will burn about 312 calories per kilogram per hour, whereas a young human might only burn about one three-hundredth this amount. A very active small bird, such as a flying hummingbird, consumes calories at a tremendous rate; since this is done by oxidation of foods, the bird must therefore consume a great amount of oxygen. If you metabolized food at the rate of a hummingbird, you'd have to eat about twice your weight in food every day.

Birds are warm-blooded—they are endotherms, generating body heat primarily internally through metabolic processes (rather than by soaking up the sun's energy), and they are homeotherms, maintaining a relatively constant body temperature of about 104°F give or take a couple of degrees. Birds may drop their body temperature when inactive, as when sleeping at night, or especially if entering torpor, an extreme state of sleeping in which body functions such as temperature, heart rate, and metabolism slow down dramatically. That hummingbird whose heart can beat up to 1,200 times per minute? When in torpor, its heart slows to 36 beats per minute.

All of this—the efficiency, the high body temperature, and the high metabolism—allows birds to live in a huge range of environmental conditions, such as very high altitudes; very hot, dry regions; underwater (for up to a few minutes at a time); and very cold areas.

Five geese—two subspecies of Canada Goose (second and third from the right) and three subspecies of Cackling Goose— stand side by side. The Cackling Goose is a tiny look-alike that was reclassified as a separate species in 2004.

GETTING AROUND

TO FLY OR NOT TO FLY

Flight is great. But at some point a flying bird has to land. Once out of the air, a bird might perch, walk, run, grasp, paddle, strut, or otherwise use that other pair of limbs they've brought along their evolutionary path from bipedal or arboreal reptiles—their legs.

BIRDS AS TWO-LEGGED CREATURES

Unlike those of bats and pterosaurs, birds' legs are not an integral part of the flight apparatus and are therefore freed up for a suite of uses from locomotion to prey capture. The wing versus leg calculus in birds covers a remarkable range. Some accomplished fliers, from hummingbirds and swifts to frigatebirds, have relatively tiny legs that are serviceable for grasping a perch but useless for locomotion.

An American Robin teases the best out of both limbs; robins fly strongly and with endurance, but they also hop and run on the ground with ease. The extinct moa of New Zealand went to the earthbound

A Greater Roadrunner hops on a branch in Arizona, showing its preference for running, not flying—up to 17 miles an hour. The large bird, up to two feet in length, is one of the few animals capable of killing rattlesnakes.

extreme. Being essentially wingless, with skeletons showing no trace of wing bones, they made a living with enormously strong hind legs and a long neck terminating in a grazing, browsing bill. Built for flight, the bird's anatomy also serves to center its weight over its hind limbs. A relatively short and stout femur is held pointed forward, between a 45-degree angle and a position parallel to the ground.

One man may take a walk and scarcely see a bird; another, with him, sees or hears, perhaps, five and twenty species.

A. J. R. ROBERTS, *THE BIRD BOOK*, 1903

From the knee joint (which we generally don't see, as it resides within the body cavity in most birds), the tibiotarsus (roughly, the "shin bone") angles down and backward to the heel (tarsal) joint. That joint is often mistaken for a "backward" knee by those unfamiliar with bird anatomy. Below this, a bird's leg differs significantly from our own.

We stand on our feet, but birds stand on their toes. The fusion of certain ankle and foot bones produces the tarsometatarsus—often called the "tarsus" by birders—which is basically the part of the bird's hind limb that we can see. The toes, usually three or four (though the ostrich has only two), extend from the distal end of the tarsus; a common toe arrangement is three forward-facing toes and, often, a rear-directed hind toe, or hallux.

Birders can't help but notice the diversity of gaits in birds. On a birding outing we might see a

Two species of southwestern quail—Gambel's (top) and Scaled—occasionally overlap in range.

scrub-jay or Blue Jay hopping on the ground. In contrast, its relative the crow walks—until it speeds up into a series of hops. A grackle walks along next to a starling that might best be said to waddle and a Lark Sparrow that seems to shuffle. A Great Blue Heron walks slowly on long, stately legs; nearby a Killdeer runs a few steps and then stops abruptly. Even within a single family, the wood-warblers, we might see a hopping Yellow-rumped Warbler, a walking waterthrush, and a high-stepping Ovenbird.

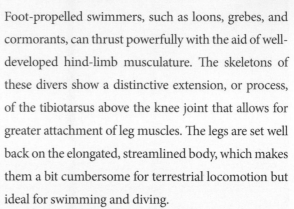

Tufted Puffin

SWIMMERS & DIVERS

Mastery of air and land are just some of birds' adaptive wonders. The ability to swim and dive opens up a bountiful set of foraging options. Webbing between birds' toes allows efficient propulsion for swimming at the surface, and webbed feet have evolved in many bird groups, including waterfowl, loons, petrels, pelicans, cormorants, boobies, flamingos, gulls, and alcids (auks, murres, and puffins). Grebes, coots, finfoots, and phalaropes have flaps or lobes along the toes that serve the same function of propulsion.

Underwater propulsion through body undulations or the movements of tails or fins are not in the repertoire of diving birds, whose body plans are a legacy of the evolution of flight. Rather, birds use their feet, their wings, or some combination of the two.

Foot-propelled swimmers, such as loons, grebes, and cormorants, can thrust powerfully with the aid of well-developed hind-limb musculature. The skeletons of these divers show a distinctive extension, or process, of the tibiotarsus above the knee joint that allows for greater attachment of leg muscles. The legs are set well back on the elongated, streamlined body, which makes them a bit cumbersome for terrestrial locomotion but ideal for swimming and diving.

Wing propulsion is best developed in three groups of aquatic birds: penguins, alcids, and diving petrels.

A young Brown Booby peers underwater for prey while swimming near Bikini Atoll. The large-bodied boobies, cumbersome at takeoff, usually dive into the sea to catch small fish or squid.

A King Penguin swims effortlessly underwater, although it is flightless and waddles on land. Kings, second to Emperors in size, weigh 24 to 35 pounds. Their dives after small fish often take them more than 300 feet down in Antarctic waters.

In these groups the wings are reduced in area to facilitate up- and downstrokes through the water. Carried to the extreme, the wings are modified as flippers and their small surface relative to body weight renders them useless for flight. This is the case not only with penguins but also with several groups of extinct flightless alcids. Living alcids, all capable of flight, have a distinctive rapid, whirring wingbeat to compensate for the heavy load the small wings must bear. Some diving birds, including many ducks and shearwaters, use both their wings and feet for underwater propulsion. Many other adaptations facilitate life in the water for birds. Deep-diving birds such as loons, penguins, and cormorants have relatively dense bones, and some reduce buoyancy with wettable plumage. Deep divers must expel air from their lungs and air sacs, and while diving they show reduced heart rates and the ability to operate muscles anaerobically (by building up lactic acid). Some divers (such as loons and large penguins) can remain underwater for 15 minutes or more. Emperor Penguins can dive as deep as 870 feet.

Bird Brain

At midnight on the second Saturday in May, hundreds of birders around New Jersey begin a 24-hour quest to see (or hear) more birds than their rivals. The single-team, all-time high total was 231 species in 2003. Participants in the World Series of Birding are on a mission to help environmental causes—raising more than nine million dollars since 1984.

Soaring effortlessly on wingspans of approximately three feet, Sooty Terns glide above Rocas Atoll in the Atlantic Ocean just off Brazil. Seabirds of the tropical oceans, they are also known as "wide-awake terns" because of their constant calling.

FLIGHT & FLIGHTLESSNESS

Colonies of Sooty Terns dot the tropical oceans. In places this is the most abundant warm-water seabird, and the cacophony of their nesting grounds leaves a lasting impression for those fortunate enough to visit. Young Sooties make their first flights when eight weeks old or so and a few weeks after that leave the colonies for the ocean, where they make a living feeding on small flying fish, squid, and other seafood at the water's surface. They fly seeking food. And fly. And fly.

These terns are slow to mature and rarely breed before they're a few years old—some may not return to breed until they're ten. Before returning to breed, usually in their natal colony, they're not likely to settle down on land anywhere else. They're not good swimmers and are almost never seen to alight on the water.

◆ **TURKEY VULTURE** ◆

CATHARTES AURA: "Vulture" comes from the Latin *vultur* "to pluck or tear" and refers to the bird's feeding habits. The word "turkey" is used possibly because a vulture's bare head suggests that of a Wild Turkey. *Cathartes* comes from the Greek *kathartes,* "purifier," as in cleansing the surroundings of carrion, and *aura* from the Latin *aurum,* "gold."

Occasionally an individual might put down on some flotsam, or even on the back of a sea turtle, but it seems an inescapable conclusion that Sooty Terns stay airborne nearly all of the half dozen years or so prior to their first breeding. This is bird flight at its most extreme. In the coastal chaparral regions from the Columbia River south through Oregon and California to northwestern Baja California, a long-tailed brown sprite called the Wrentit works through the dense twiggery in short hops and quick flaps. It's neither a wren nor a tit; in fact, the latest molecular studies suggest it's closest to a group of Asian babblers known as parrotbills. Staying on the wing for six years is something a Wrentit might dream of, but launching for five or ten seconds is about the best it can do. A Wrentit's flight gets it from shrub to shrub, but not much farther.

Flight gives birds many advantages, all of which are high on their to-do list: escaping predators; momentary, daily, or seasonal travels to productive habitats; reaching and capturing food; finding and displaying to mates. But flight is costly, and birds engage in it only as much as their lifestyles require. As discussed, that's a lot in the case of the Sooty Tern, but not in the Wrentit's. Flightlessness has evolved many times in birds, and all flightless birds had flying ancestors. Many flightless birds were (or are) very large, including running birds of open plains like ostriches and fruit-eating forest birds like cassowaries. They also included fearsome predators like the "terror birds" (phorusrhacids), relatives of the present-day seriamas, which lived in South America between 5 and 50 million years ago and stood as tall as ten feet. But small birds can become flightless as

Bird Brain

Bird-themed operas include Messiaen's *Saint François d'Assise*, Stravinsky's *The Nightingale*, Rossini's *The Thieving Magpie*, and Hans Werner Henze's *The Hoopoe and the Triumph of Filial Love*. The Birds (*Die Vögel*) by Walter Braunfels is based on the ancient Greek drama *The Birds* by Aristophanes.

well. A great many oceanic islands throughout the world were home to flightless rails; these birds dispersed widely, but over the millennia populations on distant islands often lost the power of flight through the evolutionary reduction of the energetically expensive accoutrements of flight. Sadly, most of these rails—perhaps many hundreds of species—are now extinct, blinking out with the first human contact on these islands.

A Flightless Cormorant, found only in the Galápagos, is an excellent swimmer, but it has lost the ability to fly.

CLIMBERS & CREEPERS

Flying, walking, running, swimming, diving—most birds do some or all of these things well. But consider what it takes to climb a vertical surface and how woodpeckers and some other groups of birds have mastered this. The 215 or so species of woodpeckers are distributed over most of the world where there are at least a few trees or shrubs, though they haven't managed to cross an invisible boundary known as Wallace's line, which stretches from Indonesia into the New Guinea and Australian region. A few woodpecker species even make a go of it in dry treeless plains or high mountains above the tree line. But most are birds of woodlands that specialize in climbing tree trunks.

Foraging along vertical tree trunks has its benefits; prey resides in the interstices of the bark and within living, diseased, or dead wood. Woodpeckers have the machinery to chisel into wood and get prey from deep within—including a chisel-like bill with a very hard, horny covering; skull, hinge, and jaw adaptations to diffuse the force of the blow; a long extendable tongue; and nostrils often covered with feathers, if they aren't

How Big Can a Bird Get?

The upper and lower limits of the size a bird can attain are determined by physiology, but a number of things combine to determine the maximum size of a flying bird.

The largest known flying bird was a South American Teratorn known as *Argentavis magnificens* that lived about six million years ago; it had a wingspan of some 22 feet and weighed in at 175 pounds. Researchers theorize that *Argentavis* was at or near the upper limit in size for a flying bird and almost certainly needed dependable stiff winds to get and remain airborne.

To fly, *Argentavis* also needed huge flight feathers, which, like all feathers, needed to be replaced regularly through molt. But feathers can only grow so fast—in the largest living birds that have been studied the longest wing feathers grow less than half an inch a day—and *Argentavis* might therefore have had to undergo periods of flightlessness in order to replace its flight feathers. One suspects also that the time it would have taken for a developing chick of this species to attain the powers of flight would have meant a very slow reproductive rate—perhaps at most a single chick every two to three years.

EXTINCT GIANT TERATORN

Townsend's Warbler

just lateral slits. Woodpeckers have relatively short, stout legs with strong curved claws on their toes. They're yoke-toed: That is, they have two toes pointing forward and two rearward, although the outer rear toes, in practice, are brought around to the side. A few species, scattered in four genera, have only one rear-directed toe, having lost the hallux.

Notably, the woodpecker's tail is strong and stiffened. The central shaft (rachis) of the tail feathers is broad and strong, and the barbs are stiff. This stiff tail acts as a prop, supporting the bird as it hitches up a vertical trunk. The large and laterally expanded pygostyle (Pope's nose) allows attachment of increased musculature.

When woodpeckers replace their tail feathers through the molting process, they maximize the efficiency of tail support by dropping and regrowing the strongest central pair of tail feathers only after the others have been replaced. This contrasts with the more typical replacement of the tail feathers—from the central pair outward—in most birds.

Perhaps not surprisingly, other groups of birds have independently evolved climbing, or scansorial, adaptations. Tree creepers of the northern temperate forests and woodcreepers of the neotropical forests hitch along tree trunks and limbs, probing into crevices for invertebrate prey; like woodpeckers, they have long, stiffened tails and strong, curved claws for support. They even molt their tail feathers in the so-called woodpecker pattern to preserve the tail's role as a prop. Remarkably, one group of starlings also possesses stiff-

To avoid injury from hammering, woodpeckers have well-protected brains and thick neck muscles to absorb shock waves.

ened tails for support while climbing: These are the oxpeckers, and their climbing surfaces are the sides, backs, and necks of large African mammals, from which they pick ticks and other ectoparasites for food.

Bird Brain
The Harris's Hawk, native to the American Southwest, has become one of the most popular falconry species because of its temperament and abilities. Often captive bred, it is especially adept at pursuing rabbits and hares. In the wild, Harris's Hawks live in groups, hunt cooperatively, and maintain a social hierarchy.

Peacocks and swans. From the Album de la Décoration collection, Paris (published ca 1900)

THE PLUSES OF PLUMAGE

FEATHER FORMS & FUNCTIONS

No single word better expresses the essence of what makes a bird a bird than "feather." Yes, it's tempting to say that flight defines birds, but feathers, not flight, are unique to class Aves. The protofeather fuzz of theropod dinosaurs that might or might not be the progenitors of birds aside, complex vaned feathers, which cover the exterior of the body, are the hallmark of all birds and only birds. It is well worth reflecting on all that feathers do for birds.

THE INDISPENSABLE FEATHER

Most notably, feathers enable flight. They contour the body into an aerodynamic form, and flight feathers provide the lift and thrust of powered flight. Tail feathers add lift and aid in braking, steering, and maneuvering. And being featherlight, this epidermal coat adds little to the overall weight of a bird.

No less important is the role of a bird's feather coat in thermoregulation. Downy feather bases trap a layer of air, which holds the bird's metabolically generated heat within and helps maintain a warm, constant body temperature. This air layer also protects against intense solar radiation and the chilling effects of water. Many birds, particularly some waterfowl, use plucked down feathers in the nest to provide insulation for their clutch of eggs. Humans long ago learned the insulating properties of avian down, as anybody who has donned a down jacket or used a down comforter or sleeping bag can attest.

Feathers are also a canvas on which a diverse array of colors and patterns serve as social signals. Their

Metallic green distinguishes the male Splendid Astrapia, a bird of paradise found in the mountains in New Guinea.

communication function goes beyond what meets the eye: Modified wing or tail feathers in birds such as snipe, hummingbirds, manakins, and ducks produce sounds used in courtship or serve as signals in a flock. At the other extreme, the pattern and color of feathers may serve a cryptic function. Think of a white winter ptarmigan in the snow, the dead-leaf pattern of a roosting nightjar, or the bright green

Montagu's Harrier

plumage of a parrot disappearing into equally bright green foliage.

As if this weren't enough, feathers can have other specialized uses for the birds that bear them. Grebes pack their stomachs with feathers to help digest bony fish prey. Feathers in some pitohuis, a group of New Guinea songbirds, actually contain highly toxic chemicals that thwart predation. The texture and arrangement of feathers on the faces of some owls and hawks help

their sensitive ears gather sound, and facial feather patterns can also help some birds see and accurately strike prey.

Bird Brain

Composers have often drawn inspiration from birds. The flute is the bird in both Vivaldi's *The Goldfinch* and Prokofiev's *Peter and the Wolf* (where the oboe quacks like a duck). The violin plays *Cock, Hen, and Quail* by Baroque composer Heinrich Biber. Swans are played by an English horn in *The Swan of Tuonela*, by Sibelius.

Plumage the color of dry leaves camouflages a Long-tailed Nightjar of Africa as it roosts during the day. At night, it hunts on the wing, pursuing moths and other large flying insects.

In a flash of color, a Northern Flicker leaves its nest cavity near Slana, Alaska. Though they can hammer on trees like any woodpecker, flickers prefer to find ants and small insects on the ground. They inhabit most of the United States.

THE FEATHER COAT

When we look at birds, we see their quintessential bird-ness—their feathers. Birds are covered with them, and a hundred field guides rejoice in what these feathers tell us. Epidermal structures made of keratin, feathers grow from follicles in the skin. These follicles are not uniformly distributed over a bird's body, but instead are arranged in tracts. Yet they overlap to cover nearly all of a bird's body. The pattern of feather tracts, pterylography, has been useful in classification, as their distribution is generally similar among related birds.

How many feathers do birds have? An enterprising researcher counted more than 25,000 contour feathers on a Tundra Swan; in contrast, a Ruby-throated

Bird Brain

Yanks and Brits can't agree on English bird names. American birders visiting the United Kingdom sometimes think they're seeing a new bird when someone points out a Great Northern Diver, but it's the same as the Common Loon back home. Here are a few more: Goosander in the U.K. is Common Merganser in the U.S., Slavonian Grebe in the U.K. is Horned Grebe in the U.S., and Arctic Skua in the U.K. is Parasitic Jaeger in the U.S.

Hummingbird yielded only about 940 feathers. A penguin's feathers are densely arrayed, almost like scales; an Emperor Penguin would take the cake in a feather count, but who will have the patience to count the feathers? In contrast, many parrots seem well on the way to nakedness, with sparse feathering.

Besides admiring the contour feathers that cloak a bird's body, we are most apt to notice the flight feathers—longer feathers on the wing and tail that provide lift and control flight. Flight feathers are increasingly asymmetrical from the inner to the outer regions of the wings and tail, the outer feathers having most of the feather surface, or vane, inward from the hard central shaft, or rachis. Other modified feathers in birds include the loose and fluffy down that provides insulation, bristles around the face that aid in food capture or function (in hornbills) as eyelashes that would make Maybelline proud, and filoplumes that sense air movement. A look at feathers under a microscope reveals the complexity that confers such strength for an entity of such trivial weight. But there are also practical aspects of this close examination. The microscopic structure of feathers allows identification of a bird to a group, sometimes to a species. Scientists at the Smithsonian Institution and the U.S. Fish and Wildlife Service's forensic lab in Oregon have cracked cases in crime, conservation, and aviation safety using their feather expertise and comparative collections.

Wings at the downstroke, a Blue Tit flies toward the camera. A European relative of the North American chickadee, it is easily recognized by its blue-and-yellow plumage and black mask, and it has perching skills that allow it to hang upside down.

COLORS, PATTERNS, STRUCTURES

Volumes have been written about the complexities of bird coloration and the underlying physical and chemical basis for the colors birds display. The colors you see in a bird's feather can come from molecules of pigment that absorb some wavelengths of light and reflect others back. Some pigments are ubiquitous in birds, but others are unique to certain bird groups. For example, most turacos, forest and savanna birds endemic to Africa, have remarkable copper-based green and red pigments in their plumage that are known in few other birds. A feather's colors can also be produced when the microscopic structure of a feather and tiny pockets of air trapped within it scatter the impinging light. Most of the blues, greens, and iridescent colors shown by birds are the result of feather structure, either alone or acting in concert with pigments. Some birds even show patches of structural color that reflect in the ultraviolet range—a realization that has ushered in a whole new wave of research as ornithologists dust off the black lights that shone on their psychedelic posters a few decades back.

Some of the colors we see are actually applied cosmetically by the bird or are the result of environ-

A male Red Bird of paradise displays to win the attentions of a female. More than three dozen species of birds of paradise inhabit the forests of New Guinea and nearby islands, and most have elaborate plumage.

A close-up of the feathers of a Ring-necked Pheasant—an Asian species well established in the United States—reveals their intricate design. The hardy birds adapt readily to the wild and are highly regarded by hunters for their beauty and taste.

mental staining. The subtle but beautiful pink wash on an Elegant Tern or Franklin's Gull comes from the bird's preen gland and shows up mainly on the white ventral plumage that is most easily preened by the bill. Water and mud rich in iron oxides can produce a reddish stain on the white or gray feathers of birds such as cranes, swans, and Bearded Vultures. The beauty of a bird's feather comes also from the patterns of deposited pigments as the feather is produced. Turning the deposition of different pigments in the growing feather on and off produces bars, spots, fringes, and other patterns. The spectacular eyespots on the back and tail of a peacock-pheasant, the understated vermiculations on a male Gadwall, and the "hearts" on a Heart-spotted Woodpecker only hint at the patterns nature paints on the unfurling canvas of a feather.

A feather's shape and texture can also make a statement, from the long tuft-tipped shafts of a motmot's central tail to the bizarre curls of a Scale-feathered Malkoha. Modified feathers can also produce courtship sounds, from the snapping of manakin wings to the pop made by the tail of an Anna's Hummingbird at the bottom of its dive.

OUT WITH THE OLD, IN WITH THE NEW

Though a marvelous adaptation, a feather doesn't last forever. Normal wear and tear can damage feather structure, especially for birds living in areas of dense brush or abrading sand. Sunlight can fade feathers, and feather mites and bacteria can degrade them. This decline in quality is inevitable despite a bird's best efforts to groom and maintain its feather coat through a frequent regimen of grooming, preening, and the application of oils from the

uropygial gland at the dorsal base of the tail. A bird's trip to the spa might also include taking a water bath, "bathing" in dust, and even allowing—passively or actively—ants to crawl through its plumage. (It is theorized that the formic acid released by ants repels ectoparasites.)

Bird feathers harbor quite a fauna, mostly benign. Flat hippoboscid flies travel about, sandwiched among the feathers, and various lice, mites, and ticks also take up residence. Sometimes the associations are quite

A Blue-winged Pitta enhances its colors by freshening up in a forest pool in Thailand. This passerine is found in Southeast Asia, occasionally drifting to northeast Australia. It lives on a diet of worms, insects, and snails found on the ground.

CHEMICAL DEFENSE

Of all the defenses birds have mustered against predators and parasites, one of the most bizarre is found in a group of New Guinea songbirds in the Whistler family known as pitohuis. Especially in their skin and feathers, two pitohui species in particular (the Hooded Pitohui and the Variable Pitohui) possess a toxin known as homobatrachotoxin, akin to that found in poison-arrow frogs. Much remains to be learned about the metabolic source of these poisons—they may derive from certain beetles that the birds consume. Similarly, their function has not been studied in detail, but they undoubtedly afford protection against some predators and ectoparasites. Perhaps tellingly, the two most toxic pitohui species are also the ones with a feather coat most boldly patterned in orange and black—classic "warning" coloration in nature.

A HOODED PITOHUI IN A FIG TREE

specific, with a particular parasite having co-evolved with a particular host bird species.

What is the solution to the problem of old, worn feathers that are losing their functionality? It's molt—the growth of new feathers from a feather follicle. In all but a bird's first molt, this means replacing old feathers from a previous molt cycle. The production of new feathers in a molt consumes a lot of energy; birds minimize further energetic costs, such as declines in flight and thermoregulation efficiency, by molting in an orderly, symmetrical, and prolonged fashion. Replacing all the primaries—the longest flight feathers of the wing—can take anywhere from a month to several months. A few birds have evolved a strategy of dropping all of their flight feathers simultaneously and therefore replacing them relatively quickly, but this requires movement to an area that is both safe from predators and replete with food resources.

Molting is an evolved, hormonally orchestrated phenomenon that has to fit economically within a bird's annual cycle. Usually, birds molt most of their feathers once per year, but many species insert another molt before the breeding season, often taking on a brighter breeding plumage. But molting strategies can be very complex—especially in very large birds—and scientists are still trying to understand the relationships of various partial and complete molts that birds undergo and the sequence of feather replacement within these molts. Field guides and bird banding guides are frequently refined with more accurate and comprehensive terminology to describe molt—simultaneously bewildering and fascinating the birder.

TOP 12 BIRDS WITH THE BEST PLUMAGE

Who are the best dressed of the avian world? This array of examples displays the breadth and variety of bird feather colors and patterns around the world.

❶ Golden-breasted Starling
Cosmopsarus regius Males and females of the sub-Saharan African beauty feature the unique "oil sheen" gloss to the dark plumage, yielding green and blue highlights.

❷ Lady Amherst's Pheasant
Chrysolophus amherstiae Male pheasants of many species are gaudy, but few combine the bold colors and intricate scaling patterns of this species of the forested hills of southwestern China.

❸ Lilac-breasted Roller
Coracius caudatus A favorite of travelers to the acacia savannas of eastern and southern Africa, this is arguably the most gorgeous of a dozen species in the colorful Old World Roller family.

❹ Mandarin Duck
Aix galericulata With tertials flared like sails, a puffy mane, and intricate patterning, the male Mandarin's beauty has led to the introduction of this species to Britain and California wine country.

❺ Indian Peafowl
Pavo cristatus The male "peacock" is the most spectacular of the pheasants. The huge "train," fanned in full display and amply adorned with "eye spots," is formed from elongated upper tail coverts.

❻ Rainbow Lorikeet
Trichoglossus hametodus These nectar-feeding parrots of Australia, New Guinea, and Indonesia vary geographically—up to 20 subspecies are recognized—but are consistently striking in their bold colors.

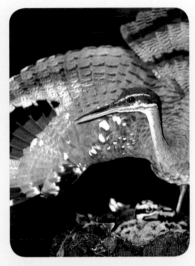

7 **Resplendent Quetzal**
Pharomachrus mocinno The long uppertail coverts of this spectacular cloud-forest trogon trail up to two feet beyond the tail tip. The bright red belly color fades in specimens.

8 **Sunbittern** *Eurypyga helias*
This unassuming bird of tropical American riverbanks transforms into a striking vision when it spreads its intricately patterned gray, buff, chestnut, black, and white wings in flight or display.

9 **Black-and-yellow Broadbill**
Eurylaimus ochromalus One of many colorful Asian broadbills, this species not only sports bold patterning but also has colorful yellow eyes and a unique blue-and-turquoise bill.

10 **European Bee-eater**
Merops apiaster The 25 species of bee-eaters, aerial insect-eaters of the Old World, are spectacular in plumage; this northernmost species has nested as far north as Scotland and Scandinavia.

11 **Gouldian Finch**
Erythrura gouldiae Endangered in its native northern Australia range, this green, blue, plum, and yellow finch occurs in three color varieties: red-faced, black-faced, and yellow-orange-faced.

12 **Red-crowned Crane**
Grus japonensis Stately and magnificent, this revered species of northeast Asia is all the more striking against a winter's backdrop. In Korean and Japanese culture it symbolizes happiness and longevity.

Eating Like a Bird

THE MANY WAYS OF SECURING A MEAL

A group of shorebirds feeds on an estuarine flat, various species going about their business in different ways. A Long-billed Curlew's seven-inch down-curved bill eases into the mud and emerges with a juicy worm as an American Avocet strolls through the nearby shallows, sweeping its upturned bill back and forth. A Semipalmated Plover runs a few steps on the mud and picks up a morsel with its short, stout bill. A Ruddy Turnstone nudges some flotsam with its stout and slightly uptilted bill to get at a small invertebrate. On a nearby clump of rocks, an oystercatcher slips its oddly compressed, knifelike bill under a limpet to dislodge it.

No matter where we go to watch birds, we're struck by the diversity of their bills' shapes and uses. Bird names reflect this: grosbeak, conebill, wrybill, shoebill, boatbill, broadbill, flatbill, hornbill, thornbill, frogmouth, and so on. Tool, weapon, signal, sense organ—a bird's bill (or beak) is key in its battle for survival. Reaching, gathering, and manipulating food is the first priority, but the bill is also a key tool in nest construction. For some birds, it is also a colorful signal of identity and status.

An American Avocet prepares to sweep its upturned bill in the shallows for insects and small crustaceans in this print by John James Audubon. Although the adults are attentive parents, the chicks of the large wading birds feed themselves.

FITTING THE BILL

Strong yet lightweight, the underlying bones of a bird's bill are fused versions of the upper mandible or maxilla (premaxillary bones) and lower mandible (dental bones), with a keratinized (fingernail-like) covering called the rhamphotheca. This covering is what we see—it bears the colors and fine specializations of the bill. The rhamphotheca is constantly renewed and can change with age and seasonally. Some jays have bright

Lining up fish in its beak, an Atlantic Puffin takes home dinner after diving off the United Kingdom's Farne Islands.

> *Even the stork in the sky knows her seasons*
> *And the turtledove, swift, and crane*
> *Keep the time of their coming.*
>
> JEREMIAH 8:7

yellow bills as juveniles but black bills as adults; and puffins are adorned with a colorful and high-ridged bill covering in the breeding season.

We often forget that the bill is hardly a static, dead structure. Bill tips of many birds are flexible: For instance, a long-billed sandpiper such as a dowitcher will seize food with the flexible bill tip after probing into the substrate. Bill tips can be highly sensitive: A Wood Stork feels for prey as it probes in murky bayou waters, and a kiwi probing for earthworms is aided by a keen olfactory sense and nostrils located near the bill tip.

Inside the bird's mouth are additional foraging accoutrements. Many seabirds that take slimy, slippery fish and squid have not only hooked bills to help grasp prey, but also rear-directed spikes on the palate that usher the prey down the hatch. Different populations of Red Crossbills have palates specialized for handling seeds of different conifers, a fascinating co-evolution of morphology and food. Like bills, tongues can also be highly specialized—from brush- or tubelike structures in nectar-feeders and prickly tongues in woodpeckers to chubby aids for filter-feeding in flamingos.

Bird Brain
The Crested Bellbird, a small, vulnerable songbird of the Australian outback, defends its nest with a ring of living-dead caterpillars—paralyzed moth larvae covered with hollow hairs that sting whatever touches them. The bellbird knows how to pinch the caterpillar bodies so they remain alive but can't crawl away.

Fruit may entice a Baltimore Oriole to come to eye level, like this male astride an orange.

NOT ALL FOOD IS EQUAL

Occupying such a wide variety of habitats and dining with such diverse utensils, birds choose their food from a vast and varied menu. Animals, seeds, fruits, and nectar are especially common in the diets of birds, but more exotic and more pedestrian

fare finds its way into the digestive tracts of some birds. From leaves and beeswax to bones, animal dung, and garbage, different diets call for different digestive capabilities, and the crops (esophageal pouches), glandular stomachs, gizzards, and intestines of birds reflect this.

Bugs, worms, seeds? Boring fast-food, really. The avian family tree is populated with gastronomic outliers with fascinating ecologies. A Phainopepla's weakness? Mistletoe berries, of which it can eat a thousand or more in a day; its digestive journey from bill to dropping can be as little as 12 minutes. The

A light broke in upon my brain,—
It was the carol of a bird;
It ceased, and then it came again,
The sweetest song ear ever heard.

LORD BYRON, "THE PRISONER OF CHILLON," 1816

mistletoe's evolutionary mission is accomplished as well: The indigestible seeds become incipient mistletoe plants when deposited as sticky droppings on trees and shrubs.

Tropical American cotingas feed largely on fruit, in a cozy co-evolutionary relationship with trees that rely largely on these fruit-eating birds for seed dispersal. Rich fruit is abundant, so male cotingas, freed from chick-raising duties, have lots of time

◆ OSPREY ◆

PANDION HALIAETUS: "Osprey" derives from the Latin *avis praede,* "bird of prey." *Pandion* refers to the King of Athens (whose daughters were turned into birds) and the nobility of the bird; *haliaetus* is Greek for "sea eagle," a combination of *hals* ("salt") and *aetos* ("eagle").

to compete with other males to attract mates—and many have evolved spectacularly ornamental plumages toward this end.

The Hoatzin, a bizarre South American bird of uncertain affinities (it may be a distant cousin of Africa's turacos) is a leaf-eater, digesting copious quantities of preferred leaves in a greatly enlarged crop. A salty diet is no problem for seabirds, whose salt glands, usually nestled in paired recesses in the skull above the eyes, concentrate and excrete the excess salt.

How much food does a bird need to eat? This depends a great deal, of course, on environmental conditions and on a food's availability, caloric value, and digestive requirements. It's not a stretch to say that the average bird eats about a quarter of its body weight each day. As metabolic rates scale inversely with size,

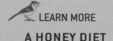 LEARN MORE
A HONEY DIET

One of the more unusual diets in the bird world is that of the honeyguides, a primarily African family of 17 species whose members dine largely on beeswax. They feed at abandoned or inactive hives, and have been known to guide humans and other mammals such as ratels ("honey badgers") to beehives to feed on the wax after the hive has been broken apart for the honey and the bees have departed. This "guiding" behavior (hence the family name Indicatoridae) involves a distinctive chattering call and quick flashes of the white tail patches, alternating with short flights toward the source of the honey. Honeyguides are particularly thick-skinned, a protection against bee stings, and their digestion of beeswax is aided by special enzymes rarely found in other birds. Of course, they also avail themselves of honeybee eggs and larvae in the hive.

small birds generally need to eat a greater percentage of their body weight daily than do large birds.

Neither feasting nor famine is rare in the world of birds. The crop can rapidly fill when food is readily available, allowing the feeder to take advantage of a large but ephemeral food source and then move off to a safe area to digest.

On the other hand, an incubating male Emperor Penguin may fast for up to 115 days before it is finally free to ship out and forage. A hummingbird deprived of food and water would die within hours, but hummers often enter into a torpid state at night, turning down their internal thermostat to survive until the next morning's meal.

William De Morgan (1839-1917) depicts a Peacock taking a meal away from a fish—an unlikely scenario.

Trolling for small fish, a Black Skimmer flies low over water near Long Island, New York. The bird uses its slender beak to slice through water turned orange by the setting sun. When the longer lower mandible contacts a fish, the bill snaps shut.

THE MANY WAYS OF FORAGING

Every one of the 10,000 modern bird species has a unique diet and its own way of finding, attacking, and manipulating food. True, most birds find their way into one or more of the general categories ornithologists use to describe foraging: gleaners, grazers, plunge-divers, chiselers, probers, scratchers, aerial insectivores, and so on. But each species has a distinctive way of combining anatomical features, occupying habitats, and exploiting ecological niches. A bird's anatomy is devoted to more than foraging, of course; the equipment needed to escape predators, migrate, build a nest, and carry out other activities coexists with foraging tools. A bird's bill is clearly its prime utensil, but its locomotory adaptations help it swoop, climb, run, or swim after its food.

◆ WHIMBREL ◆

NUMENIUS PHAEOPUS: "Whimbrel" is the diminutive form of the Middle English word "whim," as in "whimpering," which describes the bird's call. *Numenius,* Latinized Greek for "new moon," refers to the bird's curved bill shape. Greek *phaeopus,* "gray-footed," is for the color of its legs and feet.

Swifts forage on the wing for most or all of the daylight hours. Their large gapes catch their aeroplankton prey, but without long, narrow wings supremely adapted to prolonged, fast, maneuverable flight they'd certainly starve. Diving birds can't catch up with their prey without adaptations to reduce buoyancy and propel themselves underwater with their feet or wings. A raptor's hooked bill is just the thing for killing, holding, and dismembering prey, but strong legs and sharp talons are necessary adjuncts, as are wings for pursuit and keen vision for locating a meal.

Since a bird's time is largely devoted to foraging, we can't help but notice birds as they seek and obtain food. But quantifying and analyzing foraging behavior are not simple tasks; they require patience, keen observational skills, and pragmatic sets of behavioral

Bird Brain
The calming effect of birdsong may be the reason that the crime rate dipped in Lancaster, a high desert city near Los Angeles. In 2011, the town installed 70 speakers along half a mile of its main thoroughfare and piped in a dulcet chorus of songs, chirps, and tweets—minor crime fell 15 percent and major crimes were down 6 percent.

A chick half hidden by plumage reaches for a feather offered by its parent, a Great Crested Grebe nesting along England's Thames River. Many species of grebes eat small feathers, which may help protect their digestive systems from fish bones.

Passionate for fruit, a Cedar Waxwing (left) hangs upside down to eat berries. The North American bird is named for waxy secretions on its wings. A Blue Jay's powerful beak will make short work of the acorn it holds.

categories to record. Quantification aside, it's just plain fun to watch some birds forage. Herons can be the picture of patience and stateliness. Just watch a Great Egret stalk the shallows at a glacial pace, eventually leaning forward and catching a fish with a rapid grab. A Reddish Egret is not content to wait. It jumps, dances, flaps, runs, and pursues. The Snowy Egret has a varied repertoire of patient stalking, foot shuffling, bill dipping, shading, and running—all different means to the same end: catching a fish. Other birds employ still different fishing strategies. An Anhinga spears its fish, while an American White Pelican scoops its fish up in its pouch. Loons pursue fish underwater, but a Red-footed Booby grabs flying fish out of the air. Most improbably, a skimmer fishes by dragging its long knifelike lower mandible through the water until it contacts a fish, at which point it snaps its head back underneath its

◆ HUDSONIAN GODWIT ◆

LIMOSA HAEMASTICA: "Godwit" may come from the Old English *god wiht* for "good creature" and refer to its savory taste. "Hudsonian" means native to Hudson Bay. *Limosa* is from the Latin *limus,* "of the mud," mudflats being a habitat; *haemastica* is from the Greek for "bloodred," the color of the adult male's underparts.

body as the shorter but stronger upper mandible clamps down. The skimmers' tactile foraging works fine at night when small fish are closer to the surface and few other birds can find them.

Bird species' diets and hunting techniques can be highly specialized. Sporting a supreme escargot utensil as a bill, the Snail Kite feeds almost exclusively on freshwater marsh snails of the genus *Pomacea*. The African Harrier-Hawk, or Gymnogene, is adept at reaching into nest cavities and other tight spaces with a heel joint that bends laterally and backward (as well as forward)

to catch nestlings, roosting bats, and other prey to supplement its other favorite food—the fruits of oil palms. Studies of the Palila, a bird with a tenuous existence sadly typical of its Hawaiian honeycreeper tribe, show that 90 percent of its diet comes from the seeds and other parts of a single species of tree, the māmane. Some birds manage to find food in myriad ways. The comical Acorn Woodpecker's name gives away two of its foraging traits, consuming acorns and pecking wood for grubs. The specific epithet of its scientific name, *formicivorus*, describes another tactic—eating ants.

An African Harrier-Hawk in Kenya's Masai Mara Reserve uses its flexible jointed legs to probe into cavity nests as it hunts for fledglings of other birds to eat.

Dodo bird and guinea pig. Hand-colored print by George Edwards (published 1757)

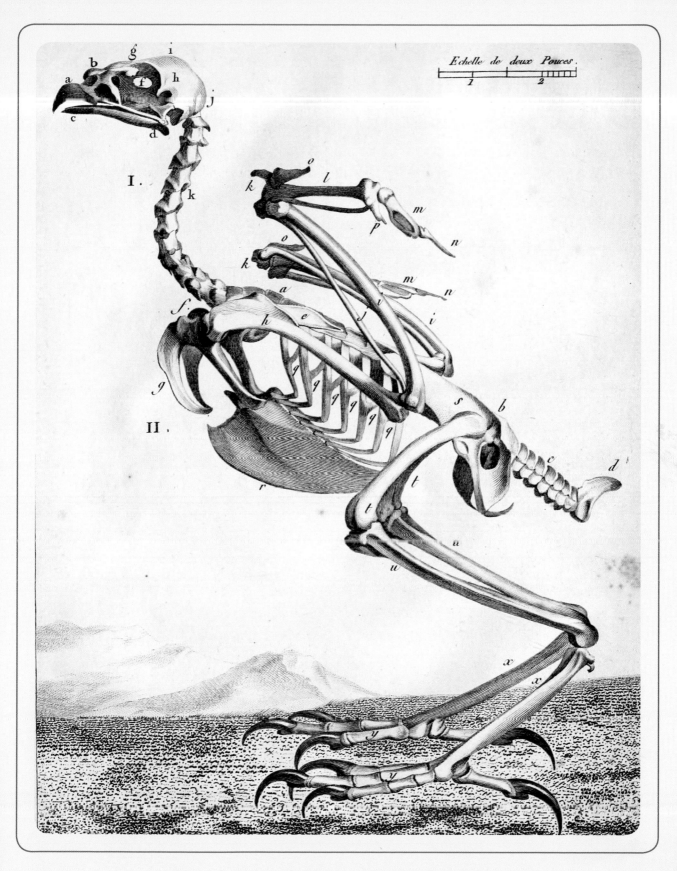

Skeleton of a falcon. Engraving by Jacques Barraband (published 1800)

THE SENSORY WORLD OF BIRDS

ON THE SAME WAVELENGTH

Why are we humans so fascinated by the wild birds around us? Why are there tens of millions of bird-watchers in the United States, while only a fraction of that number go out of their way to observe fish and mammals? The answer has much to do with how similar birds' and humans' sensory worlds—what the Germans term *umwelt*—really are. In short, we're pretty much on the same wavelength.

Birds hear and produce sounds in roughly the same range as humans do, and they communicate with visual signals using colors and patterns that we, too, can usually perceive. Like us, they de-emphasize smell (olfaction) as a key way of finding their way around their environment. We've got a lot more in common with a robin than a rat when it comes to the senses.

A KEEN EYE

Eyesight is supremely important to birds, and as you'd expect, their eyes have evolved in response to this need. They're big, for one thing. The eyes of an ostrich are larger than those of an elephant, and an examination of any bird skull shows the dominance of the eye sockets. The visual acuity of birds is due not only to their large eyes, but also to the dense concentration of visual cells on the retina. A *Buteo* hawk may have a million visual cone cells per a thousandth of a square

The male Yellow Weaver is named for the woven nests built by some members of the family.

inch on the most sensitive part of its retina, the fovea. Nature has bestowed a lot of megapixels on birds.

A bird never rolled its eyes at a birder who misidentified it. It can't, actually, since a bird's eyes are practically fixed within their sockets. But a bird can easily turn its head 180 degrees or more, and the visual field of most birds is far greater than ours—up

◆ **ATLANTIC PUFFIN** ◆

FRATERCULA ARCTICA: "Puffin" refers to the swollen or puffed-out appearance of its belly; this seabird occurs only in the North Atlantic. *Fratercula* is from the Latin, meaning "little brother" or "little friar"; *arctica* is an allusion to its northern range.

to 360 degrees and some even have binocular vision both in front and behind. The forward placement of the eyes in owls and bitterns increases the range of forward binocular vision, though it makes them unable to see behind them unless the head is turned.

Birds generally have excellent color vision, and many can perceive light in the near-ultraviolet range. Nectar and berry feeders might key in on ultraviolet signals, and researchers have shown that rodent-eating kestrels can gauge areas of high prey abundance by seeing the ultraviolet reflectivity of the urine that marks rodent scent trails. Bird irises are remarkably variable in color, from blackish to bright white and sometimes yellow, red, green, or blue. Iris color can vary by sex (yellow in adult female Bushtits but dark brown in all males) or age (a dark-eyed young Herring Gull won't develop its pale yellow iris until it is a year or two old). Even pupil shape can vary, being nicely round in most birds but vertical in skimmers. A ring of dark pigment around the pupil of a female Blue-footed Booby gives the impression of a pupil larger than the male's.

Easily recognized by the white tips on its blue crest, a Victoria Crowned-Pigeon fixes its red eye on the camera. This native of New Guinea was named for Queen Victoria of the United Kingdom and is easily tamed.

Short-eared Owl

THE LISTENING BIRD

Just as a bird-watcher quickly learns that detecting birds in many habitats is largely a matter of listening, birds augment their visual prowess with a lot of listening of their own. To detect potential mates, territorial intruders, alarm signals, predators, and even prey, a bird relies on its sense of hearing. The optimal hearing range of birds and humans is quite similar, in the range of 1,000 to 5,000 cycles per second. Of course birds can detect a much greater range of frequencies: Some can discern sound as low as ten or fewer cycles per second and as high as 29,000 cycles per second, though a given species will have a smaller range of audible frequencies. It is little surprise that most of the sounds birds make are within their optimal hearing range.

THE MUSIC OF BIRDSONG

MUSICAL REPRESENTATION OF THE SONG OF A WHITE-THROATED SPARROW

Birds make a variety of percussive and mechanical signals (think of a woodpecker's drum or the whistling of a goldeneye's wings), but their most frequent and complex sounds involve the wind instrument known as the syrinx. Located at or near the junction of the trachea and the two bronchi, the syrinx consists of muscles, cartilaginous rings, and membranes, and varies greatly in structure and placement among different groups of birds. Birds like storks and Turkey Vultures that can barely muster a hiss have poorly developed muscles around a simple syrinx. But in songbirds, the complex syrinx with numerous pairs of muscles yields much more complex vocalizations; some songbirds produce different sounds simultaneously in the bronchial portions of the syrinx. Syrinx function is further influenced by the air sac that surrounds it, and the sounds produced are amplified in the long windpipe.

The scoop face of the Barn Owl helps to funnel sound to its ear openings, placed near its eyes. The night hunter detects scurrying rodents at night by sound. Its typical call is a raspy, hissing screech.

The avian ear is much like that of mammals, though it lacks an elaborate external appendage and has only a single bone in the middle ear. Feathering over the ear openings (auriculars) helps to reduce interference from passing air as a bird flies and to keep water out in diving birds. In owls, the keenest listeners, facial feathers form a disk that helps gather sound, and the flaps of skin that rim the ear within this disk are expanded to funnel sound into the middle ear. Owl ear openings are also asymmetrical, with one "funnel" oriented slightly upward and the other slightly downward. Combined with the horizontal offset of the two ears, the effect is an ability to readily pinpoint a sound source in three dimensions.

Laboratory studies have confirmed a Barn Owl's ability to capture a mouse in clinical darkness by virtue of its supreme hearing. Some birds also have a crude echolocation system, detecting echoes from short sound clicks to navigate through dark caves, though these sounds are not in the ultrasound range used by bats. Certain swiftlets of Southeast Asia and the remarkable Oilbird of South America are echolocators, but unlike many bats they cannot locate and capture their food using echolocation.

OLFACTION & OTHER SENSES

It's not like a bird to sniff its way through its environment, relying on olfactory clues. Birds clearly have a poorer olfactory sense than that found in many organisms, including mammals such as rodents and carnivores. Even insects can be hypersensitive to the most diffuse chemical odors. Nevertheless, many birds have a serviceable sense of smell, and in a few bird groups olfaction is key to locating food and nest sites.

A keen seabirder learns that tube-nosed seabirds—storm-petrels, fulmars, shearwaters, and their relatives—have a distinctive musty smell. More than once a birder has sniffed out a stowaway petrel hiding on a boat. The fact that tubenoses give off a

O Nightingale, that on yon bloomy Spray
Warbl'st at eeve, when all the Woods are still,
Thou with fresh hope the Lovers heart dost fill…

LORD BYRON, "THE PRISONER OF CHILLON," 1816

scent might be a clue that they also detect smells better than the average bird. Experiments at sea have shown that fulmars and some other tubenoses will zigzag upwind and zero in on a point source of fish oil that is virtually invisible. Some storm-petrels and petrels might also use their keen olfaction to help locate their breeding colonies and nest sites within the colony. Kiwis use their well-developed sense of smell to locate earthworms and other prey in the forest floor litter of New Zealand, aided by external nostrils located near the tip of the long bill.

 LEARN MORE

THEY MAY BE UGLY, BUT THEY SURE SMELL WELL

We know from experimental studies that Turkey Vultures use their highly developed olfactory sense to locate rotting carcasses upon which they feed. Not surprisingly, the vultures' anatomy hints at this profound ability. The large transparent external nares, or nostril openings, are easily visible in the field; the nostril openings of the Turkey Vulture are larger than even those of the giant condors. Similarly, the olfactory lobe of the brain is far larger in the Turkey Vulture than in the condors or the Black Vulture, and the complex microanatomy of the olfactory chamber also hints at the vulture's extraordinary sense of smell. These anatomical adaptations are also found in the other two members of the Turkey Vulture's genus *Cathartes*: the Lesser and Greater Yellow-headed Vultures. The extraordinary King Vulture also seems to possess the anatomy to detect its food by smell, and indeed an enterprising field biologist in Costa Rica found that a King Vulture was able to find a dead sloth wrapped in a plastic bag and buried under two inches of forest leaf litter.

Rotting flesh is the food of choice for carrion feeders such as vultures. Some New World vultures, which are only distantly related to the vultures of Africa and Eurasia, locate carrion with their sense of smell. Chemicals emitted by rotting flesh include compounds very similar to the ethyl mercaptans used by gas companies to give an odor to otherwise undetectable natural gas. Not only have Turkey Vultures been shown in experiments to hone in on point sources of ethyl mercaptans as well as hidden rotting carcasses, they have even been used to locate leaks in natural gas pipelines.

The sense of touch, or mechanoreception, is of great importance to many birds. Birds are aided by sensitive corpuscles on the skin, tongue, and bill as well as by filoplumes—hairlike feathers that detect airflow and allow flying birds to make adjustments to the position of their flight feathers. Birds' ability to detect fine changes in atmospheric pressure helps them navigate their world. And increasingly, scientists are researching birds' ability to detect the properties of the Earth's magnetic field and to use this information in orientation and navigation.

Bird Brain

How common is the Common Sandpiper in North America? Not very. Almost half of the 23 birds on the North American checklist whose names start with "common" are, in fact, rarely seen here. Among the shorebirds, Common Greenshank, Common Redshank, Common Sandpiper, and Common Snipe are all vagrants from Europe or Asia.

A kiwi, New Zealand's iconic symbol, forages at night for worms, grubs, and insects. The chicken-size flightless kiwis—there are five species—lay eggs a fourth their weight and are the only birds with nostrils at the end of their long bills.

Soaring on rounded wings over a Florida wetland at dusk, a Snail Kite looks for its preferred meal of apple snails.
Excellent eyesight allows many birds of prey to see food from great distances and streak toward it.

A BRAIN BUILT FOR SPEED

The pejorative "bird brain" might just be a compliment, really. Since birds get around their environment differently than we do, their brains emphasize different functions, too. We can't pretend to understand everything that goes on in a bird's brain, but we can deduce which functions predominate by looking at the anatomy of the different regions of the brain.

The cerebral hemispheres of the forebrain lack the extreme development and folding of the human brain, and it isn't a stretch to posit that birds don't think very deep thoughts. The forebrain includes the olfactory lobes (variable in birds) and centers for learning, memory, and complex behavior. It's where the superior spatial memory shown by so many birds resides. The bird's relatively massive optic lobes reflect

◆ ROCK PIGEON ◆

COLUMBA LIVIA: "Pigeon" is from the Latin *pipio,* "young, chirping bird," and is echoic in origin. "Rock" refers to the rocky cliffs preferred by nesting wild birds (buildings replace cliffs for city pigeons). *Columba* is Latin for "dove or pigeon"; *livia* is Latin for "bluish," the hue of its plumage.

the importance of vision. Particularly well developed and hardworking is the cerebellum, governing rapid and complex muscle movements involved in flight, maneuverability, and rapid reactions.

In addition to demanding effective and redundant ways of sensing their environment and instantaneous reactions, a bird's high-speed lifestyle requires unfailing balance—controlled by the inner ear's semicircular canals. Taken together, the sensory and nervous systems of birds allow for remarkable abilities to analyze and react to their environments. Like us, birds rest their brains through sleep. Although bird sleep resembles that of humans in that deep sleep alternates with rapid eye movement sleep, birds spend much of their sleep time resting only one cerebral hemisphere: In essence, half the brain remains awake, and one eye stays open and vigilant.

Bird Brain

Famed choreographer Kenneth MacMillan's ballet *House of Birds* is based on a macabre Grimms' fairy tale. Other bird-theme ballets are Stravinsky's *Firebird;* *Swan Lake* by Tchaikovsky; and *The Dying Swan,* set to Saint-Saëns's "Le Cygne" from *Carnival of the Animals.*

Familiar worldwide, two Barn Swallows bicker in Bulgaria, although they are also found in Asia, Africa, and the Americas. Barn Swallows often build their cuplike nests of mud in barns, where their insect-eating habits make them welcome guests.

A Multitude of Avian Variations

EVOLUTION SHAPES THE BIRD

The long path to the development of the birds we see today began in earnest in the Jurassic period. Their reptilian progenitors evolved forelimbs that might have been suitable for maneuvering, capturing prey, gliding, and ultimately powered flight.

CONVERGENT EVOLUTION

Few testaments to the power of natural selection are more convincing than the concept of convergent evolution. Simply put, this concept says that simi-

The formidable bill of the Toucan seen in this 19th-century lithograph is mostly for picking fruit from small branches.

lar characteristics may evolve in unrelated groups of organisms that are shaped by selective pressures in similar environments.

Think of the similarities, for example, between filter-feeding whale sharks and huge filter-feeding baleen whales—highly modified mammals only some 50 million years removed from some hippo-like ancestor. Convergent evolution within birds is common and often striking. That this should be so evident is not surprising, as similar niches exist in different regions of the Earth that have different groups of dominant bird families, and components of those avifaunas have evolved characteristics similar to those of their counterparts elsewhere. The notion of convergent evolution is reinforced in some of the group names we apply to birds, such as flycatcher, warbler, honeycreeper, sparrow, and grosbeak. These names convey a general suite of adaptations, often related to foraging architecture and behavior, but are applied to only distantly related taxa, or taxonomic groups. For example, the birds called warblers—small, thin-billed insectivorous songbirds, only some of which actually warble—exist in nine different families of songbirds. Some of these families are closely related to one another, but others are quite distinct.

Another striking convergence involves the small, active iridescent nectar feeders of the New World (hummingbirds, whose closest relatives are the swifts) and Old World (sunbirds, which are songbirds). Although differences among the two groups

Honeycreeper vs. Sunbird

WHAT IS THE DIFFERENCE? These two species—a Shining Honeycreeper (left) and Greater Double-collared Sunbird (right)—share many structural similarities, but they are not closely related. The honeycreepers belong to the neotropical family of tanagers, and the sunbirds are a family found in tropical and subtropical areas of the Old World.

are great, particularly in flight apparatus and style, one can't help but be impressed by the superficial similarities in plumage and general structure when looking at a Purple-throated Carib (a hummingbird from the Lesser Antilles) and an Amethyst Sunbird from Africa. If something works, evolution will certainly repeat it in a new arena.

Another notable example of convergence is seen in the similar weaponry used by terrestrial hunting birds to catch animal prey. The strong grasping talons, sharp hooked bills, and other hunting adapta-tions found in the hawks and eagles of the family Accipitridae are largely repeated in the very distantly related falcons (Falconidae) and owls (Tytonidae and Strigidae).

Bird Brain

The War Hawks were a group of early 19th-century southern and western congressmen who urged the United States to go to war with Britain in 1812. In the mid-1960s, the hawks—supporters of the Vietnam War—and the doves—those who opposed the war—were embodiments of the social upheaval of that era.

ADAPTIVE RADIATIONS

Under the right conditions, evolution can proceed as if on steroids, molding a diverse array of organisms out of a single common ancestor. Nature's most effective and striking laboratories for this rapid evolution of diversity—what we call adaptive radiation—are island archipelagos, rife with opportunities for evolutionary divergence through isolation.

Most schoolchildren know of the radiation of "finches" (actually tanagers, as it turns out) on the Galápagos Islands, wherein a finchlike colonist became established, dispersed to other islands, evolved differences in isolation, and recolonized the original island having attained sufficient differences to be reproductively isolated from its ancestor. The process repeated, with diversity driven by different niches on the various islands, and this radiation resulted in a suite of some 14 species ranging from impressively billed ground finches to dainty warbler finches. The fame of these finches is Charles Darwin's legacy—but even more striking adaptive radiations can be found on the Hawaiian Islands and on Madagascar.

The Hawaiian birds in question were christened honeycreepers and given the family name Drepanididae. (Sadly, though we speak of them in the present tense, many are now extinct.) They show an amazing diversity of bill forms: stout, hooked, thin, curved, and so forth. They include hammerers, probers, nectar lappers, seed crushers, and even snail munchers. It had been well established that their progenitor was a finch from the family Carduelidae—and the Drepanididae have in fact been subsumed into that

The Iiwi, a common Hawaiian honeycreeper, lives in mountain forests and sips nectar from flowering trees.

family by taxonomists—but recent molecular sleuthing has suggested that a Common Rosefinch (an unassuming Eurasian bird) or one of its close relatives made that fateful journey some five and a half

Bird Brain

Ostrich meat has a flavor profile that's reminiscent of beef. This may be because both animals spend a lot of time walking and foraging, and eat lots of greenery. Ostrich eggs weigh three and a half to five pounds each. To soft boil a fresh egg would take about one hour.

million years ago to Kauai or Niihau, when those islands were in their infancy.

As tectonic forces spit out new islands from a deep-sea hot spot and inched them northwestward, opportunities for speciation abounded. Wet forests, dry woodlands, high forests, low woodlands—a diversity of habitats existed on the many tall, complex islands, laboratories for a burst of newly evolved taxonomic groups within a relatively short geological time period. Mai-tai sipping tourists in the lowland resorts of the Hawaiian Islands, surrounded by introduced birds and plants, are almost completely unaware of the archipelago's unique terrestrial birdlife and the tragic human-caused environmental changes that have lead to the extinction

of the majority of the 50 descendants of a long-ago wayward flock of rosefinches.

On the large, isolated Indian Ocean island of Madagascar another group of songbirds has undergone a similarly impressive adaptive radiation. Vangas (family Vangidae) have a lineage that appears to trace back to an ancestor from an Australasian group such as the butcherbirds or woodswallows rather than to birds on the nearer African continent. The 15 or so extant species show foraging behaviors and bills resembling those of shrikes, nuthatches, sallying flycatchers, or gleaning warblers; one hunts insects and lizards with a large swollen bill, and another probes woodpecker-style with a sickle-shaped bill.

A Helmet Vanga, found only in Madagascar and the Comoros, raises its distinctive bill above its nest. Most species of vangas are shrike-like with smaller hooked beaks and eat reptiles and frogs, but the Helmet Vanga feeds mostly on insects.

Coastal Sage Sparrow vs. Desert Sage Sparrow

WHAT IS THE DIFFERENCE? Two different Sage Sparrows—the coastal subspecies (left) and the desert interior subspecies (right)—show subtle but distinctive differences. The resident coastal birds are smaller, darker, and shorter-winged than their migratory desert relatives. Where the populations overlap, there is little evidence of hybridization. Studies may reveal that the Sage Sparrow group represents two or possibly three separate species.

ECOGEOGRAPHIC RULES

Adaptive radiations on the scale of the Hawaiian honey-creepers or Malagasy vangas are impressive, but the keen birder will notice variation even within species or among closely related species that still reflects adaptation to local environments. The Song Sparrow is one of the most familiar, widespread, and best studied of all North American birds, and its distinctive calls and song, which evokes Beethoven's Fifth Symphony, are recognizable throughout its range. But Song Sparrows in New York, Phoenix, San Francisco, and Anchorage look quite different from one another—their variation

Bird Brain

British author Ian Fleming was an avid bird-watcher who lived in Jamaica for a time. He had a copy of *The Birds of the West Indies* on his bookshelf and, in 1953, borrowed the name of its ornithologist-author, James Bond, for his intrepid spy protagonist. At a meeting in 1964, Fleming presented Bond with a first edition, signed, "To the real James Bond, from the thief of his identity."

in size, hue, and color saturation reflect evolutionary adjustments to these widely different environments. Song Sparrows on Alaska's Aleutian Islands are dark, dingy, and the size of a towhee. On the Pacific coast, they're still dark but more rufous and smaller overall. In the Colorado desert, they're remarkably pale and reddish. Over much of the rest of the continent they are distinctly streaked but vary subtly in color, size, and bill size. In many ways sparrows are the poster children for geographical variation.

Hail to thee, blithe spirit,
Bird thou never wert!
That from heaven or near it
Pourest thy full heart
In profuse strains of unpremeditated art.

PERCY BYSSHE SHELLEY, "TO A SKYLARK," 1820

The Sage Sparrow, a shrubland bird of western North America, is pale gray, large, and long-winged where it breeds in the northern Great Basin; it migrates to the southwestern deserts in winter. Resident populations in coastal California, in contrast, are smaller, shorter-winged, and much darker (see opposite). Fox Sparrows are also famously variable: reddish across the boreal regions, dark brown on the northwestern coast, and gray in the montane west—where some

A mosaic from an ancient Roman building celebrates an unknown bird perched amid foliage.

populations have small bills and others have large bills.

These variations often follow predictable ecogeographic "rules." It is generally, though hardly universally, true that individuals at high latitudes tend to be larger and have shorter extremities than their relatives at lower latitudes. Similarly, those residing in humid regions tend to be darker than their arid-land cousins. Migratory populations often have relatively longer wings or more pointed wing tips than sedentary ones, even within a species. The sedentary Tropical Pewee, for example, is readily differentiated from the highly migratory Eastern and Western Wood-Pewees by its much shorter wing tips.

◆ **ALLEN'S HUMMINGBIRD** ◆

SELASPHORUS SASIN: "Hummingbird" refers to the sound made by the bird's wings. "Allen's" is for Charles Andrew Allen (1841–1930), an ornithologist who collected birds. *Selasphorus* comes from the Greek for "light bearing," describing the bird's plumage; *sasin* is from the Nootka Indian word for this bird.

CONFUSING THE TAXONOMISTS

Those who watch birds can be frustrated when taxonomists—those scientists who tease apart the evolutionary relationships of organisms and then classify and name them appropriately—fail to settle on a fixed set of bird names. Bird lists are always being adjusted as species are split or grouped, family assignments are reconsidered, and scientific binomials, which are supposed to be stable monikers, change with each transfer of a species from genus to genus.

These reshufflings really are neither cruel jokes played on birders by bespectacled feather counters nor a way for ornithologists to entertain themselves.

A painting shows Snow Buntings (bottom two), Lapland Longspurs (middle two), and Lark Buntings (top).

Instead, they reflect both the confounding effects of evolutionary intermediacy—trying to pigeonhole taxa into defined categories when evolution and speciation are slow, haphazard processes—and the flourishing new technologies and intellectual frameworks brought to bear in modern taxonomy. Early taxonomists scrutinized morphological characteristics that could be examined and measured on skins and skeletons as well as in "pickled" specimens that preserved soft tissues. Rarely were these workers familiar with a species when it was alive. In contrast, modern taxonomists meld evidence from morphologists' detailed and valuable work together with information on behavior and vocalizations gained from observing the living bird. For decades now—and with increasing sophistication each year—taxonomists have also used molecular data to examine the genetic relationships of birds. Today, DNA can be sequenced not only from freshly collected specimens and preserved tissue samples, but also from molted feathers, blood samples, and often tiny bits of material from old specimens, bones, and eggshells. This wealth of information has corroborated many relationships postulated long ago from anatomical data, even as it has called other traditional taxonomic treatments into question.

Some closely similar groups now turn out to be only distantly related, their likenesses a result of evolutionary convergence. For example, longspurs, which appear sparrowlike, have proved to be quite distinct from the North American sparrows and Old World buntings with whom they were always classified within the family Emberizidae. It also turns out that morphologically divergent groups can have a

Collections of bird study skins, such as these buntings at California's Western Foundation of Vertebrate Zoology, are invaluable to ornithologists studying taxonomy. Each specimen is labeled with data on where and when it was collected.

closer relationship than predicted by appearances. The recently extinct Bishop's 'Ō'ō of Kauai and its close relatives in the genus *Moho,* also extinct, were thought to be honeyeaters from the Meliphagidae family, implying a colonization of the Hawaiian Islands from Australasia. With their black-and-yellow plumage, curved and probing bills, tubular tongues, and overall shape, they certainly resembled many honeyeaters; but recent genetic work suggests they are in fact relatives of the quite dissimilar silky-flycatchers and waxwings—shifting our understanding of their biogeographic history to a Northern Hemisphere and perhaps even New World origin. Modern analyses also seem to confirm a relationship between two groups of waterbirds that could hardly look more different from one another—the grebes and the flamingos.

◆ **LEWIS'S WOODPECKER** ◆

MELANERPES LEWIS: "Woodpecker" came to be the name for obvious reasons. "Lewis's" is for Captain Meriwether Lewis (1774–1809) of the Lewis and Clark Expedition, who collected the first specimen in 1805. *Melanerpes* is coined from the Greek *melas* ("black") and *herpes* ("creeper").

Rhinoceros Hornbill of Southeast Asia. Hand-colored print by Johannes G. Keulemans (published 1882)

CHAPTER TWO

BIRDS THROUGH THE AGES

Catherine Herbert Howell

A miniature of a 17th-century falcon resides in a museum of Asiatic art in Paris.

FLYING THROUGH TIME

BIRDS AS WORLDVIEW

From our earliest days, humankind has contemplated the nature of the bird. Birds hold close so many secrets, from the sorcery of flight to the mystery of migration. Precisely what early humans thought about birds is not known, but their fascination is evident in the depictions of birds that appear in the oldest prehistoric art.

THROUGHOUT ANCIENT CULTURES

The walls of the Lascaux Cave from the Upper Paleolithic period in southwestern France include the image of a bird-headed man as well as a drawing of a bird on a stick. Neither bird is recognizable as a species,

although it has been suggested that the man might be masked, like a shaman. An even older cave in Chauvet-Pont-d'Arc, dating back some 30,000 years, contains the carving of an owl in soft rock near the entrance. With its pronounced ear tufts, it appears similar to the Eurasian Eagle-Owl. The recent discovery of a rock painting in northern Australia depicts what may be the giant bird *Genyornis,* which became extinct some 40,000 years ago. Verification of that particular subject and the date would make this painting the oldest known example of a bird in art.

Figural representations of bird-headed women appear throughout Europe—a variation of the small

This pendant of a falcon decorated with semiprecious stones and colored glass was found in the Egyptian tomb of Tutankhamun.

An unidentified feathered flier carved into stone raises its wings on a rock wall at Petroglyph National Monument near Albuquerque, New Mexico. The scene indicates that prehistoric humans had a relationship with birds.

female forms with exaggerated sexual characteristics known as fertility figures. Many archaeologists attribute them to a mother-goddess tradition. Later, Celtic culture would span an even larger area of Europe, bringing with it art that incorporated bird images into intricate designs. Among the many birds that figured in Celtic lore was the wren, which lived in close association with humans. The parade of costumed wren boys, young men who sing from house to house in Ireland on the day following Christmas, derives from a Celtic tradition in which a wren was hunted and captured to bring good luck in the new year.

◆ LOGGERHEAD SHRIKE ◆

LANIUS LUDOVICIANUS: "Shrike" refers to a bird with a shrill call. "Loggerhead" means "large or block-headed." *Lanius* is Latin for "butcher," an allusion to how the shrike impales its prey on a thorn before dismembering it; *ludovicianus* is a Latinized reference to Louisiana and this species' southerly range.

Lesser Spotted Eagle

IN THE EARLY AMERICAS

Groups of people from Siberia traveled over a land bridge connected to North America and began to populate the Americas perhaps as many as 20,000 years ago. Over time they kept moving on, reaching all the way to the tip of South America. What we now regard as the native cultures of North and South America took different forms based on environmental and existential concerns, but a number of mythologies united large areas. Many of these, not surprisingly, involved birds.

The thunderbird, a supernatural megabird based on the eagle or vulture, occurs in Native American myth and art from the Pacific Northwest to the Great Plains to the eastern woodlands. Considered the messenger of the Great Spirit, the thunderbird flapped its monstrous wings, creating thunder, and shot bolts of lightning from its eyes or flung lightning snakes from its talons as it flew. Representations of the thunderbird appear remarkably standardized—with head often in profile and wings outstretched—and are found in art forms from petroglyphs to pottery. The raven also captivated the minds of ancient Americans. Like the thunderbird, it is seen in cultural artifacts over much of the continent. Native American mythology celebrates the raven as a trickster figure, like the coyote—one who often manipulates events for selfish ends. In one prominent story, the raven insinuates himself into the life of an old man and his daughter so

A winged thunderbird tops a totem pole in Vancouver, British Columbia. Birds ranked high in Native American cultures.

A Bald Eagle screams, showing the hooked upper mandible that tears apart prey. The symbol of the United States is not really bald; the older meaning of the word is "white-headed."

that he can steal the light the man has locked up in a box and illuminate the world. Pacific Northwest groups took raven imagery to great heights, literally, in the construction of totem poles. Raven figures appeared prominently on these poles, especially those of the raven clan, and on accessories used in rituals, such a rattles, and they continue to be seen in native artwork to this day.

Eagles also held great significance throughout the Americas. In North America the Golden Eagle stood for war. Its feathers often decorated weapons, and its claws were considered potent charms. Eagle feathers conferred great status when worn as personal adornment. The traditional feathered bonnets of the Plains tribes, which displayed feathers that were added for individual feats of bravery or merit, adorned the heads of warriors and chiefs. Bonnets typically were works in progress that grew fuller and longer along with an individual's status.

Birds permeated the myths and cultures of ancient Mesoamerican cultures as well, with a good deal of overlap with the species honored in North America. A Golden Eagle figured in the founding myth of the

Aztec city Tenochtitlan, which rose in 1325 in what is now Mexico City. The Aztec, or Mexica, people stopped their search for a capital when they found a spot where an eagle sat atop a cactus devouring a snake in the middle of a lake. Today, this event features prominently on Mexico's official seal. The Aztecs also sacrificed Golden Eagles. In a 2006 discovery, buried eagles formed the top layer of offerings to the goddess Tlaltecuhtli in the excavation of a monolith at the Aztec Templo Mayor site in Mexico City.

On the journey to their new capital, the Mexica were led by another of their sacred birds, the god Huitzilopochtli (which means "left-handed hummingbird" or "hummingbird of the left"), who became the capital city's patron. Farther east, in the Maya city of Chichén Itzá, carvings of Harpy Eagles, an enormous species with an eight-foot wingspan, appear along the panels skirting the Platform of the Eagles on El Castillo, or The Castle. Aztec and Maya both revered the Resplendent Quetzal, associated with the feathered serpent-god Quetzalcoatl. Its exquisite iridescent tail plumes adorned the headdresses and capes of the cultures' elite. These groups used the hummingbird for

The figure of a bird sewn into cotton dominates a mola, *which adorns blouses of the Cuna women of Panama and Colombia.*

A male Resplendent Quetzal peers from its nest in a hollow tree in Guatemala. The weak flier, known for its colorful plumage, is the national bird of Guatemala and was considered divine by pre-Columbian civilizations.

adornment as well, fashioning capes from its feathers and ornamenting ears and hats with entire birds. Every culture around the world has responded to the presence of birds through sacred practices, art, myth, or folklore. And each has attempted classification of local birdlife based on observation and cultural criteria.

At times these indigenous systems varied widely with scientific classification, and at others they were spot-on. Ornithologists exploring a remote New Guinea mountain area learned that native peoples there classified their birdlife into 137 species. When the ornithologists did their own scientific survey, they came up with 138.

◆ BELL'S VIREO ◆

VIREO BELLII: "Vireo" derives from the Latin *vivere*, "to be green"; olive green is the predominant color of most vireos. "Bell's" is for John Graham Bell (1812–1889), a taxidermist and close friend of Audubon, who collected several new species in California. The scientific name mirrors the English name.

IN THE FIRST CIVILIZATIONS

Early civilizations in the Old World further elaborated the mythic and symbolic roles of birds. A terra-cotta plaque known as the Burney Relief was found randomly in Iraq, not associated with any known archaeological site, and resides now in the British Museum. Up to 4,000 years old, the high relief shows a winged goddess with legs ending in raptor claws, flanked by two owls. The figure may depict a known Sumerian goddess or even Lilith, the demoness from Jewish folklore, who took on an identity as Adam's first wife, made from muck and debris at the time of Adam's creation. From a slightly older period, the ancient Sumerian text *The Epic of*

Gilgamesh recounts a creation story—similar to that found in Genesis—of the birds sent out to find dry land following the great flood. In the Bible a raven flies out first, followed by a dove. In the Gilgamesh account, the dove precedes a swallow. The similarities attest to the millennia of cross-cultural influences that define the Middle East.

The ancient Egyptians' worldview was populated with mythological, symbolic, and sacred birds. Worship of the falcon-headed god Horus reaches far back in time, predating even the pharaohs. Considered god of the sky and of war, Horus was the son of Osiris and Isis, who avenged his father's murder by the desert god Set. Horus also symbolizes the unification of Upper

A mosaic from Kom El-Dikka in Alexandria, Egypt, features a bird amid a geometric design. The Roman site includes an ancient villa with well-preserved animal mosaics.

BIRDS AS WORDS

EGYPTIAN HIEROGLYPHICS

Bird images played an important role in the ancient Egyptian writing system known as hieroglyphics. The use of hieroglyphs (sacred carvings, from the Greek) dates back some 5,000 years, but by the Greco-Roman period in Egypt it was used mostly on buildings and monuments. The characters were not pictograms (what you see is what you get) or ideograms (symbolic representations), but a combination of ideograms and phonograms (representations of sounds). It required knowledge of hundreds of different hieroglyphs to read and write the language. At least 14 different birds are represented in the hieroglyphic system as phonograms, ideograms, and determinatives. They include two different vultures, a buzzard, an owl, three ibises, a cormorant, a swallow, a sparrow, a goose, standing and flying ducks, and a quail chick.

and Lower Egypt and wears the pharaonic double crown. His image appears everywhere, and the heads of his sons top the canopic jars that store the preserved organs of mummified individuals. Real falcons got the royal treatment after death; hundreds of thousands of linen-wrapped falcon mummies have been found at Egyptian burial sites. But even these great numbers of falcons represent a fraction of the millions of mummified ibises—symbolic of Thoth, the god of wisdom—that were prepared for the afterlife.

◆ **WHITE-BREASTED NUTHATCH** ◆

SITTA CAROLINENSIS: "Nuthatch" refers to the bird's technique of wedging a nut or seed into a crevice and hacking (or hatching) it open. *Sitta* is from the Greek for a bark-pecking bird; *carolinensis,* "from Carolina," refers to where the first specimen was obtained.

Eurasian Hoopoe

AMONG THE GREEKS & ROMANS

Birds of land and sea are ubiquitous on the labyrinthine islands forming the Greek archipelago. Not surprisingly, the most ancient cultures there incorporated birds into their rituals and art. The bird-goddess traditions of prehistoric Europe emerged similarly in the Minoan culture on the island of Crete, beginning some four millennia ago. The bird-goddess took form on vases and plates and as votive figurines.

Fabulous birds flourished in the culture as well. The Greeks gave name and form to the mythology of the phoenix as well as the Stymphalian birds—those man-eaters thought to populate a lake in Arcadia in central Greece. Heracles destroyed them in his sixth labor, as depicted on a painted amphora from the sixth century B.C. And last, but not least, is the Little Owl, whose delicate, wide-eyed features came to represent Athens in its Golden Age.

While the Romans did not view all birds in a good light, they viewed birds in general as essential to human happiness. In their estimation, a world without birds was considered a bleak and cheerless place. They took this concept to the extreme in calling the underworld Avernus, which came from a Greek word meaning "without birds." Avernus originally referred

THE PARADOXICAL OWL: GOOD OR EVIL?

World cultures typically regard the owl in love-hate terms: Either they accord it respect as a figure of wisdom and benevolence, or they fear it as a dark and sinister force.

Ancient Egyptians equated the owl with death. When the pharaoh wanted to give a pink slip to an underperforming minister, he would pass along the image of an owl, with the expectation that the recipient would dutifully dispatch himself. The Romans were also leery of the owl, associating it with death and the work of witches. By tradition, the hoot of an owl foretold the deaths of Julius Caesar and Augustus.

The Greeks weighed in on the other side of the coin—literally. They revered the owl, a favored companion of Athena, goddess of wisdom. They even put the bird on the reverse side of their coins (Athena was on the obverse), which became known as "owls."

Native American groups also had varied views of the owl. The Apache associated it with death, whereas the Inuit looked to it for guidance. The Hopi saw the Burrowing Owl as the keeper of the underworld, helping souls navigate death—known as "crossing the owls' bridge."

ATHENA AND HER OWL

Heracles, known as Hercules to the Romans and to today's Western world, shoots waterfowl with a slingshot in this painting on an ancient Greek vase. Defeating the mythic Stymphalian Birds was the sixth Labor of Heracles.

to a lake west of Naples believed to emit toxic fumes that killed any birds flying over it. In time, Avernus came to be synonymous with Hades.

The nature of birds also significantly influenced Roman institutions. Quite aware that cocks crow well before dawn, Romans called the third division of the night, commencing around 3 a.m., the *gallicinium*—which translates as "of the cocks." Like other ancient cultures, the Romans regarded the eagle as epitomizing characteristics of strength and power, and they appropriated it to proclaim the strength of their state and empire. Around the first century B.C., the Roman

military adopted the eagle as the emblem on their imperial standard. A pole bearing a bronze or gilt spread-winged eagle was carried into battle by every Roman legion.

This practice fixed the eagle in military, national, and imperial iconology from that point on. Charlemagne took the eagle as the symbol for his shield some nine centuries later, and the bird appeared in a nationalistic or imperial capacity all over Europe. The Bald Eagle, having won the right to be called the national bird, emblazons the Great Seal of the United States.

Partridges. Woodblock print commissioned by Japanese official Seki Mitsubumi (published 1790)

鷓
鴣

Birds Sacred & Profane

FEATHERED MYTHS & LEGENDS

In many mythologies, gods and goddesses take on associations with different birds that symbolize their powers or do their bidding. Roman and Greek mythologies, which share many personnel and plot lines, are replete with these connections.

MYTHS TAKE WING

The rooster, for example, is associated with the Greek and Roman god Apollo in one of his many roles—as sun god. The connection extends to Apollo's son Asclepius, the god of medicine. At times of serious illness it was considered prudent to sacrifice a cock to Asclepius, as Socrates reputedly acknowledged on his deathbed: "We owe Asclepius a cock." Zeus's bird was the eagle, which often carried out his justice. One of the eagle's tasks was to catch thunderbolts hurled at the god by his enemies. An eagle also performed the punishment that Zeus imposed on Prometheus for stealing fire from heaven—being chained to a rock and having his liver pecked at for eternity.

Goddesses had their bird associates as well. For example, the goose is sacred to Aphrodite, the Greek

Emblems of Thailand, golden effigies of the winged deity Garuda guard a temple in Bangkok. Leaders of the Ayutthaya Kingdom—which dominated Southeast Asia for more than four centuries—considered Garuda the symbol of their power.

Japanese Cranes: Folded Birds of Hope

For the Japanese, the graceful courtship of the Red-crowned Crane and its habit of mating for life have made the bird the ultimate symbol of marriage, fidelity, and longevity. Magnificent crane designs often are woven into traditional wedding kimonos, and crane motifs appear in Japanese art. The crane more generally represents prosperity and in recent centuries has become a universal symbol of peace. Recently, the tradition of creating a thousand origami (folded paper) cranes to ensure fulfillment of a wish has been renewed in a global show of support for earthquake victims in Haiti and Japan.

Japanese folklore features the story of the crane wife, part of a universal folktale pattern of enchanted, shape-shifting wives. In the Japanese version, not long after a man nurses an injured crane back to health, a beautiful woman comes into his life. He marries her and she begins to weave beautiful cloth

ORIGAMI CRANE

for him to sell. At the start, the wife exacts a promise that he never will watch her weave. He agrees, but curiosity ultimately gets the better of him and he spies on her, only to learn that his wife is a crane who plucks her own feathers to use in the beautiful weavings. The promise broken, the crane wife flies off, leaving the man with nothing.

goddess of love, and to Juno, the Roman goddess of marriage. In both cases it served as a symbol of fertility.

In a well-known myth, Zeus even took the form of a bird to seduce the wife of the king of Sparta. Zeus desired Leda, and to get his way he became a swan who visited her the same night she had been with her husband. From the two unions came four children: the beautiful Helen, over whom the Trojan War would be fought; twins Castor and Pollux, destined to become stars in the constellation Gemini; and Clytemnestra, who became the wife of King Agamemnon.

In the Hindu-based mythologies of South and Southeast Asia, there is the tradition of the *vāhana*. The word translates as "vehicle," and often a god or goddess associated with a particular bird or other

animal is depicted riding on its back. But the vāhana also symbolizes the deity more directly, and some vāhanas have mythological histories suggesting they were once considered deities in their own right. Bird vāhanas include Garuda, the eagle that serves Vishnu, one of the three deities of the Hindu trinity; the owl-associate of Lakshmi, the goddess of prosperity and wisdom; and the peacock that represents Saraswati, goddess of knowledge, the arts, and music.

Norse myth tells of a pair of ravens, favorites of the warrior-god Odin. Every day Odin dispatched the birds Huginn (thought) and Muninn (memory) to the corners of the world to pick up information. When they returned each evening, the birds perched on Odin's shoulders and whispered their findings into his ear.

THE GREATEST BIRD THAT NEVER LIVED

Ancient cultures from Egypt to China embraced the notion of a vividly colored bird with flaming gold-and-scarlet tail feathers, which lived for 500 or 1,000 years before building a nest of twigs that it set on fire—only to emerge reborn from the ashes. In some versions, it then fashioned the ashes into a sacred egg that it flew to the Egyptian city of Heliopolis, to be deposited with the sun god there.

Only one such bird existed at any one time, adding to its mystique. This was the phoenix, whose back-

Ubi aves, ibi angeli—
Where there are birds, there are angels.

THOMAS AQUINAS (1225–1274)

story so intrigued the ancient world that it blurred the boundary between myth and reality.

As with today's spottings of Sasquatch or the Loch Ness Monster, reports of phoenix sightings were commonplace. Herodotus acknowledged never having seen the bird himself, but wrote with great certainty of its habits, as did the Roman poet Ovid: "They do not live on flowers and fruit but on frankincense and odiferous resins."

Christianity wholly embraced the phoenix as a symbol of the resurrection. Clement, a first-century

Mythical bird that never dies, a phoenix rises from flames in a medieval book about real and imaginary animals.

pope, firmed up the connection in his First Epistle, guaranteeing it prominence in art and literature going forward into the Renaissance. Modern writers such as C. S. Lewis and J. K. Rowling incorporated it in their own myth-building. In Rowling's Harry Potter series, Fawkes the phoenix ferries young heroes out of dire situations and heals them with his tears. His name references rebel Guy Fawkes, whose plot to blow up the Houses of Parliament in 1605 is celebrated annually with bonfires and fireworks—a nod to the phoenix's pyrotechnic (temporary) end.

Cities, countries, and institutions rebuilt after fire or other discontinuities often choose the name or

◆ BUSHTIT ◆

PSALTRIPARUS MINIMUS: "Bushtit" is a combination of "tit" for a small animal or object and "bush," the species' preferred habitat. *Psaltriparus* is a combined term: *Psaltria* means "one who plays the lute" and *parus* is Latin for "titmouse"—the result is hard to fathom; *minimus* is Latin for "smallest."

symbol of the phoenix for their relaunch. Among countless examples, Phoenix, Arizona, rose on the remains of the indigenous Hohokam culture; Atlanta adopted the phoenix after its Civil War conflagration; and the Greeks reconnected with the bird for their modern independence movement.

Bird Brain

Bird names often contain helpful color clues, like red, yellow, and brown. Lesser known color terms include ferruginous = rust-colored; cerulean = azure blue; fulvous = yellowish brown; glaucous = pale bluish gray; hepatic = dull red; plumbeous = gray or lead-colored; and rufous = bright reddish brown.

Popular in mythologies of Arabs, Persians, Greeks, Romans, Egyptians, Chinese, and Phoenicians, the phoenix is a mythical firebird that arises from its own ashes. Its cry is said to be a beautiful song.

A wicked queen forces 11 brothers whom she has turned into swans to fly away in this watercolor of a tale by Hans Christian Andersen. "The Wild Swans" ends happily, as did most stories by the 19th-century Danish writer.

ONCE UPON A BIRD

Many folkloric bird characters have ancient lineages, and the motifs of their tales are found over a large region. Northern European cultures share many folkloric traditions, one being the notion of enchanted swan maidens. Details differ, but in most tales the swan maidens go to a lake to bathe, where they take off the cloaks or other garments that transform them into swans. Then a hunter spies on the maidens and steals a garment to keep one from changing back into a swan after her bath. He hides the cloak, marries her, and they have children. A lingering remembrance of her true nature remains with her, until one day she finds her swan cloak—often with the help of her children—dons it and flies off. A variant of this tale forms the basis of the celebrated ballet *Swan Lake*.

Fairy tales differ from folktales in certain ways. A fairy tale usually comes from a literary tradition and

◆ **AMERICAN ROBIN** ◆

TURDUS MIGRATORIUS: "Robin" (a diminutive form of Robert) is the English name for a common European songbird, which is similar in coloration to the American Robin. *Turdus* is a Latin word meaning "thrush"; *migratorius* comes from the Latin *migro,* meaning "moving from one place to another."

can often be traced to a single author. While they frequently are crafted on characters or motifs from folklore, fairy tales at times are just a figment of the author's imagination. Hans Christian Andersen's "The Ugly Duckling" falls into this category: It is believed to be his creation. More than that, Andersen sometimes referred to it as his autobiography. An awkward man from a poor background, Andersen sought constant validation from the upper reaches of Danish society. When his books became extremely popular, he had the wealth to climb the social ladder, although unlike the duckling, his appearance did not improve.

German brothers Jacob and Wilhelm Grimm published tales they collected on trips into the countryside. Bird motifs ran through many of these stories, often with an element of enchantment. Frustrated parents and evil stepmothers uttered curses that transformed young men into swans or ravens. In one tale, "Jorinda and Joringel," a witch turns every maiden that comes her way into a bird, until she accumulates 7,000 of them in cages. Joringel, the hero, finds the witch's hut and restores his sweetheart Jorinda, an enchanted nightingale, and all the other birds back into maidens.

THE MORAL OF THE STORY

The fable is a type of instructive tale featuring anthropomorphic animals instead of humans, who nevertheless display human foibles. A fable often sums itself up with a catchy maxim at the end, but at times it is left to the audience to figure out the lesson.

Aesop's fables, well known in the Western world, are attributed to a Greek writer thought to have lived in the sixth century B.C. About a third of Aesop's 500 fables feature a bird character or characters. One of the best known is "The Crow and the Pitcher," in which a thirsty crow figures out that he can raise the water in a pitcher by throwing in stones.

A famous fable tradition featuring birds came out of India. The Panchatantra (five principles or doctrines) are attributed to a second-century B.C. Hindu writer and designed to instruct princely brothers in morality and statecraft. "Of Crows and Owls," one of the five sections, expands on the themes of war and peace through the skirmishes of the two enemy groups.

AESOP'S FABLE, THE FOX AND THE CROW

BIRDS FOR WORK & PLAY

MEETING HUMAN NEEDS

As soon as humans became hunters, birds became part of their quarry. Birds on the ground, on the wing, on the sea, and in the nest were stalked, killed, and gathered up for food using a variety of techniques throughout the ages.

HUNTING FOR FOOD & SPORT

An action as simple as throwing a rock could stun, if not kill, a bird. A rock on either end of a string, similar to the Argentine cowboy's bola, could wrap around a large bird's neck and bring it down. A solid launch of a spear or a dart-chucking device known as an atlatl also accomplished the goal, as did true aim with a bow and arrow. Early bird hunters hunted for subsistence. Waterfowl and game birds such as pheasants and grouse—as well as wading birds and large, flightless species—were taken not only for their meat, but also for all the useful products found

Hunting coots and other waterfowl is central to this 17th-century painting in a pastoral setting of the Flemish School.

THE ART OF DUCK HUNTING

To hunt waterfowl in the United States, you need to buy an annual stamp featuring fabulous waterfowl art; the proceeds from stamp sales go to the conservation of waterfowl habitat, so that current and future generations can hunt more waterfowl. The stamps cannot be used for postage.

This is all part of a program managed by the U.S. Fish and Wildlife Service, which sponsors an annual art contest to pick a standout image to go on each year's stamp. The best wildlife artists in the country, many of them also avid hunters, vie for the chance to be a winner by submitting their paintings of waterfowl. Some winners have won in multiple years. Winning can also run in families: The Hautman brothers of Minnesota have won among themselves a total of ten Federal Duck Stamp contests.

Any licensed hunter older than 16 needs to have a current federal stamp, which serves as a hunting license

THE FIRST FEDERAL DUCK STAMP (1934), ARTWORK BY J. N. "DING" DARLING

and currently sells for $15. The stamp can be used for free admission to any national refuge. The program raises about $25 million a year for the Migratory Bird Conservation Fund, which purchases acres of wetlands to enlarge the National Wildlife Refuge System.

---

on their bodies, including feathers, skin, down, bones, and sinew.

As agriculture developed around the world, assuring a more consistent food supply, the hunting of birds tended to become more of a sport, often the privilege of royalty or aristocracy. At the least, the hunting of certain species, such as swans, often became a royal prerogative. Modern bird-hunting began with the appearance of the shotgun in the 17th century. It was far more efficient to fire a load of shot at a rising flock than to release only a single projectile. This is what the

"shoot to study" naturalists did for centuries, using fine shot to cause minimal damage to the specimens.

Hunters often take specialized bird dogs with them on the hunt. Some breeds excel at finding downed birds, others at retrieving them. Breeders work on developing traits such as a "soft" mouth in a retriever, which means the dog will carry the bird lightly, avoiding further damage. The charming habit of many golden retrievers to walk around with a stuffed toy loosely clenched in their jaws displays this selected trait.

◆ BENDIRE'S THRASHER ◆

TOXOSTOMA BENDIREI: "Thrasher" probably derives from "thrush," not "thrash." "Bendire's" is for Charles Emil Bendire (1836–1889), an officer in the United States Army who discovered this species. *Toxostoma* was coined from the Greek *toxon* ("bow") and *stoma* ("mouth"), a reference to the thrasher's curved bill.

FANCY FALCONRY

Few sights are as thrilling as watching a magnificent raptor climb thousands of feet into the air and then drop like a bullet in a controlled dive, or stoop, to catch its prey in midair—a feat that Peregrine and other falcons perform with effortless aplomb. When they do so under the direction of a human handler, who releases the falcon and summons it back on command, they are part of one of the many ancient rituals that make up the sport of falconry.

Falconry was practiced thousands of years ago in Egypt, the Middle East, and Asia. Raptors other than falcons were also used. In Central Asia, handlers released Golden Eagles to take down antelope on the

And the raven, never flitting,
still is sitting, still is sitting
On the pallid bust of Pallas just above
my chamber door.

EDGAR ALLAN POE, "THE RAVEN," 1845

A falcon in this 17th-century painting wears a cord called a halsband, which steadies the bird when launched.

ground. Falconry, a sport of kings and aristocrats, was expensive: There were birds to procure and train, handlers to work with them, and all the custom equipment necessary for both bird and falconer. In Europe, a general hierarchy emerged around who hunted with which bird. The king was accorded the Gyrfalcon, the prince a Peregrine, and so forth, down to the yeoman with his Goshawk and the servant with the lowly Kestrel. Women could hunt larks with a ladyhawk, the delicate Merlin.

In the 13th century, Holy Roman Emperor Frederick II of Hohenstaufen wrote a comprehensive treatise on falconry called *De arte venandi cum avibus (The Art of Hunting with Birds)*. Hailed as a masterwork when discovered by ornithologists centuries

Bird Brain

Escaping from a tough eggshell can be quite a struggle. Baby birds have evolved a neat solution: They grow an egg tooth near the tip of their bill. It's not a true tooth—birds don't have teeth—but a hardened, upward-facing point of bony material that falls off soon after hatching.

Snow Bunting

later, it describes the sport in great detail and also contains astute observations of bird behavior based on the author's lifetime of experience.

Falconry still enjoys a wide popularity in different parts of the world, including the United States, within the confines of laws designed to protect both predator and prey. The sport is highly regulated in one of its ancient strongholds, the United Arab Emirates, to give the populations of both Peregrine and Saker Falcons time to recover from migratory disruption, habitat destruction, and pesticide use. The regulations also protect their typical prey, the Houbara Bustard, an endangered desert species.

Falconry exposes captive birds to a significant amount of wear and tear, and communicable diseases. Since opening in 1999, the Abu Dhabi Falconry Hospital has treated tens of thousands of birds in a state-of-the-art facility that outshines human health care in many parts of the world. In Britain, modern falconers get called in to fly their Harris's Hawks at the pigeons of Trafalgar Square on a regular basis. The goal is not to take out the pigeons (although occasionally an unexpected catch occurs), but to encourage pigeons to seek handouts elsewhere and leave Lord Nelson in peace on his column.

Aerial ambush: A wild Peregrine Falcon nabs a Willet, a stocky shorebird, near La Jolla, California.
The piercing talons of a bird of prey kill more often than its hooked beak.

Domestic chickens forage in the outdoors in Wiltshire, England. Domestication of birds and the advent of firearms turned falconry into a sport instead of the subsistence role it once had.

BIRDS ON A PLATE

From the first wild bird taken down by a hunter to plastic-wrapped trays of factory-raised chicken, birds have always been part of the human diet. Which kinds of birds and which parts of those birds are considered palatable is a product of culture, economy, and now conservation. The ubiquitous barnyard chicken descends from the Red Junglefowl of Southeast Asia, which was domesticated about 8,000 years ago. It is kept throughout the world for its meat and eggs, although from the start its combative nature was encouraged in cockfighting.

European explorers became excited about the culinary possibilities of North American wild turkeys and brought them back home, probably in the 16th century. Confused with the guineafowl—known as the turkey fowl in Europe—this New World species became known as the turkey. Today, as is increasingly the case with chickens, many people are beginning to prefer a more flavorful, free-range variety of turkey—closer in taste to the wild form than to a factory-raised, broad-breasted behemoth—for their holiday bird.

In ancient Greece and Rome, individuals who wished to improve their singing voices consumed the tongues of songbirds, particularly nightingales. They also ate nightingale flesh to stay awake, making it antiquity's answer to today's energy drinks. Until quite recently, slow-to-speak children in parts of Europe were fed the tongues of talkative birds to improve vocal development. In modern times, laws to protect endangered and threatened species reduce the kinds of birds eaten throughout the world. Food shortages after the two World Wars in Europe, though, caused a striking increase in the capture and consumption of wild birds. Neighbors often shared tips on how to make stringy or foul-tasting birds palatable. Gastronomes today often flout modern laws to feast on bird delicacies, such as the tiny Ortolan Buntings that are roasted and eaten whole, especially in southern Europe.

The force-feeding of geese to make a paste of their rich liver dates back to at least Roman times. Confined geese often had their feet nailed to the ground and endured having a slurry of milk, flour, and honey poured down their throats. Animal rights activists today deplore the treatment of geese in the traditional pâté de foie gras industry.

Where birds are kept and eaten, so, too, are eggs. In the not-too-distant past, the smaller eggs of wild birds were served as delicacies, until laws made them off-limits. On the other hand, the very large, farm-raised ostrich and emu eggs enjoy a faddish popularity. The contents of a three-pound ostrich egg make a spectacular statement as an omelet, if you can find a pan big enough to cook it in.

FOUR & TWENTY WHAT?

Few people who dip into a piece of pie are likely to think about the origin of the word "pie," or to consider that it might have something to do with birds. Most think about fruit and delicious crust. But pies of old were more likely to have been made from birds than berries. And the bird in the filling could well have been that abundant corvid, the European Magpie. These birds were known originally as "pies" (from the Latin *pica,* their genus name today), and the word came to signify something that was black and white in pattern.

In Middle English, "pie" could also connote an assortment of objects, like the hoards collected by magpies, jays, and other corvids. The culinary pie, then, could reference the edible bits and pieces that went into pies, stews, and soups.

And what about the "four and twenty blackbirds" of nursery rhyme fame? That probably spoke to a practice favored by Italians and others of hiding live birds in a crust to startle guests when the crust was cut and the birds flew out in all directions.

BELOVED BUDGIES & OTHER PET BIRDS

Early on any given morning in Beijing and other cities across China, people young and old stroll to parks while lightly swinging elaborate birdcages. When they arrive at their destination, they hang the cages on the lower branches of trees and begin to socialize with their human friends. Daily bird-walking is a Chinese pastime that dates back to the founding of the Qing Dynasty in 1611, when elites gathered in teahouses with their birds, sharing bird-care tips and knowledge of new species. Modern bird-walkers claim the stroll

benefits the bird as well as the human. The bird gets fresh air and also must grip its perch tightly during the swinging, keeping itself toned and trim.

The Chinese hold the record for the number of pet birds residing in one country: about 71 million. But keeping birds as pets is an ancient tradition all over the world. Parrots ranked as favorites with the Egyptians, who kept African Grays; chatty mynahs were popular pets in India. The Greeks and Romans also favored parrots. Some Romans even procured the ser-

> It was the nightingale, and not the lark,
> That pierc'd the fearful hollow of thine ear;
> Nightly she sings on yon pomegranate tree:
> Believe me, love, it was the nightingale.
>
> WILLIAM SHAKESPEARE, *ROMEO AND JULIET*, 1595

vices of a personal attendant for their pampered birds. Sailors and pirates made pets of the parrots they discovered on their voyages. Very sociable and satisfied with a simple diet of nuts and seeds, parrots proved excellent traveling companions.

Throughout Europe, just about every local songbird has been kept as a pet at one time or another. The

Bird paintings were a favored adornment in the 19th century. This painting decorated an English home in 1870.

Bird Brain

Steeped in tradition, duck hunters have their own nicknames for ducks that are often more descriptive than the official names: Mallard = greenhead; American Wigeon = baldpate or baldy; Bufflehead = butterball; Common Goldeneye = whistler; Ring-necked Duck = marsh bluebill; Greater Scaup = big bluebill; and Lesser Scaup = little bluebill.

Birdcages dangle outdoors in China. At about 71 million, the nation holds the record for most pet birds, but people in countries around the world join in this ancient tradition of making pets of birds.

canary, brought to Europe from the Canary Islands in the 16th century, immediately became a highly prized songbird, and the Harz Mountain region of central Germany emerged as a center of not only canary breeding but also training.

Bird conservationists work constantly against illegal trade in wild birds, especially in the tropics. The European Union has banned the sale of all but captive-bred exotics as pets. Sometimes captives escape, forming unusual colonies of colorful exotics in non-typical habitats. London, for example, provides a home for some 30,000 Rose-ringed Parakeets, while a large population of Monk Parakeets exists in Brooklyn, following escapes and breakouts from the pet trade.

◆ PEREGRINE FALCON ◆

FALCO PEREGRINUS: "Falcon" comes from the Latin *falc,* "curved or sickle-shaped," which refers to the bird's curved talons or possibly the shape of its wings in flight. "Peregrine" is from the Latin *peregrinari* "to wander" or "to travel abroad"; many of these birds are highly migratory.

European Turtle-Dove

A PASSION FOR PIGEONS

All over India and Pakistan, men come home from a day's work and head straight to the roof of their home for an assignation. There, waiting in a shady, crowded coop, are the many objects of their affection—all of them domestic varieties of the species *Columba livia,* the Rock Pigeon. Each pigeon vies for attention to be fed, admired, and cared for. Favorites may be cuddled for a while, like a kitten or puppy. The flock is an owner's pride and joy, his second family, and, he hopes, the source of bragging rights after the next race.

Pigeon racing is an ancient sport still practiced in many parts of the world. South Asia has a racing pigeon tradition that goes back centuries. In this sport, pigeons are not raced head to head from point A to point B. Instead, coops vie against each other in a long-distance endurance contest. Owners transport their birds to a location up to hundreds of

1. Französische Paggadotten-Taube, 2. Maltheser-Taube, 3. kleine Maltheser-Taube, 4. Hühnerscheckige-Taube, 5. Nönnchen-Taube, 6. Englische Tafel-Taube, 7. Römer-Taube, 8. Montauban-Taube, 9. Almonds Tümmler-Taube, 10 Tümmler.
Nach d. Nat. ges. v. G. Neumeister.

*The selective breeding of Rock Pigeons has resulted in many plumage variations;
a few are depicted in this German print from 1876.*

miles away and release them. The goal is to have one of your birds be the first to arrive back home and enter its own coop, where it may trip a timer. The journey is quite a feat; a homing pigeon can travel up to 600 miles in a day at an average of 50 miles an hour.

Some owners race brooding females who fly frantically to reach the eggs in their nest. Others trick females into thinking they have a clutch by placing plastic eggs in the nest a few days before a race. All racing birds are tagged and registered for the race, and their data are checked carefully before and after. Even with a win, an owner usually suffers losses. It is not uncommon for more than 10 percent of one owner's birds to be lost to predation, tall buildings, or disorienting signals from cell phone towers during the course of a single race.

Homing pigeon racing also remains a strong tradition in New York City, where rooftop coops, though not as commonplace as they once were, are still an iconic feature in certain neighborhoods. A century

> *Mir Nihal went to the kotha where his flying pigeons were kept. He released the birds . . . They were ever so many, black ones and white ones, red ones and blue ones, dappled and grey, beautiful wings stretched out in flight.*
>
> AHMED ALI, *TWILIGHT IN DELHI*, 1940

ago, pigeon racers avoided the trouble of having to transport their own birds to the release point by being on friendly terms with railroad conductors who would make some extra money by accepting

Feathers fly as keepers release pigeons from their carriers at the start of a race in the United Kingdom in 1953.

the pigeons as cargo and releasing them at an agreed destination. Older racers are heartened whenever a younger person shows interest in carrying on the sport. There are signs that the sport is catching on with younger inner city residents, who sometimes share the news from the coop with other homing pigeon enthusiasts via the Internet.

Bird Brain

During the 1890s, a single aigrette—a long, white plume grown by the Great Egret and other herons during the breeding season—was worth twice its weight in gold. The millinery trade created most of the demand for plumes to decorate stylish hats. It is estimated that in those years 200 million birds a year were killed for their feathers.

Ceylon Junglefowl. Hand-colored print by A. Prevost (published 1849)

WINGED SYMBOLS

FINDING MEANING IN BIRDS, FROM THE ANCIENTS TO MAO ZEDONG

If you've ever taken one end of a wishbone from a turkey, chicken, or goose and pulled with a partner until the wishbone broke, you've taken part in a kind of divination. By tradition, the person left with the larger piece is granted a wish.

BY BIRDS FORETOLD

The wishbone, or furcula, was one of several bird parts traditionally used in divination to get a read on the best course of action to take in a certain situation.

The breastbone also came under scrutiny. In 15th-century Bavaria, peasant diviners examined goose breastbones to determine what kind of a winter to expect. And all over the world diviners have looked at the entrails of a slaughtered chicken to evaluate a proposed plan. The ancient Etruscans and Romans also looked to nature, and especially to birds, for clues about favorable actions ultimately tied into the will of the gods. The founding of Rome is credited to this kind of divination, called augury. Romulus

Harbingers of doom, Black Vultures are silhouetted in a tree at sundown in Belize. Maya hieroglyphics often connect Black Vultures with death, but the bird performs a service by eating carrion that might be a breeding ground for disease.

THE BIRD MAN OF ASSISI

Born into privilege in 1182, the son of a wealthy cloth merchant of Assisi, in today's Italy, Giovanni Bernadone lived a medieval celebrity lifestyle, partying with his entourage and using his father's money to fund his fun. A stint in the cavalry, though, led to a year of captivity in a hostile city, where Giovanni had a life-changing epiphany. He ended up rejecting his wealth and worldly ties, and entered the religious life, founding both a brotherhood and sisterhood devoted to the poor. Known thereafter as Brother Francis, he also ministered to four-footed and winged creatures, and was especially fond of birds. Sometime around the year 1220, he preached his famous avian sermon, in which he urged them to sing praises for their wondrous birdness. The text is often rendered in this way:

FRANCIS OF ASSISI AND WILD BIRDS

> My little sisters, the birds, much bounden are ye unto God, your Creator, and always in every place ought ye to praise Him, for that He hath given you liberty to fly about everywhere, and hath also given you double and triple raiment; moreover He preserved your seed in the ark of Noah, that your race might not perish out of the world; still more are ye beholden to Him for the element of the air which He hath appointed for you; beyond all this, ye sow not, neither do you reap; and God feedeth you, and giveth you the streams and fountains for your drink; the mountains and valleys for your refuge and the high trees whereon to make your nests; and because ye know not how to spin or sow, God clotheth you, you and your children; wherefore your Creator loveth you much, seeing that He hath bestowed on you so many benefits; and therefore, my little sisters, beware of the sin of ingratitude, and study always to give praises unto God.

and Remus, the legendary twin founders of the city, were both considered accomplished augurs, and they looked to the flight of vultures to determine the best site for their settlement. Roman augury became very formalized. State-appointed augurs took themselves to high ground, where they held aloft their curved staffs to divide the heaven into quadrants. They looked carefully at the birds entering the different sections of the sky, paying attention to details of flight and voice. Only certain species qualified for this kind of divination; foremost was the eagle, the bird associated with Jupiter. Divination by observing bird flight or voice featured in many cultures through the ages.

The Roman military also made its battle plans by observing the feeding behavior of chickens. If they ate greedily, the signs were right to take the action under consideration. If they didn't eat or tried to get away, then the plan was a no-go. Some generals tried to manipulate the circumstances to be able to carry out their favored battle plans.

THE TOWER RAVENS: MONARCHY INSURANCE

TWO RAVENS IN FRONT OF
THE TOWER OF LONDON

If you believe the legend, six canny corvids hold the future of Britain in their sharp little claws. Were they to leave the Tower of London, the Tower would fall and along with it, the British monarchy. Some insist that a group of Common Ravens has lived on the Tower grounds since Roman times. Others assert that Charles II decreed perpetual protection for the imposing birds. Modern historians support a less-dramatic notion that the ravens' presence dates only to late-Victorian times, perhaps starting out as pets of the Yeoman Warders stationed at the Tower.

In addition to the Crown Jewels, most visitors to the Tower want to see the six ravens who live in comfort on its grounds. The ravens patrol four territories on the Tower grounds, cocking an eye at visitors and sometimes mimicking a startling, deep-voiced "Hello!" Despite having clipped wings, they have been known to pop out of their enclosures to snatch food from unsuspecting tourists. One, appropriately called Grog, even made it as far as an East End pub, before being taken into protective custody by vigilant Londoners.

The continuity of the raven presence was broken during the Blitz in World War II, when bombing killed some birds and left others to die of shock. Yet when the Tower reopened on the first day of 1946, six shiny birds were back on the job.

MESSENGERS IN PEACE & WAR

For millennia, long-distance flight capabilities and strong homing instincts made the Rock Pigeon the go-to bird for message delivery. Egyptian pharaohs used them; so did King Cyrus of Persia, who needed to keep tabs on his empire. Taken into battle zones during the two World Wars, pigeons were dispatched to command posts behind the lines with urgent messages tied to their legs. They flew quickly, eager to return to coop and companions. Other pigeons harnessed with time-delayed lightweight cameras flew aerial reconnaissance missions. Both Allied and Axis forces used carrier pigeons. The English trained Peregrine Falcons to counter German pigeons that aided spies sent to

European Bee-eater

scope out invasion possibilities. The falcons patrolled vulnerable areas, such as the Cornish coast, knocking enemy pigeons from the skies. If they survived, the pigeons became POWs, like their human counterparts.

Many individual carrier pigeons distinguished themselves in military service. In the waning days of World War I, a pigeon known as Cher Ami lost a leg delivering a critical message to the American command from a battalion trapped by the Germans near Verdun. For this valiant effort, the French government awarded the bird a Croix de Guerre with Palm. Both Cher Ami and his medal are now on display at the Smithsonian's Museum of American History.

Bird Brain

Birding slang: "I dipped on that mega neotrop. Would've been a lifer tick, but I'm terrible at IDing LBJs. Cool bins!" Translation: I missed finding that super-rare neotropical migrant. It was a species I've never seen before, but I'm not good at identifying little brown jobs (birds). Nice binoculars!

The Dickin Medal went to a Rock Pigeon named "G.I. Joe" in 1946. The only American war pigeon to win the medal, "Joe" carried a message preventing a bombing that saved the lives of a thousand Allied soldiers in Italy.

MAO'S ANTI-SPARROW CAMPAIGN

In the late 1950s, amid concerns about diseases and increasingly poor crop yields in heavily populated China, Mao Zedong decided unilaterally—the way dictators often do—to put in place a program to eradicate what he believed were the main cause of China's woes. The Four Pests Campaign of 1958 targeted the mosquito, fly, rat, and Eurasian Tree Sparrow, the latter being an abundant species that had adapted easily to agricultural areas of the sprawling country. The eradication of the Eurasian Tree Sparrow expanded into a separate agenda. Chairman Mao charged Chinese peasants with the task of wiping out these pests quickly and by any possible means. The bird was wholly blamed for widespread seed loss, never mind that a change toward better agricultural practices, such as mulching and cover-cropping, might have reduced the problem. Better to have a public enemy number one in the form of a sparrow as a national scapegoat.

> *So you ask what the birds say?*
> *The sparrow, the dove,*
> *The linnet and the thrush say,*
> *"I love and I love!"*
>
> S. T. COLERIDGE, "AN ANSWER TO A CHILDE'S QUESTION," 1802

Whipped by propaganda into a fervid collective killing machine, Chinese of all ages became mass executioners. Children wielding slingshots pinged birds out of the air, joining adults who knocked nests to the ground and smashed eggs. At night whole villages banged pots and pans to keep the sparrows from settling in to roost. Exhausted from continuous flying, the birds fell from the sky. Day in and day out, the eradica-

"Eliminating the Last Sparrow" was a poster distributed in China in 1959, when the birds were considered vermin.

Bird Brain

The feathers of the female Common Eider have been used by humans for millennia to keep warm. Eider down has the best thermal insulating qualities of any known natural substance—no synthetic has been able to match its combination of warmth and lightness. Today, true eider down is an extravagant luxury product. A single pillow can cost $3,000.

A Eurasian Tree Sparrow sits on an ornamental cabbage in China. Mao's eradication campaign of the crop-damaging birds in 1959–1960 resulted in a plague of locusts, pests eaten by the sparrows in previous years.

tion continued until there were no more sparrows. In the absence of the tree sparrows—their natural predators—locusts thrived. The voracious insects swarmed the fields in 1959 and 1960 and devastated crops, causing far more damage than the sparrows ever had. By the time the effects played out, 30 million people were dead. The locusts weren't the only culprits, but they certainly were key players in the mega-catastrophe known as the Great Chinese Famine.

Mao finally listened to agricultural experts and stopped the campaign against the Eurasian Tree Sparrow. But rather than downsize from four pests to three, he nominated the ubiquitous bedbug to take its place.

◆ **YELLOW WARBLER** ◆

SETOPHAGA PETECHIA: "Warbler" derives from the Old French *werbler,* "to sing with trills and quivers." *Setophaga* was coined from the Greek words *setos* ("insect") and *phagein* ("to eat"); hence "insect eater." *Petechia* is Latin for "skin with red spots," a reference to the male's red-streaked breast.

FINE-FEATHERED ARTS

THE BIRD AS MUSE

Birds offer writers so much fodder for their craft. They lend themselves to all literary forms and characterizations and to every sentiment that needs expressing, from sheer joy to abject terror and everything in between.

LITERARY WORKS TAKE WING

The Bible is replete with allusions to birds. They are used to describe the beauty of the beloved in the Song of Solomon ("Your eyes are doves behind your veil"), and they form the basis of parables in the New Testament ("Behold the birds of the heaven, that they sow not, neither do they reap, nor gather into barns; and your heavenly Father feedeth them"). Key scenes in Bible narratives also feature birds prominently: the dove sent out by Noah to determine whether the floodwaters had receded and the cock that crowed after Peter's betrayals of Jesus on the night before his Crucifixion.

A Holy Spirit fresco in Serbia has the biblical dove at the very center of the painting. Doves have long been symbols of peace and purity because of their sweet dispositions, but white doves are only a color variation, not a species.

A multitude of bird species crowds a 17th-century painting by Flemish artist Carl Wilhelm de Hamilton (1668–1754) called "The Parliament of Birds." The painting illustrates Geoffrey Chaucer's dream poem titled "The Parliament of Fowls."

Writing his comic play *The Birds* in 414 B.C., Greek playwright Aristophanes created a Utopian society where birds ruled, and they controlled all communications between mortals on Earth and the gods on Mount Olympus. Aristophanes demonstrated a keen understanding of birds and transposed them to the habits and foibles of ancient Greek society and politics. Shakespeare referenced birds in nearly all of his plays. Some played important roles: A lark signals to Romeo that it's time to be leaving Juliet's chamber, and an owl foretells the assassination of Julius Caesar.

Perhaps more than other writers, poets draw inspiration from birds. Chaucer wrote his 700-line "Parliament of Fowls" in the 14th century around the notion of a conference of birds eager to choose mates on St. Valentine's Day. From the rhapsodic murmurings of Browning to Poe's unsettling images in "The Raven," birds have left an indelible mark on poetry. It has been said that Poe got his inspiration from the raven character Grip in Dickens's historical novel *Barnaby Rudge,* who was based on the Dickens family's pet raven of the same name. Poe apparently had remarked that Grip deserved a bigger role in the work, but whether his own poem was an actual homage to the Dickens raven is not known.

European Honey-buzzard

PAINTED PINIONS

From a mural on an Egyptian tomb to the delicate renderings in the margins of a medieval psalter to a raucous cartoon in the *New Yorker,* birds are everywhere in world art. Before field guide and wildlife art came to define the modern image of the bird, birds were looked at aesthetically and symbolically and celebrated as a defining element of nature.

In some artistic traditions a specific kind of bird was elevated to artistic icon, as was the case for cranes in Japan. In medieval and Renaissance art, birds appear mainly in works with classical themes and as symbols in the religious art that characterized those periods. Birds retained symbolic value in the Baroque period, but they also became an important element in sumptuous still lifes, especially in northern Europe.

Five thousand miles away, birds flourished in the tradition of Mughal miniature paintings. The artists took inspiration from the novel flora and fauna in the Indian environment, celebrating all its native creatures and those brought to the subcontinent by the inquisitive and acquisitive Mughal emperors. The fourth emperor, Jahangir, the father of Shah Jahan of Taj Mahal fame, was a gifted naturalist. The paintings he commissioned are known as much for their delicate aesthetics as

SYMBOLISM IN A TINY PACKAGE

The tiny European Goldfinch held a prominent place in Christian symbolism that belied its small size. The bird's preferred diet of prickle-covered thistles lent it a natural association with the crown of thorns that represented the passion of Christ. The goldfinch appeared in many depictions of Madonna and Child, especially during the Renaissance, often firmly clutched in the child's hand. Despite its charming aspect, the chubby bird in the baby's grasp served to foreshadow the passion and Crucifixion of Christ to come. The goldfinch also symbolized less ominous attributes, such as endurance and fruitfulness.

The goldfinch is only one of a long list of birds with important roles in Christian symbolism and art. Among them, the dove represents purity and peace, while the peacock stands for immortality, based in part on the mistaken belief that its flesh does not decay. The old European notion that the stork brought babies may tie into that bird's role as a symbol of the Annunciation to Mary of her impending motherhood.

EUROPEAN GOLDFINCHES

German Renaissance artist Albrecht Dürer (1471–1528) painted this exquisitely detailed watercolor of the wing of a European Roller in 1512. This species is one of the most colorful European birds.

they are for the faithful reproduction of species, recognizable at a glance. He is credited by modern ornithologists with the foresight to procure a faithful rendering of the Dodo, hunted to extinction in the 17th century by sailors who visited Mauritius, the Dodo's Indian Ocean island home.

Pablo Picasso turned the art world on its head with his experiments in cubism in the early 20th century, but he is equally known for a simple line drawing that was transformed into a lithograph and reproduced over and over. Picasso, who had Communist leanings, donated his Peace Dove to the 1949 Soviet-backed Paris World Peace Conference. Since then, it has been liberated from its ideological associations and adopted as a universal symbol of peace.

Bird Brain

Although it may look like a tiny straw, the hummingbird's bill is not a hollow tube. This bird uses its long, grooved tongue to obtain nectar. Brushy "hairs" on the tip of the tongue lap up nectar at a rate of about 13 times a second. Some species consume up to three times their own body weight in nectar each day.

INSPIRED BY BIRDSONG

Most musicians inspired by birds attempt to imitate their effortless tones. One of the earliest pieces of written music that survives in Britain, "Sumer is icumen in," contains a passage mimicking the song of a cuckoo. Indeed, the trio of the cuckoo, nightingale, and lark can take much of the credit for avian inspiration in Western music: J. S. Bach set up a counterpoint between a chicken and a nightingale in his Sonata in D Major, while Handel composed a similar duet in his organ concerto, "The Cuckoo and the Nightingale."

Beethoven invoked a cuckoo, nightingale, and quail in his *Pastoral* Symphony, and Respighi incorporated the nightingale and cuckoo with the hen and the dove in "The Birds." Russian composer Igor Stravinsky centered his short opera *Le Rossignol* on the Hans Christian Andersen tale "The Nightingale," and composed the startlingly modern *Firebird* ballet based on the mythology of the phoenix. Britain's Ralph Vaughn Williams took inspiration for his ode to summer, "The Lark Ascending," from a poem of the same name by George Meredith.

Contemporary music and even rock-and-roll gather inspiration from the birds. Beatle Paul McCartney's gentle touch with the quietly acoustic "Blackbird" displays the strong pull of nature

You must have the bird in your heart before you can find it in the bush.

JOHN BURROUGHS, "SHARP EYES," 1879

on the British imagination. At the other end of the spectrum, the avian images found in Lynyrd Skynyrd's "Freebird" help it stake a claim as the modern anthem of the commitment-phobe. A recent commercial for public broadcasting shows a frustrated composer as he receives insight for a melody from the natural arrangement of birds on a wire outside his window.

A Brazilian musician and filmmaker has taken the concept even further, transcribing the "notes" formed by a flock of starlings on power lines in a newspaper photograph and arranging them using computer

MENURA SUPERBA.

Tail feathers of the male Superb Lyrebird gave the Australian fowl its name; the bird is also an excellent mimic of sounds.

Mozart's Starling

Wolfgang Amadeus Mozart purchased a starling from a Viennese pet shop in May 1784. He noted in his expense book that the bird sang a tune fragment resembling a composition of his, though the bird sang a G sharp where Mozart had written a G natural. While seeming precocious, the starling was doing what starlings do. They possess an extremely flexible vocal capability and can reproduce a wide range of sounds—from human speech to a dog's bark to the sound of rattling keys.

The starling lived with Mozart until it died three years later, and the composer held an elaborately staged funeral and read a poem he had written himself. Some thought the tribute and the ceremony over the top. And while few doubted the sincerity of Mozart's feelings for the bird, a more modern, psychological spin suggests that the fuss might have represented conflicted emotions Mozart had on the death of his overbearing father, an event that had occurred the same week.

software and the synthesized sounds of xylophone, bassoon, oboe, and clarinet. Of course, the composer made the decisions of which birds to transcribe as single notes and which as chords, but the result is a very pleasing—and uncontrived—tune that has gone viral on the Internet.

◆ HEPATIC TANAGER ◆

PIRANGA FLAVA: "Tanager" comes from the Tupi Indian (South America) name *tanqara* for these birds. "Hepatic" comes from the Greek *hepatikos* for "liver" and means "liver-colored"—the color of the male's plumage. *Piranga* is another Tupi Indian word for "bird"; *flava* is Latin for "yellow," the color of the female's plumage.

Blue Magpie of Asia. Hand-colored print by John Gould and Henry C. Richter (published 1850–1883)

Blyth's Hawk-Eagle of Southeast Asia. Hand-colored print by Joseph Wolf and Henry C. Richter (published 1850–1883)

CHAPTER THREE

THE LIFE OF A BIRD

Kimball Garrett

✦✦✦✦✦

Two Red-tailed Comets attend to their nest in the central Andes in this painting by American artist Martin Johnson Heade (1819–1904).

CHICKEN OR EGG?

AVIAN LIFE CYCLES

Hardly staid and detached, biologists aren't immune to the aesthetic appeal of birds. They revel in birds' beauty and diversity, in their magical powers of flight, and in their complex and often ethereal songs. But biologists also have to admit that when you reduce things to the barest essentials, a bird's evolutionary directive—which it shares with all living things—is to reproduce.

THE DRIVE TO REPRODUCE

Taken even further, an individual bird is essentially a vehicle—a container of DNA looking to recombine its genetic material with that of a mate to produce another generation of slightly different DNA containers. Every bird's life's work, so to speak, is to settle into an appropriate breeding habitat, attract potential mates, and produce and nurture young, but this simple imperative is played out in an incredible array of avian reproductive strategies. An individual bird is a collection of inherited traits that impact the bird's fitness, and its fitness is measured by its success at surviving and reproducing. Varying expressions of these genetically based traits affect a bird's fitness differently. Bill size, plumage color, the number of eggs in a clutch,

Wandering Albatrosses gather on South Georgia Island in the southern Atlantic Ocean. These largest of albatrosses take many years to breed. The white male on the left and younger female may be a breeding pair; the bird in flight is younger.

An adult male Orange-breasted Pigeon of Asia covers two chicks with its wings. The chicks feel no allegiance to the nest, a flimsy platform of a few twigs onto which the two eggs were laid.

the ability to recognize a predator—all these traits are shaped by natural selection.

Natural selection also influences when a bird reproduces and how many young it has. Scientists often classify the extremes of reproductive strategies as "K-selection" and "r-selection," named after symbols for population-carrying capacity (K) and for the intrinsic rate of population growth (r). To oversimplify, K-selected species exhibit a take-it-slow approach, with delayed reproductive maturity, long reproductive life, low reproductive rates, and well-developed parental care that results in high rates of survival among the young. Consider the albatross: The largest species,

which might live to be 50 years old or more, may not breed until about ten years of age and will raise only a single chick every other year, which will take more than 12 months to go from egg to fledging.

This strategy contrasts with r-selected species, which reproduce early and with great fecundity, though they have low survival rates and reduced longevity. Nutmeg Mannikins, southern Asian songbirds introduced in southern United States, may begin to breed when less than a year old, can raise three broods a year, require only a month from egg-laying to fledging, and rarely live more than five years. However, 90 percent of the young probably die during their first year of life.

DOVETAILING WITH NATURE

Imagine yourself in California on the winter solstice for the Christmas Bird Count. Winter groups of migrant Audubon's Warblers and White-crowned Sparrows are all around, so it seems a bit incongruous to glance up and see a female Allen's Hummingbird nestled on a clutch of two eggs in her quarter-size felt cup of a nest. But it's not surprising, really. Winter rains mean a profusion of nectar-rich flowers are just around the corner, and a wealth of exotic flowering plants augment the natural food supply. Birds so often defy our notions of the calendar: A "spring" migrant Willow Flycatcher can be winging its way to northern breeding areas on June 20, a week after the first flock of southbound "fall migrant" female Wilson's Phalaropes have passed through the same spot.

Breeding, molting, and sometimes migrating—all of these energetically expensive undertakings have to fit into the avian calendar. Day length, or photoperiod, which predictably and inexorably waxes and wanes through the year, is the determining factor. It mediates hormonal changes that trigger migratory urges, molting, and reproductive behavior and physiology. Many avian annual activities are almost strictly governed by photoperiod, from the onset of migration to the date the first egg is laid or the first primary feather is molted. South American Monk Parakeets, now established in many parts of the United States, have a breeding and molting schedule that is shifted six months from their natural Southern Hemisphere cycle—demonstrating the power of the sun's calendar.

Birds have a Feng-shui of their own—an unwritten and occult science of the healthy and unhealthy places of residence.

JEROME K. JEROME, *SECOND THOUGHTS OF AN IDLE FELLOW*, 1890

But fascinating exceptions remain, and annual cycle events are sometimes triggered by more proximate factors such as rainfall or food availability.

A common pattern might be to breed, molt, migrate, maybe molt again, migrate back again, and start over with reproducing. Of course there are many variations. Some birds are completely sedentary, whereas others migrate astonishing distances. A species may have one discrete molting period each year while others have two or more molting periods; in large birds, molt cycles are lengthy enough to overlap. Reproductive efforts may take only a few weeks or may continue over many months.

Interesting multitasking strategies have evolved in some birds. The female of some hornbill species

Pale gray, adult-like feathers of a molting Mediterranean Gull are replacing the gull's dark juvenile wing feathers.

A large flock of American Flamingos—in the shape of a giant flamingo—gather in a shallow lagoon in the Gulf of Mexico. The gregarious, long-legged wading birds gather in huge colonies to avoid predators, use scarce nesting sites, and feed.

undergoes a complete molt while safely sealed within a nest cavity, fed by the male as she incubates and cares for the young. Phainopeplas may breed in early spring in southwestern deserts and then migrate to coastal or more northerly regions to breed again later in the spring. Some hypothesize that this double-breeding strategy occurs in certain woodland songbirds of western North America that may nest a second time in the summer monsoon rain regions of northern Mexico.

Rain is the stimulus for breeding in many arid-land birds in interior Australia, Africa, and southwestern North America, because it translates to a profusion of resources that will peak as the young are fed and after they fledge. The nesting season of the Eleanora's Falcon of the Mediterranean region is shifted to the fall, timed to coincide with the peak fall passage of migratory birds, the falcon's preferred prey.

Bird Brain

Listen closely and some birds will tell you their names. The Eastern Phoebe calls out *fee-be*, the Eastern Wood-Pewee says *pee-a-wee*, and the Blue Jay shrieks a piercing *jay, jay, jay*. Other self-identifiers are the Dickcissel, Eastern Towhee, Eastern Whip-poor-will, Great Kiskadee, Northern Bobwhite, and Willet.

TURF WARS, BIRD STYLE

A common lament from those who maintain hummingbird feeders is that a single "bully" male hummingbird has laid claim to the entire area, instantly pouncing on any unfortunate visiting hummer that had its eye on the provided nectar source. Under the right circumstances—when enough feeders are scattered over a big enough area, or during a migration peak when large numbers of hummers are in the area—defending feeding territory becomes just about impossible for the territory owner. In short, the energy the bully male spends traveling among well-spaced feeders or dealing with multiple simultaneous intruders becomes greater than the energy he gains from having the food source to himself. This cost-benefit equation is the basis for feeding territories that birds maintain.

Territories can encompass more than defended food resources. The classic all-purpose territory will include all resources needed for procuring food, locating and building a nest, and raising young. Yet another bird's defendable territory may be as small as the space a nesting bird can reach with its bill—a personal space of sorts within a dense breeding colony. A bird can consume considerable energy when establishing and defending territories; asserting its rights to a chunk

Australian Gannets cluster on Cape Kidnappers, New Zealand, annually for nesting. Pairs stay together for several seasons and perform elaborate greetings, stretching their necks skyward and tapping bills together.

of space can occupy much of a bird's waking hours. So why would a bird bother to defend an area? Put simply, its goal is to reduce competition for resources from other birds of the same species, also known as conspecifics, although sometimes it is hoping to prevent individuals of other potentially competing species from gaining ground. We're familiar with nesting season territories of songbirds because of the reach of their message: Song after song carries over their territory from dawn through much of the day, proclaiming space and attracting a potential mate. Punctuated by chases and sometimes a minor brawl or two, holding territory is a lot of work.

Territoriality can be a strong imperative in the non-breeding season as well. Just watch a Northern Mockingbird chasing Hermit Thrushes and other berry-eaters away from a productive patch of fruiting shrubs. Wood Thrushes and some warblers fiercely maintain territories when on their wintering grounds. And as you'd expect, territories can be ephemeral and shifting. For instance, Sanderlings defend spaces around them that are redefined as they move along beach tidelines to probe for food.

For many birds, breeding in dense colonies works far better than in well-spaced, defended territories. Breeding colonies of seabirds are a legacy of the tiny amount of available breeding space—in the form of oceanic islands lacking terrestrial predators—relative to the wealth of feeding areas in the vast oceans. In some species, massive colonies form when there is a boom of an unpredictable food source. Red-billed Queleas will gather in the millions when conditions are right in the African savannas, nests packed tightly

Declaring his territory, a burrow from the previous year, a Magellanic Penguin brays in a voice his mate will recognize.

together. How do so many birds get along? In colonies, inter-individual aggression is stifled; colonies are predicated on the availability of abundant food in surrounding areas.

Bird Brain

Patronyms are bird names that honor a particular person. Bachman, Baird, Botteri, Brewer, Cassin, Harris, Henslow, Le Conte, and Nelson have North American sparrows named for them. All these men were scientists working in the 19th century, when many new species were being discovered.

HOME IS WHERE THE HABITAT IS

Extreme birding isn't everyone's cup of tea, but those smitten by the sporting aspects of bird-watching may, on occasion, engage in an activity known as the Big Day—a quest to find as many bird species in a single calendar day as possible. Planning a "Big Day route" means considering (whether consciously or unconsciously) how bird species fit into the continuum from habitat "generalist" to habitat "specialist." Looking for a Red-tailed Hawk or Mourning Dove? No problem, we'll find them anywhere and everywhere. A Mallard or a Great Blue Heron? We might have to find some water first, but those birds will be there. A great many birds will be predictably found within their general habitat type: a coniferous forest, river edge woodland, or freshwater marsh, for example.

The challenge is to find the specialists, which dwell in unique or limited habitats. Plan a detour to just the right wooded mountain stream for a singing Louisiana Waterthrush and then travel to a wet sedgy marsh for a Sedge Wren. Fields and pastures are everywhere, but you'll need to drive 30 miles to just the right hayfield to find that Henslow's Sparrow. A perusal of the range maps and habitat descriptions

A bird-watcher scans a cloud forest in Ecuador, a small South American country with more than 1,600 species of birds. Endemism is high in the world's cloud forests because "specialist" species have adapted to different feeding niches and plant types.

Perching on a spruce in Germany, a male Red Crossbill shows a bill whose upper mandible twists over the lower. The bill shape supplies leverage for prying open tough cones. Crossbills wander large distances in search of a good cone crop.

In a good field guide will reinforce how variable bird species are in the extent of their geographical distributions and the breadth of their habitat preferences.

Even within general habitat types, birds can show extreme specialization. Some 270 species of antbirds make a living in woodlands and forests of the New World tropics. In parts of the Amazon basin, 40 or more species may occur in the same area. But they exploit different microhabitats within the lowland forests. Some are specialists at finding insects in clusters of dead leaves, others search only tangled vines, and still others feed almost exclusively around army ant swarms. While some antbirds are rarely seen away from stands of *Guadua* bamboo, others are tied to vegetation growing on white-sand soil.

The ornithological literature is replete with quantitative measures of bird habitat requirements, whether for breeding, wintering, molting, or refueling in migration. Scientists measure climatic variables and plant associations and construct statistical models of canopy cover, snag abundance, leaf litter, prey density, and so on. The predictive power of these models helps us conserve specialized species and estimate impacts of climate change.

Northern Catbird nest and eggs. Hand-colored print by Virginia Jones (published 1880)

SEALING THE DEAL

COURTSHIP PRACTICES IN THE BIRD WORLD

Even before the first hints of light in late spring, the sounds of birdsong begin to fill the cool air, first augmenting, then smothering, the chirps of insects. This crescendo of exuberant song is known as the dawn chorus, and experiencing this natural symphony is always exhilarating. A New England chorus might begin with an American Robin, but soon White-throated Sparrows, Eastern Bluebirds, Eastern Wood-Pewees, and Song Sparrows will contribute, and the Wood Thrush is the star of the second movement. In the high mountains of California, Western Wood-Pewees and Violet-green Swallows are the early players in the score, with Green-tailed and Spotted Towhees, Fox Sparrows, American Robins, and Thick-billed Fox Sparrows soon joining the chorus.

SONG & DANCE

Why do birds sing? Many books have been written about the different layers of answers to this question. A less poetic explanation is that they sing because

The male Vogelkop Bowerbird of New Guinea makes up for its dull appearance with an elaborate bower. The bird arranges decorations leading to a hutlike structure, hoping that a female will be attracted to his treasure and mate with him.

A male White-throated Sparrow sings from a conifer branch in New York. Studies show that birds sing to convey messages of territorial proclamation and to attract mates.

they're pumped up with hormones that tell the brain to send messages to the muscles that change the pressure of the cartilage and the shape of the vocal membranes of the syrinx, the sound-producing organ at the junction of the windpipe and the bronchi. They sing because song conveys messages of territorial proclamation and mate attraction.

Songs, relatively complex vocalizations largely related to mating and territoriality, are but part of the vocal repertoire of most birds. A variety of other vocalizations, usually simpler and shorter, might convey information about the caller's location to a mate or flock members, express alarm or warning, or indicate aggression or hunger, as in the begging calls of nestlings. Most birders have discovered that location calls are important to learn, as they are species-specific and given during most of a bird's waking hours through the annual cycle. Even at night migrants overhead can often be identified to species by the contact calls they give—the night sky in May can ring with the *quee?* flight calls of Swainson's Thrushes as they wing northward.

Not only do birds produce songs of every description, but also they have evolved behaviors to make

What female Indigo Bunting could resist this vibrant blue male, singing during breeding season? The sparrow-size songbird, common across half of the United States, sings not only to attract females but also to mark his territory to other males.

those songs better heard. A singing bird may seek out a high branch or shrub top from which to better broadcast its song; in flat expanses of grassland or tundra, many species perform flight songs over their territories. The timing of song delivery and the frequencies and patterns of the notes are evolutionary accommodations to the sonic environment in which a bird lives. Species of dense understory, for example, generally sing songs lower in pitch than those of open forest canopies. Because they're never heard by most birders and ornithologists, the eerie nocturnal songs of many petrels, shearwaters, and storm-petrels on their nesting colonies go underappreciated.

A few hundred species, including many wrens and bush-shrikes, are known to engage in song duets, in which each member of the pair provides elements of a seamless song. This synchronized singing maintains contact between the pair in dense habitats and strengthens the pair bond.

Even more fascinating are the mimics—species appropriating vocalizations of other bird species into their own song. Well-known mimics include Northern Mockingbirds and several thrashers, European Starlings, European Marsh Warblers, and the extraordinary lyrebirds of Australia; Lawrence's and Lesser Goldfinches of North America and the Lawrence's Thrush of South America are outstanding mimics as

Wilson's Storm-Petrel

well. One study of Marsh Warblers determined that the warblers imitated 99 European species plus another 133 African species whose calls they had learned on the wintering grounds. Mimicry is an extension of the song-learning process of many passerines: Normally songs are learned from conspecifics, but the larger repertoire gained through mimicry may be a signal of the fitness and desirability of the singer.

Birds produce a great many nonvocal sounds, from the whistling of a goldeneye's wings in flight to the explosive "pop" at the bottom of an Anna's Hummingbird's display dive, which is produced as its tail feathers are spread to decrease speed, much like applying a car's brakes. Modified wing feathers of courting manakins produce snapping and rattling sounds. A woodpecker's rapid tapping of its bill against a hard, resonating surface produces the drums that substitute for vocal songs.

Augmenting the sounds they produce, some courting birds also engage in intricately choreographed dances on the ground, in the trees, and in the air. Cranes dance on the ground and jump in the air; birds of paradise and manakins dance among the twigs and branches in arboreal display sites; and terns and tropicbirds engage in synchronized aerial glides and maneuvers.

The Willow Warbler prefers low foliage for nesting as it sings in England during breeding season. Although it is one of the first birds to appear each spring in northern Europe, it winters in the sub-Sahara.

Red Phalarope

STRUTTING THEIR STUFF

A monogamous reproductive partnership with a long-term pair bond is a common strategy in birds and one we humans tend to idealize. Strong pair bonds and close cooperation are obligatory in cases where the participation of both parents is critical to the survival of the young; this is true for most seabirds, large wading birds, birds of prey, and a great many other birds. But it isn't the only option for birds. The interplay of habitat and diet can free up birds from the need for biparental care, and this is where it gets interesting. Polygyny, polyandry, full-fledged promiscuity, and other mating strategies have arisen many times in the world of birds. For sheer reproductive exuberance, there isn't much that matches the avian lek, an arena where multiple males gather to display—strutting, dancing, vocalizing, exhibiting sometimes outrageous ornamentation, and basically behaving like a bunch of guys cruising at a singles bar.

We find leks only in those species in which males are freed from parental duties, whether because abundant rich resources allow females to adequately feed themselves and their developing young without male investment or because young are well-developed (precocial) upon hatching and can quickly fend for themselves. Females visit leks solely for the mating opportunities.

Declaring his love from a strutting ground called a lek, a Greater Sage-Grouse in Montana fans its tail and rapidly inflates and deflates air sacs in its throat, creating a bubbling sound that it hopes will attract a mate.

Within these leks, males spar and jostle for dominance, either physically or through possession of the biggest, baddest badges—various plumage or bare skin ornaments, for example. Dominance translates, roughly, to increased vitality and fitness, and this is what interests females coming to the leks. So a male might gain most or all of the mating opportunities with the females that wander in either by dominating the other males or by possessing traits most attractive to females—"honest advertisements" of gene quality.

Most dedicated North American birders eventually will spend a frigid early spring dawn at the lek sites of prairie-chickens or sage-grouse, the latter being among the best known birds with display arenas. The surreal strutting of sage-grouse—accompanied by popping and swishing and whistling noises, fanned tail spikes, and ballooned breast skin—is something to behold. Female sage-grouse apparently agree, seeking mating opportunities at the leks whether or not they're ogled by birders.

Ruffs, shorebirds breeding in northern Eurasia, also engage in arena behavior. Between three and as many as 50 male Ruffs will gather at the lek site—sites that can persist for a century or more. Different males have different status, occupying more central or more peripheral parts of the lek. Younger males or those otherwise of low status are marginalized and may not gain any matings. Many males never even visit leks, instead attempting to intercept females elsewhere for mating. Birds of paradise (from the New Guinea region) and many cotingas and manakins (in the neotropics) have spectacular displays and highly developed ornamentation. These males gather in leks that are often more

As part of its courtship display in Norway, a Ruff flares the ornamental neck feathers that gave the sandpiper its name.

dispersed than those of Ruffs or grouse and thus are given the irresistible term "exploded lek."

Most hummingbirds use patchy but abundant resources; males control a patch of flowers and have access to mates in that territory. One group of hummers, the hermits, feeds instead by what is referred to as trap-lining—traveling over large areas and visiting scattered nectar resources. Hermits can't economically defend a territory and control access to mates there. They gather in leks instead, singing, hovering, and pumping their tails. By clumping together at these leks, they increase the chances a female will encounter a male for mating.

DESPERATE NEST-WIVES

Perhaps 90 percent of bird species are monogamous, a mating behavior that is actually rather rare in the animal kingdom. But long-term studies of marked birds and modern genetic techniques that establish paternity and maternity reveal that even among monogamous species there is a great deal of fooling around in bird neighborhoods. The plot lines of avian soap operas are varied and sometimes downright tawdry. Extra-pair copulations are the avian equivalent of an extramarital affair, and they're hardly unheard of.

Copulation for birds is generally a perfunctory thing. The cloacas—the common external opening of the urogenital and digestive systems—of the male and female are briefly pressed together in what ornithologists allude to as a cloacal kiss. A few hundred million sperm may be passed to the female in a single copulation event. A lot of the attentive behavior a monogamous male lavishes on a female is, bluntly, an effort to ensure that the only sperm received by his mate is his own. Guarding behavior and aggression toward neighboring or itinerant males are means by which a

THE FAMILY JEWELS: WELL-ENDOWED WATERFOWL

MALE MUSCOVY DUCK

Among a few birds, particularly waterfowl, game birds, and ostriches and their relatives, an erectile extension of the cloaca serves as a copulatory organ. Going beyond the cloacal kiss, many male waterfowl have especially well-developed copulatory organs. Particularly well endowed is the Muscovy Duck, a large duck that is native to Mexico and Central and South America. It has an organ that can measure up to eight inches in length and extend at blinding speed.

male can avoid being cuckolded. There's no limit to the trickery some birds will try to gain a mating. Sneaky "floater" males are always looking for the right opportunity. In those lekking Ruffs, some males (referred to as she-males) even have a female-like plumage that can allow them to slip in under the radar, so to speak, to gain copulations.

We can't prove that "marriages" among birds are happy, but we do have some idea of their longevity. Some swans and albatrosses have lifetime bonds, in which the pair may remain together for several decades. Other species with multiyear pair bonds have "divorce" rates documented to be about 5 percent per year—not bad by any standards. In a great many songbirds, however, it is the rule, not the exception, to have a new mate every year.

Mating scenarios in which a bird of one sex takes two or more mates of the other sex occur in some bird groups under certain ecological conditions. Marsh-nesting Red-winged Blackbirds and Marsh Wrens are generally polygynous. The males holding and defending the highest quality territories have the most mates; males with poor territories—often young, inexperienced birds—are not likely to attract any mates at all.

From the female's standpoint, the advantages of a mate's high-quality territory outweigh the downside of sharing the resources, and the mate, with other females. Polyandry, in which a female has multiple

America's largest game birds, male Wild Turkeys strut to impress hens, fanning tail feathers.

male mates, occurs in some shorebirds: A female Spotted Sandpiper will lay up to four clutches of eggs on a territory that she defends, each attended by a different male (though she may attend the last clutch). Jacanas and phalaropes have similar polyandrous mating systems.

◆ **NORTHERN CARDINAL** ◆

CARDINALIS CARDINALIS: From the Latin *cardinalis*, "important" or "principal," hence the name for the senior bishops of the Catholic Church, who wear robes that match the male bird in color.

HOME SWEET NEST

LAYING EGGS & RAISING YOUNG

Those in the lay public who know little about birds often assume that a bird's entire life is centered around its nest: a retreat during the day, a sleeping spot at night, a place to raise young—a "home" that is in use all year long. In fact, it isn't the usual bird modus operandi to be tied to a single spot, although most must be when raising young. Predictable residence and frequent visitation at a nest can put a bird at great risk of predation. So nests are used almost exclusively for a portion of the reproductive effort, from some phases of courtship through the egg stage and variably into the young life of the developing chicks. Beyond that, a bird's life is lived almost entirely independent of a nest site.

NESTING CHECKLIST

It's fairly simple to run through the benefits a nest provides, but the achievement of those advantages has spawned the evolution of a huge spectrum of nest types, from no structure at all to some of nature's most elaborate architecture. First and foremost, a nest must provide a safe place for the development of the eggs and the hatched young. Safety from predators is key. This is often achieved by building a small, well-hidden nest, constructed of cryptic material and attended by adults made inconspicuous through their appearance or stealthy behavior. Safety may also come from inaccessibility: Consider an oriole or weaver nest hanging from a branch tip or a seabird's burrow on a small island free of terrestrial predators. Sometimes safety comes from fortification, as in the hard mud structure

A nest with eggs, concealed in foliage, is used mostly for reproduction. A bird spends most of its life elsewhere.

of a South American ovenbird, or proximity to nests of large birds of prey or wasps that discourage other predators from hanging around. A nest must also provide an optimal environment for the developing eggs and young. Indeed, the nest and the attending parent together form a complex that, through nest architecture and placement as well as the behavior and physiology of the adult and developing young, will ameliorate environmental extremes and assure a precise temperature range for growth and development.

And because it provides safety and a developmental environment, the nest also plays a key social role. Nest site selection and sometimes the initial stages of construction may be integral to courtship: For instance, male weavers attract mates through their weaving handiwork, and the female will complete the nest interior once a bond is established. Yet despite the mates' best efforts, failure rates for nests are high. Songbirds in North America experience nest predation rates between 25 and 80 percent, and failure rates are even higher in the tropics. Snakes, mammals, other birds, and even ants may prey on eggs and nestlings.

Bird Brain

Alfred Hitchcock's 1963 film *The Birds* was inspired by real-life events around Monterey Bay, California, in 1961, when dying and disoriented seabirds flew into homes. The cause was a mystery, but scientists now blame the seabirds' behavior on a bloom of toxin-producing algae that concentrated in the birds' natural food and poisoned them.

A Gentoo Penguin hovers over a days-old chick, which still has the egg tooth at the end of its bill that helped it hatch. For a nest, this parent in the Falkland Islands probably constructed a platform made of stones and pieces of vegetation.

Nests differ as much as the birds that make them. Some fashion cups from mud and grass, some create a sphere of twigs, and some place sticks randomly. The smaller the bird the more care it seems to devote to a nest.

FROM MINIMAL TO MAGNIFICENT

In spring, when bird nestbuilding is in full swing, the diversity of bird nest types becomes evident to the keen observer. On a walk through a vacant gravelly lot, we spot a Killdeer running ahead, calling, and occasionally flailing as if injured. Wise to this distraction display, we look for and soon find the nest—nothing more than a scrape in the gravel, actually, with four well-camouflaged eggs. Stealth and guile are the Killdeer's only nesting defenses.

Around the bend, we spy a mass of sticks partly visible high in a tree, which proves to be occupied by a Great Horned Owl and its nestlings. That stick nest was constructed, it turns out, by a Red-shouldered Hawk last year; the owl, which builds no nest of its own, has taken over the perfectly acceptable site for this year's breeding effort. A flash of color a few trees away reveals a neatly woven hanging pouch attended by a pair of orioles. And

◆ **BALTIMORE ORIOLE** ◆

ICTERUS GALBULA: "Oriole" derives from the Latin *aureolus* "golden." The "Baltimore-bird" was named by the early naturalist-painter Mark Catesby (1682–1749) for the black and yellow colors of the Baltimores, the colonial proprietors of Maryland.

as we reach the highway bridge over the river, dozens of gourdlike structures made of mud are plastered at a right angle to the bridge overhang; a coursing swarm of Cliff Swallows identifies the builders.

The nests we've seen on this virtual walk are but a fraction of the diversity of bird nests we find in nature.

Another approach, the "no nest" strategy, is famously used by the Emperor Penguins. In their

That's the wise thrush; he sings
each song twice over
Lest you should think he never could recapture
The first fine careless rapture!

ROBERT BROWNING, "HOME THOUGHTS FROM ABROAD," 1845

icy colonies the "nest" is a nook between the belly skin and feet of the incubating male. White Terns of the tropical oceans and neotropical nightjars known as potoos lay their single eggs directly on a branch or stump. Nest complexity and construction effort may be as simple as a ground-nesting bird's scrapes to simple platforms or cups made of vegetation. A Mourning Dove's simple nest platform is a minimalist affair of small twigs, often loose enough to barely contain its two eggs. The platform nests of grebes

Bird Brain

Every year, 2,000 Northern Gannet chicks are harvested on Sulasgeir, an uninhabited island in the Outer Hebrides. Men from the Ness district of Lewis, a nearby island, spend a fortnight on Sulasgeir harvesting and salt curing the "gugas." This centuries-old hunt is sanctioned by the EU and has little effect on the flourishing population of gannets.

THE INCREDIBLE EDIBLE NEST

The Edible-nest Swiftlet has a remarkable, refined way of using saliva—as a cement for building a nest. The entire nest cup created by this small brown southeast Asian swift consists of sticky globs of saliva, which harden into a small cup to support the eggs, the attending adult, and eventually the developing young.

These nests, daringly harvested from rope ladders within large caves, form the basis for the Chinese delicacy known as bird's nest soup.

SWIFTLETS IN THEIR EDIBLE NESTS

and Black Terns actually float on the water's surface in ponds or marshes.

Constructed nests can be tiny—an inch in diameter among the smallest hummingbirds—to massive. An African Hamerkop's globular nest with a side entrance is up to six feet in diameter and may weigh more than a hundred pounds. Bald Eagles augment nests annually, with the cumulative nest weighing as much as two

The Bald Eagle, like this one in Yellowstone National Park, adds sticks each year to its nest, the largest in North America.

Noise proves nothing. Often a hen who has merely laid an egg cackles as if she had laid an asteroid.

MARK TWAIN, "PUDD'NHEAD WILSON'S NEW CALENDAR" IN *FOLLOWING THE EQUATOR*, 1897

or three tons after many years. Compound nests, used by multiple pairs can also be huge: A Sociable Weaver condo complex can be used by up to a hundred pairs and reach 25 feet in a single dimension.

The most accomplished nest weavers are the African ploceids (called weaver finches) and the New World orioles, caciques, and oropendolas in the blackbird family. Besides placing these long woven pouches near the tips of small branches, some weavers construct long entrance tubes to thwart predation by snakes. Male ploceids have an innate drive to weave, but well-constructed nests require much practice; the various sections of the domed nest, from roof to egg chamber to entrance tube, are built in a sequence using precise loops, tucks, coils, and knots. Several warbler-like birds of the Old World family Cisticolidae stitch leaves together to form a pouch, within which a soft nest cup is then placed. Many swifts build small platform nests using their sticky saliva to cement sticks together and affix the platform to a vertical surface, such as the interior of a hollow tree trunk or chimney.

◆ CORMORANT ◆

This name traces back to the Latin *corvus marinus,* "sea crow," for the bird's black plumage and large size. "Cormorant" entered English in the 14th century from the Old French *cormarenc.*

TOP 10 AMAZING BIRD NESTS

Nests come in all kinds of shapes and sizes. Some are more unusual than others.
Here's a sampling of some of the most amazing:

1 Orange-footed Scrubfowl: These Australian birds build a huge mound of soil and organic material within which the female buries her eggs. The eggs are warmed by the heat of the decomposing mound.

2 Edible-nest Swiftlet: Swift saliva is great material for cementing together small sticks to form a platform for the egg and chick. This species from Southeast Asia skips the sticks, using its saliva, which dries and hardens into a shallow cup.

3 Rufous Hornero: Mud is used in nest construction by many birds, but the hornero of South America uses copious amounts of mud to build a palatial adobe structure that may weigh ten pounds and last for years.

4 White Tern: For some birds no nest is the best nest of all; the White Tern carefully situates its egg on a tree limb, and the risks of this precarious choice are apparently more than compensated for by the reduced exposure to arthropod parasites.

5 Black-throated Malimbe: These African birds skillfully fashion a nest chamber and entrance tube that may be up to three feet in length; snakes, feared nest predators, find it almost impossible to negotiate this tube to reach the nest.

6 Sociable Weaver: These African weavers build a giant communal nesting condominium, up to 12 feet by 20 feet, that houses up to several hundred nests and provides an ideal thermal environment as well as safety from predators.

7 Baya Weaver: Predator-thwarting entrance tubes are part of the nests of several weavers, including the Baya Weaver of India; further safety is afforded by the long woven attachment, which allows the nest to be suspended below a tree branch.

8 Long-tailed Tailorbird: Certain Old World warblers in the family Cisticolidae, including the aptly named tailorbirds, place their nests within a pocket that they construct by stitching together large leaves with plant fibers.

9 Grebe: Grebes (e.g., Eared Grebe, Pied-billed Grebe, or Western Grebe) never venture far from water. Even their nests float on the water's surface; the platform of aquatic vegetation is usually in a foot or more of water and is anchored to marsh vegetation.

10 Marbled Murrelet: The nest of this species is remarkable on two accounts—not having been verified and described until the 1970s, and often being placed high in mature trees in old-growth forests, which is unusual for a marine bird.

A male Vitelline Masked-Weaver weaves its nest in Kenya.

NESTS BY EXCAVATION

One of the safest places for birds to nest is deep within a burrow or cavity, beyond the reach of many predators. Burrow-nesting is practiced in many bird families, from petrels and storm-petrels to bee-eaters, kingfishers, owls, and swallows. Some of these birds excavate their own burrows, while others use existing burrows originally dug by mammals. Soil soft enough to burrow into yet firm enough not to collapse is not available just anywhere. Earthen river banks are especially popular for kingfishers and colonial bee-eaters and Bank Swallows.

The master excavators are woodpeckers, whose chisel-like bills can drill into decaying wood or even living wood—or, in some species, adobe-like termite nests—in order to create nesting cavities. Starting with an entrance hole a little greater than the bird's girth, continuing inward toward the center of the trunk or branch, and then turning downward into the heart of the trunk or branch where the main nest chamber is excavated, the woodpecker's finished product may be a foot or two deep, with a comfortable bed of wood chips. A suite of adaptations of the skull, jaw and neck musculature, and hinge at the base of the mandible protect the drilling woodpecker from headaches or, worse, brain damage.

In wooded habitats throughout the world—except in the region comprising New Guinea and Australia, where woodpeckers are inexplicably absent—these

The Red-knobbed Hornbill of Sulawesi nests in a tree hole, and the female seals herself in to tend the chicks.

resilient carpenters are key homebuilders not only for themselves but also for a great variety of species that later use their abandoned cavities. The list of these secondary cavity nesters is long even just within North America. Titmice and chickadees, nuthatches, House Wrens, bluebirds, and *Myiarchus* flycatchers (such as Great Crested and Ash-throated) will use woodpecker cavities for nesting, as will Tree and Violet-green Swallows. Among wood-warblers, Prothonotaries and

◆ GOOSE ◆

Indo-European *gha* and *ghans,* "to yawn or gape," evolved into early Germanic *gans* and *gons* and Old English *gos.* "Gosling" is a baby goose (diminutive ending), and "gander" is a male goose.

Lucy's are unusual in their use of such cavities. Small owls and kestrels use cavities drilled by the larger woodpeckers, and even some ducks such as Bufflefheads will avail themselves of such sites. The relative safety of nest cavities has led to the evolution of larger clutch sizes and longer developmental periods of cavity nesters.

Aggressive European Starlings, having invaded nearly all of North America after their introduction to New York in 1890, are well known for their tendency to evict other cavity nesters, even to the point of seriously depressing local populations of species such as bluebirds and Tree Swallows. The starlings' impact on native secondary cavity nesters underscores how the availability of suitable nest cavities in many woodland habitats is a factor that influences the population sizes of many bird species.

Bird Brain

Garuda is a mythical birdlike divinity in both Hindu and Buddhist mythology. He carries the god Vishnu on his back and is depicted with the body of a strong man with red wings and an eagle's beak. Garuda is known for feeding on snakes, behavior perhaps inspired by the Short-toed Eagle of India.

A colony of Red-throated Bee-eaters cluster outside their nests on a riverbank in Senegal. All bee-eaters nest in holes, either dug in banks, which can flood, or level ground, which is sometimes trampled.

NATURE'S PERFECT CONTAINER

EGGS, EGGS, EGGS: A TINY CENTER OF LIFE

Most of us probably think little of bird eggs, apart from those laid by domestic chickens for our consumption or those we see when we encounter a nest while bird-watching, eggs that will eventually hatch into real birds. We rarely consider that egg-laying is an ancestral trait of birds: Archosaur ancestors from crocodiles to dinosaurs were egg-layers, a trait that is found through much of the animal kingdom. It's little wonder, then, that the egg-laying habit has

> *A bird's nest is a bedroom, dining-room, sitting-room, parlor, and nursery all in one.*
>
> LEANDER S. KEYSER, *IN BIRD LAND*, 1897

persisted among birds, since the early development of young outside the mother's body makes a lot of sense for a creature built for flight. Apart from parental care and a protective environment, everything necessary for development of the embryo (up to hatching) is contained within the egg.

THE KALEIDOSCOPIC VARIETY OF EGGS

Formulation of the egg is fascinating: It begins as an enlarging follicle in the female's ovary; it is fertilized; develops yolk, albumin, membrane, and shell; and, once laid, it proceeds from embryo to hatchling. There's a whole field of science that studies the nest environment, embryonic development, nutrients within the egg, and the interplay of eggshell

Variation of design and size can be seen in the collection of the Western Foundation of Vertebrate Zoology in Los Angeles.

structure, gas exchange, and water vapor loss. Because this is all pretty inscrutable to the bird-watcher, we tend to key in on the visible part: the size, shape, color, and pattern of the egg and its calcified shell. And on close inspection, the variation in these characteristics is remarkable.

At only about a quarter of an inch long, a Bee Hummingbird's egg wouldn't stand out in a tin of breath fresheners. Ostrich eggs, in contrast, are nearly seven inches long and can weigh more than three and a half pounds. That's nothing compared to the egg of the extinct Elephant Bird *(Aepyornis maximus)* of Madagascar, which were more than 13 inches long and had a volume of well over two gallons. Just as interesting is the size of a bird egg relative to the size of the female producing it. An ostrich egg is only about 2 percent of its mother's body weight, though she'll eventually lay a clutch of up to eight eggs. The flightless kiwis of New Zealand lay relatively huge eggs that approach a fourth of the female's weight. European Cuckoo eggs are quite small relative to size of the female, better matching the size of the eggs of the host species whose nests she parasitizes.

Bird eggs are, well, egg shaped, but there's lots of latitude there. They can be almost perfectly round,

Bird Brain

Because they look almost identical, it's helpful that American Crows *(caw, caw, caw)* and Fish Crows (nasal *uh-uh*) sound so different. Ask a Fish Crow if it's an American, and you get your answer—*uh-uh*. Some waggish birders refer to the Fish Crow as the "Virgin Crow"—it's always saying *uh-uh*.

Pecking its way to freedom, a Kelp Gull chick from the Antarctic Peninsula uses its egg tooth, the hardened white tip of its bill, shed soon after hatching.

as in some owls, or acutely pointed, as in cliff-nesting murres, whose long-term survival depends on having eggs that do not easily roll away. Egg shells vary greatly in texture, thickness, and microscopic structure. Looking at the outside, we are most apt to notice such differences as the smooth, glossy eggs of tinamous; the rough, pitted avocado-wannabes of emu eggs; or the chalky surface of the eggs of birds such as boobies and grebes. Larger eggs, logically, have thicker shells, and the maximum size of a bird's egg might well be determined by the greatest shell thickness a hatching bird can penetrate.

The phrase "Robin's-egg blue" brings to mind a very specific color, one of the blues and subtle greens that form the background color of many bird eggs.

Bird Brain

The U.S. Endangered Species Act was passed in 1969, and the first bird listed was the Whooping Crane, which is still on the list. The 2012 list for the continental U.S. classifies 12 species and 14 subspecies of birds as endangered. The beleaguered Hawaiian Islands are home to 26 endangered bird species.

Wood Duck chicks hatch in a high hole lined with duck down in an Ohio tree. The chicks must jump next day to the ground or water to join their mother. Despite the long fall, they are rarely injured.

A Lesser Flamingo, most numerous of the flamingos, bends to mother a chick emerging from the one egg she laid on Lake Nakuru in Kenya. In a few days, the chick will join thousands of youngsters tended by a few adults.

But pure white eggs work very well for many kinds of birds. White eggs are more visible within cavities and burrows and are therefore the norm for woodpeckers, burrowing petrels, kingfishers, bee-eaters, hornbills, owls, and many other groups. Overlaid on the light background color may be intricate patterns of spotting and squiggling, and such markings can be fine and sparse or dense and complex. An egg's colors and patterns may make them more cryptic, as in the background matching of many ground-nesting birds. In dense colonies, egg patterns may also allow parents to recognize individual eggs.

◆ DUCK ◆

"Duck" derives from Anglo-Saxon *duce* and earlier words meaning "diver" and "to go under," referring to the way some ducks dive underwater in search of food.

Eggs seem too big for a Piping Plover, which warms them on a beach on Long Island, New York. The hatchlings are soon able to feed themselves. Parents protect them from weather and lure away predators with a "broken-wing" display.

CARING FOR THE CLUTCH

Clutch size refers to the number of eggs a bird lays in a single nesting effort. There has been no lack of evolutionary theories addressing the many variations we find in avian clutch sizes, and while some important general patterns have emerged, the science behind the determinants of reproductive effort continues to evolve.

Many birds invariably lay only a single egg. Most tropical seabirds, for example, adopt this slow but steady approach to reproduction, though it should be noted that such birds are long-lived and will survive to reproduce over many years or even decades. In general, tropical birds lay fewer eggs than their temperate or high-latitude counterparts. There are many reasons for this tropical-temperate contrast—one of which relates to the higher predation pressures in many tropical forest environments. Because large clutches mean larger nests and more activity

◆ PETREL ◆

The word likely references St. Peter walking on water (Matthew 14:28) and alludes to the way some storm-petrels fly with their feet pattering on the water's surface. The Latin *petrus,* "rock" is the root for the name "Peter" and its diminutive form is "petrel."

and commotion at the nest, most tropical passerines tend very small clutches within small nests—thus likely avoiding predators' notice.

Clutch size can be conservative phylogenetically. Petrels and all other tube-nosed seabirds invariably lay only a single egg. This is so firmly established that the occasional appearance of a second egg within a nest must surely be explained as the handiwork of a second female. Nearly all hummingbirds and doves lay two eggs, though some lay only one. Most gallinaceous birds, such as turkeys and grouse, have relatively large clutch sizes—even up to 20 or more in some partridges. Most temperate-zone songbirds lay three to five eggs, but exceptions persist: Titmice, for example, can lay a dozen or more in a clutch. Terns and gulls commonly have clutches of two or three eggs, but for species breeding at lower latitudes a single egg is more frequent.

Other trends are evident as well. Birds whose young hatch in an advanced (or precocial) stage of development lay more eggs, often far more, than altricial birds, whose young hatch in a naked and helpless state. Secondary cavity nesters, having adopted relatively safe nest sites originally excavated by woodpeckers, tend to lay larger clutches than related species that nest more openly. Predatory species at high latitudes experience great year-to-year fluctuations in prey availability, and many, such as Snowy Owls, lay far larger clutches in years of plenty than in lean years.

EGG COLLECTING: MORE THAN AN OUTDATED HOBBY

As with many pursuits in natural history, egg collecting was practiced as a hobby and reached its heyday in the late 1800s and early 1900s. Hobbyists usually kept careful records of the circumstances under which an egg was found, and the aggregation of such private collections as well as those from scientific collectors have resulted in a number of important research collections of eggs.

Among the many things we learn from these collections are details of breeding seasonality, historical changes in breeding distributions, host-parasite relationships (for brood parasites), trends in clutch sizes, and basic taxonomic correlates of eggshell characteristics. Importantly, such collections also serve as a timeline to measure environmental changes. For instance, data-rich egg collections allowed scientists to trace the impacts of organochlorine pesticide residues through the 20th century, because the contaminant resulted in abnormally thin eggshells.

EXTENSIVE EGG COLLECTION

Swift Parrot

INCUBATION STRATEGIES

Images of a bird caring closely for developing eggs in a nest are familiar to us all, but this caretaking behavior is also known in crocodilians, some theropod dinosaurs, and other groups that occupy the vicinity of the avian family tree. Such care involves incubation—the provision of an optimal thermal environment of the developing eggs—as well as more general protective behaviors. Birds provide this thermal control through behavioral and physiological means. A brood patch develops in most birds, at least in the sex that incubates, on the lower breast and belly; here, highly vascularized bare skin radiates body heat to the eggs to maintain their temperature. Behaviors such as shading and egg-wetting further act to control temperatures of the eggs within a range ideal for development.

Embryonic development generally does not begin until incubation starts; it is a common strategy to delay

White Storks in Russia add fresh vegetation to their nest, which can grow to enormous proportions over years of use. Considered a good omen since the Middle Ages, storks often nest on man-made structures and forage in nearby plowed fields.

MEGAPODE MANEUVERS

Perhaps the most remarkable nests built by any bird are those of the megapodes, chickenlike fowl of Australia, New Guinea, and surrounding islands of the southwestern Pacific. Their alternative name, mound-builders, hints at their strategy.

Megapodes use external heat sources for incubation, rather than using a brood patch to transfer body heat to the eggs. Several species build large mounds of soil, sand, and decaying vegetation. A pair of Australia's Orange-footed Scrubfowl, which are about the size of coots, can build a mount eight feet high and twenty feet in diameter. Eggs are buried within the mound and warmed by the heat generated by the decaying leaves. Some megapode species constantly test the temperature around the eggs and mix decaying leaves and inert matter as needed to maintain an optimal temperature. Some southwestern

A FEMALE MEGAPODE BURIES HER EGG.

Pacific Island megapodes forego mound-building and use warm volcanic soil to provide the exogenous heat needed to incubate the eggs.

incubation until most or all of the eggs in the clutch have been laid, resulting in some degree of hatching synchrony. In species that begin incubation with the first egg, hatching dates of the young are staggered, and older chicks (from earlier-laid eggs) have the

---

All the quarrels between birds are about the best way of building nests.

J. M. BARRIE, *THE LITTLE WHITE BIRD*, 1902

---

advantage. The division of parental labor in the care of the clutch varies from uniparental to strictly biparental. A female may perform sole incubation duty (as in hummingbirds and many others), whereas in other cases (as in phalaropes) the male is on hand. Where cooperation of both parents is required, elaborate nest exchange behaviors may evolve in the interest of maintaining a strong bond of cooperation. Often a male's role will not directly involve incubation but rather be focused on feeding his incubating mate.

For most songbirds, the period of time from the onset of incubation to hatching takes about two weeks. A few woodpeckers have ten-day incubation periods; their young are poorly developed at hatching but grow rapidly within their protected nest cavities. In contrast, a small storm-petrel, weighing about the same as a cardinal, has an incubation period of about 40 days. Albatrosses, huge relatives of the storm-petrels, have the longest incubation periods—up to about 80 days.

Baltimore Oriole nest and eggs. Hand-colored print by Eliza J. Schulze (published 1879)

PL.XII.
SIALIA SIALIS.
EASTERN BLUEBIRD.

Eastern Bluebird nest and eggs. Hand-colored print by Eliza J. Schulze (published 1880)

HELLO WORLD

HOW TO PARENT A HATCHLING

Finally, emancipation from the egg. A chick hatches.

It takes some effort, chipping away at the inside of its shell aided by a calcified bump at the tip of the mandible known as the egg tooth. It might take just a few hours for a songbird to emerge, but for some large birds the hatching process can be prolonged, taking up to four days.

Helpless chicks await the return of parents to a nest in Brazil. Altricial young are not fully developed when hatched.

HELPLESS, NAKED, OR OTHERWISE?

So what does this newborn look like? As you might have suspected, it depends a great deal on the kind of bird. At hatching, a bird can appear to be little more than an embryo freed of its confinement within the egg—tiny, naked, eyes closed, largely immobile and unable to thermoregulate. It will take a lot of parental care to get this hatchling into fledging shape. Such immature birds are at one extreme of a continuum that ranges from helpless (altricial) to fairly developed (precocial) young. Highly altricial birds include songbirds, swifts and hummingbirds, kingfishers, woodpeckers, and pelicans.

The trees are in their autumn beauty,
The woodland paths are dry,
Under the October twilight the water
Mirrors a still sky;
Upon the brimming water among the stones
Are nine and fifty swans.

WILLIAM BUTLER YEATS, "THE WILD SWANS AT COOLE," 1917

Let's swing to the opposite end of the spectrum. When the eggs of megapodes hatch, chicks find themselves buried within the mounds of decaying vegetation that had served to keep the egg warm. Using well-developed legs—these chicks kick their way out of the egg—they work their way upward to the surface of the mound-nest, an endeavor that may take more than a day. Emerging strong and

Audubon depicted this family of Willow Ptarmigans in his Birds of America. *The chicks catch insects soon after hatching, but the adult is mainly vegetarian. Adults of this state bird of Alaska molt into white plumage in winter.*

well feathered, they can even fly and feed on their own. It's a good thing newly emerged megapode chicks are so precocial, since they'll receive no parental care at all. Young quail, cranes, and waterfowl are highly precocial upon hatching, able to follow a parent around and feed almost immediately after hatching.

Many birds fall closer to the middle of the altricial-precocial spectrum. At hatching, terns and gulls are cloaked in down and soon open their eyes, move around within the nest, and are able to thermoregulate to some extent. But they'll remain within the nest for a few days, an intermediate strategy sometimes termed "semi-precocial."

Bird Brain

A Red-necked Phalarope spins in the water like a whirling dervish dancer to create a liquid vortex that draws up edible creatures too deep for it to reach. This small sandpiper's lobed toes kick seven to eight times per second while the bird completes one revolution. The tiny creatures transported to the water's surface are snapped up at a rate of 180 times per minute.

Common Crane

PROTECTING THE BROOD

We can't help but marvel at the parental dedication evident in a pair of songbirds as they provide their nestlings with food. Wood-warblers feeding insects to their young may return to the nest with food every minute or so at peak times, for as many as 300 to 400 feedings in a day. Generally these birds have the advantage of foraging close to the nest site. During peak feeding times, Gull-billed Terns will bring fish, insects, or small lizards to their young

every few minutes if a flush of these prey items is available nearby. Adults often must go farther afield to forage, however, with feeding rates dropping and the energetic investment of the parent increasing.

Depending on their diet, foraging range, and the threat of predation at the nest site, some birds may feed their young only once a day. Black Swifts forage high in the sky throughout the day, sometimes traveling many miles from the nest, which is most often tucked on a vertical cliff in the zone receiving spray from a waterfall. They'll return only once, near dusk, with a large bolus of flying insects to feed the single chick.

Similarly, storm-petrels feed at sea all day and return to their nesting colony after dark to minimize the chances of being nabbed by a gull or other predator. Once safely home, they'll regurgitate a mushy, oily seafood paste to the chick.

Albatrosses may forage for several days at sea, turning famine to feast for their chicks upon their return with a bolus of fish and squid that may weigh a pound and a half or more. It's often the case that the diet of nestlings differs from that of their parents. For instance, many seed-eating sparrows switch to

Black-browed Albatross nurtures its single chick, which will stay in the nest for 120 to 130 days before flying off.

Bird Brain

The measurement expression "a quill of gold" originated during the California gold rush of the mid-19th century. Miners used the hollow and translucent quills of California Condor flight feathers to store gold dust. A full-size quill could hold a third of an ounce.

BELLY UP TO THE WATERING HOLE

Sandgrouse seem like an amalgam of pigeons, shorebirds, and partridges. Their relationship to other bird groups is still unclear, though current thought trends a bit toward the pigeon family.

The 16 species of sandgrouse live in arid regions of Africa and southern Eurasia. Faced with the problem of getting water to their developing young, sandgrouse have adopted a commuting strategy. A male will fly up to 50 miles to reliable water holes to obtain water for the young. The water is held not in bottles or even in a drooping bill. It is held instead by the specialized microscopic structure of his belly feathers—which is three or four times more effective than a kitchen sponge for holding water.

Even though up to half the water might be lost on the long commute back to the nest, what remains is a lifesaver for the chicks. The provision of shade in the hot desert sun is also a key contribution of both sandgrouse parents; but the young find their own food—a diet of seeds—under the guidance of the adults.

BURCHELL'S SANDGROUSE

arthropod prey when feeding their young. Pigeons and doves don't bring food items to their nestlings at all; they feed them instead with a rich secretion from their crop lining known as pigeon's milk.

The parent's job description includes far more than just providing food to the young, as our own experience might suggest. Small young birds can't regulate their body temperatures as well as older birds, so brooding the young for warmth is critical at night and during cold spells. Overheating can also be a problem, in which case adults may shade the young or even transport water to the nest. Nest hygiene is also on the agenda. Eggshells are removed from the vicinity of the nest after the young hatch in order to discourage scavengers and predators. Parents also dutifully remove the feces of their small young, a task simplified since the droppings are enclosed in a tough fecal sac, which can easily be carried away from the nest.

Parents of precocial young may continue to brood them and lead them to productive foraging sites for some time. In some species, the adults actively transport the young. Downy Grebes often ride on the back of a parent. Male Sungrebes can carry their poorly developed small young in a pocket of skin under each wing—even in flight.

American Redstart

INTRUDERS IN THE NEST

Can it be? You see a four-inch, one-third ounce Common Yellowthroat almost overwhelmed by a begging juvenile bird much bigger than she is and four times her weight. Undaunted, she shovels a couple of grubs into its gaping mouth and flits off to find it more food. The hungry juvenile is her adopted offspring, a Brown-headed Cowbird. A similar scene is repeated across the Atlantic Ocean where a Marsh Warbler (the same size as the yellowthroat) is dwarfed by a nestling Common Cuckoo that's even twice the size of the young cowbird.

This, the result of brood parasitism—in which adult females of one species abdicate the responsibilities of incubation and nurturing of their young by laying eggs in the nests of another, unwitting host species—is a jarring sight, even as it's

Feeding a usurper, a Great Reed Warbler in Japan stuffs insects into the bill of a larger parasitic cuckoo chick.
Many female cuckoos lay eggs in the nests of other species and let others raise them.

also an affirmation of the power of the host parent's dedication to a dependent young bird.

Brood parasitism has evolved in several bird families. Cowbirds are the best known brood parasites in North America. Brown-headed Cowbird females aren't particularly choosy about the foster parents they choose for their young; some 50 species are regular hosts, and close to 150 have reared young cowbirds at least once. A female cowbird may lay up to 40 eggs in a season, usually depositing only one in a given nest.

Parasitism fits well with the itinerant life of a cowbird. Known for following herds of bison, they're not well suited to be tied to a nest site for weeks at a time. Within the cowbird's core ancestral range, various would-be hosts have evolved strategies to minimize parasitism. Some, like robins, waxwings, and kingbirds, recognize the foreign egg and either eject it or abandon their nest and start over. Cowbirds have had serious impacts on some host species, however, because they have greatly expanded their range to encounter more naive hosts. They've also become more abundant and more sedentary in many areas, putting great pressure on populations of frequent hosts. Nestling cowbirds are generally larger than their nest-mates and grow very fast; by monopolizing food brought to the nest, they usually prevent successful

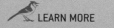

LEARN MORE
MATCHED FOR HATCHING

Astonishingly, a given female Common Cuckoo will specialize on a particular host species and lay eggs that match the hosts' own eggs in color and pattern as well as size. (The eggs are very small relative to the cuckoo's large size.)

In another impressive feat, the nestlings of brood parasitic indigobirds and whydahs of Africa (genus *Vidua*) match their estrildid finch nestmates in their begging calls and even the markings around the inside of the mouth that stimulate feeding by the adult finches.

fledging of any of the host's own young. Cowbird "control" is a key element in the management of some declining species that suffer high parasitism rates.

Brood parasitism by cuckoos has apparently evolved twice: in many Old World genera and in at least three species of the New World tropics. African honeyguides, those beeswax-eating relatives of woodpeckers, are brood parasites on barbets and other hosts. Step-siblings from hell, newly hatched honeyguides actually kill their nest-mates with lethal hooks on their bill tips. At least one duck species, the Black-headed Duck of South America, is a brood parasite, mostly using other ducks and coots as hosts. Some other ducks, including Redheads of North America, sometimes lay eggs in the nests of other duck species, and egg dumping into nests of conspecifics is not rare in waterfowl and some other birds.

Bird Brain
In 1940, unscrupulous New York City pet dealers started selling House Finches, native to the Southwest, renaming them "Hollywood Finches." When threatened with prosecution by the U.S. Fish and Wildlife Service, the dealers released their birds. The released House Finches spread west until they joined the native western population in 1995.

Begging for food, a juvenile Gentoo Penguin chases a parent in the Falkland Islands. Before long, the hungry youngster will have to seek krill and fish by itself as it swims in its southern ocean home.

FULL-FLEDGED YOUNGSTERS

Human families vary in their own fledging strategies. Some parents want the kids out of the house as soon as possible. Others can't ever accept having a son or daughter leave home.

It's not so different among birds. Megapodes might never even see their parents. Once they hatch, they're on their own. Some of the largest seabirds, in contrast, spend so long raising their chicks that they can only breed every other year. A young Wandering Albatross won't fly until 40 weeks post-hatching, receiving parental care for much of that pre-flight period.

There are really three components of fledging. The first is departure from the nest. This can happen on day one in precocial species. Not surprisingly, these highly precocial species are mostly ground-inhabiting or swimming birds and so are not strongly dependent on flight for foraging. Birds that can only feed with strong powers of flight may remain in the safety of the nest until ready to fly. For example, young swifts may remain in the nest until developed enough to fly, a period that can be as long as ten weeks. Most

◆ LOON ◆

Scandinavian words *lomr* and *lom* for "lame" probably refer to the loon's inability to walk upright on land. The Shetland name for the bird is *loom*. "Loony," short for lunatic, derives from a different Latin word, *lunaticus*, "moon-struck," although it seems an apt description of the loon's wild and eerie cries.

songbirds spend less than two weeks in the nest. A second step in fledging is the attainment of full locomotory skills, which includes flight for the vast majority of bird species. As we've seen, this can occur well after a young bird has left the nest.

Finally, the true endpoint of fledging is independence from the parents. When a young albatross finally takes flight, it won't receive any more care from its parents. Quite unlike albatrosses, young terns may follow and continue to be fed by a parent for weeks or even months after they've perfected flying. Young cranes, swans, and geese typically migrate long distances as a family unit, with the immature spending the winter honing their skills in an appren-

ticeship with their parents. Young birds launched into the world on their own during their first year of life suffer high mortality rates. First-year survival in many migratory songbirds may be as low as about 10 percent, and mass kills at skyscrapers and other structures in fall migration are overwhelmingly dominated by young birds.

Bird Brain

Ancient Egyptians revered the Sacred Ibis as a representation of Thoth, god of writing and wisdom. At one archaeological site, more than a million ibis mummies were found, well prepared for their journey into the afterlife—their stomachs packed with food. The Sacred Ibis is now a rarity in Egypt, although it is common in sub-Saharan Africa.

An owl fledgling that cannot yet fly bluffs an intruder by spreading its wings. The young bird developed the feathers to fly but left the nest too early and cannot get airborne.

LIVING ON THE EDGE

BIRDS THAT ADAPT TO NATURE'S EXTREMES

Our fascination with birds focuses on their remarkable diversity and beauty, for certain, but perhaps most importantly we are in awe of their ability to fly and the varied avenues that this evolutionary innovation has opened up for them. Because of their powers of flight, birds are found almost everywhere on Earth—at least at the surface, a bit above it, and a very little bit below it.

BIRDS, BIRDS EVERYWHERE

Cruising through the eastern tropical Pacific Ocean, at a point farther from land than anywhere on Earth, one still encounters birds—lots of them. There are petrels: White-winged, Black-winged, Juan Fernandez, and others. White-faced Storm-Petrels dance by,

I once had a sparrow alight upon my shoulder for a moment while I was hoeing in a village garden, and I felt that I was more distinguished by that circumstance than I should have been by any epaulet I could have worn.

HENRY DAVID THOREAU, *WALDEN*, 1854

and a flock of Sooty and White Terns wheels in the distance. Even the most remote of oceanic islands can host huge numbers of nesting seabirds. Birds have mastered not only the ocean but also Earth's highest peaks, with rosy-finches in the highest North American mountains and snowfinches high in the Eurasian mountains. Alpine Choughs, relatives of the crows, have been seen at elevations higher than 25,000 feet in the Himalaya.

Birds are found at other extreme places, too. South Polar Skuas have been observed over the center of the harshly frigid Antarctic continent. The driest deserts, from the African Sahara to Chile's Atacama, are not without birds, and bird diversity is very high in the

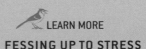 LEARN MORE

FESSING UP TO STRESS

Stress is a common thread running through the lives of humans. And it's the same for birds. Finding enough food, riding out a bad storm, staying cool, migrating, avoiding predators, bickering with a mate, dealing with incessantly begging young—it all adds up. But it's hard to get a bird to fess up about its problems, so scientists divine this by studying levels of corticosterones, hormones produced by the adrenal glands when birds are subjected to stressors.

Corticosterones mediate an adaptive response to stress, but in a world made ever more stressful by human environmental impacts, things can get out of kilter. Scientists have discovered that feathers retain a record of corticosterone levels as they grow in, so a bird can serve as a living record of its own history of stress. The detailed study of stress can help us learn how our intrusions into birds' lives affect their well-being.

Flamingos feed in a high-altitude lake in the salt flats of Bolivia. The tall wading bird sweeps through the salty water with its bill upside down, filtering food through hairlike structures called lamellae.

Earth's wettest habitats such as Colombia's Choco. Echolocating birds penetrate well into caves, and diving birds have been recorded at the equivalent of 80 stories under the ocean's surface. Even the cores of the most urbanized areas of the world host a suite of adaptable bird species.

Anatomical, physiological, and behavioral adaptations allow birds to exploit habitats we might deem prohibitively harsh. Extreme cold and heat, too much or too little water, thin air, thick smog, howling winds and intense sun—birds have managed to survive in all these challenging settings.

Bird Brain

Fieldfares of northern Eurasia organize a unique "neighborhood watch" during breeding season. When their nesting area is threatened by potential troublemakers, the Fieldfares take to the air and, one at a time, screech, dive down, and defecate on the interloper. If the predator is another bird, like a crow, its feathers can become clogged with Fieldfare feces, which can prevent flying and eventually prove fatal.

WHERE'S THE WATER?

VERDIN, A SOUTHWESTERN
DESERT SPECIES

Want plenty of backyard birds? Just add water. A reliable source of water for drinking and bathing can be a magnet for birds. But many birds inhabit environments in which reliable drinking water is scarce. Nevertheless, habitats such as deserts and arid steppes that may be parched most of the year have distinct avifaunas adapted to such limitations.

How do such birds cope? One strategy—mastered by doves and sandgrouse—is to fly long distances to find water. Other birds may be independent of free-standing water by eating animal prey, up to two-thirds of which consists of water. But an impressive list of arid-land seed-eaters can survive indefinitely without drinking water, including Black-throated, Lark, Brewer's, and Vesper Sparrows, Verdins, several Australian finches, and many larks.

Water is produced in the process of energy metabolism—in essence, a diet of dry seeds can actually produce enough metabolic water to sustain a small songbird. Conserving this water is aided by efficient kidneys and by behaviors that reduce evaporative water loss such as seeking shade and limiting midday activity.

Avoiding overheating—or even tolerating a temporary increase in body temperature—reduces the need to rely on panting to cool down, which is important because much water is lost through the respiratory system during panting.

SURVIVING THE HEAT

As one travels through the deserts of southwestern North America, an observant birder might be struck by two things. First, the desert is by no means devoid of birds. Common Ravens cruise the highways, feasting on easily found roadkill. Turkey Vultures flush off a piece of flattened interstate fauna as well. A town or rest stop might be full of Great-tailed Grackles, and scattered Horned Larks fly low over the sandy soil. Once in a while, a crested black bird, a Phainopepla, will be spied atop a mesquite. Or sometimes it turns out to be a Loggerhead Shrike instead.

Red-backed Shrike

Second, having established that there are birds in our most arid deserts, we might also notice that a great many of them are black. This seems counterintuitive: Wouldn't white feathers better reflect radiation and help a desert bird to avoid overheating? Physiological ecologists, concerned with how organisms adapt to physiologically demanding environments, point out that solar radiation does not penetrate black feathering as deeply as paler plumage. Combined with the slight erection of the feather coat and the realistic presence of a slight breeze, black plumage facilitates more efficient convective heat loss—reducing heat gain to the core of the bird.

Gray Gulls, seabirds of South America's Pacific coast, forsake the coast to nest 20 miles inland on the deserts of northern Chile, one of the driest places on Earth. The advantage they gain? A lack of predators. Adults gain a heavy heat load when shading eggs and chicks at midday, but a dependable afternoon breeze allows convective cooling. The daily commute to the ocean is an acceptable price to pay for the safety of the desert.

Colonial waterbirds in very hot environments must shade the eggs and chicks to prevent lethal overheating, so close parental cooperation and seamless nest exchanges are critical. The off-duty adult will cool off by soaking its feet in water, and many species bring water back to the nest by soaking their belly feathers. Egyptian Plovers soak themselves and return to the nest to cool the eggs and chicks.

Erecting feathers, seeking shade, fluttering bare throat skin, and foot-wetting or belly-soaking are important adaptations to lessen the effects of solar radiation. But desert birds also cope with scarce water. Some, such as the Verdin, attain virtually all the water they need from their diet of insects. The dry-seed-and-insect diet of Black-throated Sparrows would seem to be little help in quenching thirst, but very small birds can meet nearly all of their water requirements through metabolic processes rather than actual drinking.

Living in sub-Saharan Africa, the Egyptian Plover waters its chicks from moisture gathered in its belly feathers.

Bird Brain

Only 29 birds that regularly breed in North America have one-word names: Anhinga, Bluethroat, Bobolink, Brant, Budgerigar, Bufflehead, Bushtit, Canvasback, Chukar, Dickcissel, Dovekie, Dunlin, Gyrfalcon, Killdeer, Limpkin, Mallard, Merlin, Osprey, Ovenbird, Pyrrhuloxia, Redhead, Sanderling, Sora, Surfbird, Veery, Verdin, Whimbrel, Willet, and Wrentit.

POLAR PARTICULARS

Cold environments exist on the highest mountaintops and also on the figurative "top" of the world, the North and South polar regions. Birds' feather coats are an ideal survival mechanism in the coldest climates; denser feathering and thicker down are the only adjustments needed. Cold tolerance is also behaviorally driven. Seeking shelter from wind does wonders, and fluffing out feathers and reeling in exposed extremities helps a great deal. The gestalt of a bird changes radically when it's really cold; a robin may look sleek, long-necked, and long-legged on a hot day, but when temperatures fall below freezing, the same bird will appear puffed out and neckless, with feet tucked in.

At home in the snow, the high-altitude Lammergeier in Spain is a vulture not a hawk, despite its feathered neck.

> *I think that, if required, on pain of death, to name instantly the most perfect thing in the universe, I should risk my fate on a bird's egg.*
>
> T. W. HIGGINSON, *THE LIFE OF BIRDS*, 1862

Natural selection favors greater cold tolerance in species whose environments are routinely subjected to low temperatures. Within a hundred years of their introduction to North America, House Sparrows from Florida would die when subjected to temperatures below minus 10°F, whereas their counterparts in Manitoba could tolerate another 9 or 10 degrees below that.

One of the biggest drawbacks of extreme cold is the reduced availability of food or the difficulty accessing it. Birds remaining at the highest latitudes and elevations through the winter must have appropriate foraging strategies. Ptarmigan spend much time under the snow, accessing twigs and buds. Taiga and high-elevation grouse may switch from a rich diet obtained on or near the ground to a diet of more accessible conifer needles.

At the highest elevations, birds have to deal not only with extreme cold and limited foraging

◆ BOOBY ◆

Early Spanish and Portuguese sailors referred to these birds as *bobos*, "stupid fellows or buffons." Boobies nest on isolated tropical islands and had little fear of man—foolish behavior in the presence of hungry sailors. Latin *balbus* means "stammering or inarticulate."

opportunities, but also with an atmosphere relatively low in oxygen. Within a species, populations living at high elevations tend to show larger hearts and higher oxygen affinity of the blood than low-elevation populations. If a lowland bird is transported to a much higher elevation, it will—as a short-term adaptation—show a physiological response of increasing its concentration of red blood cells. The choughs, rosy-finches, snow-finches, and other denizens of the highest mountains of the world show that birds, well feathered and with efficient respiratory systems, are well adapted to life in high places. Bird diversity is low on the highest mountaintops primarily because of the lack of diverse foraging niches.

Bird Brain

Man-eating birds? So says a Maori legend. Fact: Haast's Eagle, although extinct for 500 years, lived in New Zealand alongside the Maori people for hundreds of years before dying out. Twice the size of any eagle living today, a Haast's Eagle could easily have carried off a small child in its tiger-size talons.

Related to crows, Yellow-billed Choughs, like this one flying in the Swiss Alps, are mountain experts. For what may be the highest-nesting bird, its eggs have adaptations that improve oxygen intake and reduce water loss.

THE NOMADS OF THE BIRD WORLD

Birds have settled into nearly every habitat available on the Earth's surface and have evolved myriad adaptations to fit into those habitats. But there are some birds that can't stay put. They can't even migrate seasonally between breeding and non-breeding areas. These are the nomads—itinerant birds that continually move to track resources: They settle into an area when conditions are right but move on when these change. They may wander because the food resources on which they specialize boom and bust in unpredictable fashion. Many seed-eating finches fit into this category since seed crops at any one site vary greatly from year to year, but somewhere over the horizon, more seeds are there for the taking.

Birds in arid regions where rain is infrequent and unpredictable often must be ready to respond to a sudden soaking. Many birds of the arid Australian interior follow this strategy by establishing thriving breeding colonies in ephemeral wetlands with the imperative to reproduce quickly before things dry up. Freckled Ducks, Banded Stilts, and Red-necked Avocets are among the nomadic birds that concentrate in these unpredictable wetlands.

Red-billed Queleas of relatively dry Sahel and savanna regions of Africa can occur in flocks of several million, gathering at roost sites and flooding like feathered locusts into grasslands and cultivated areas to feed on grass seeds and cereal grain crops. Their pest status has sparked major control

LIFE IN AN URBANIZED WORLD

Our human population continues to grow, and bird species continue to disappear in a clear case of cause and effect. Natural habitats with their unique avifaunas are converted for our own ends or suffer the insults of pollution, invasive species, or fragmentation. At the same time, urban centers inexorably expand. Most bird species cannot survive in heavily urbanized areas. A very few seem to thrive in a commensal relationship with people—Rock Pigeons and House Sparrows are classic examples—but many others adapt to varying degrees to the modifications of citified landscape for at least part of their annual cycle. Red-tailed Hawks occupy the center of Manhattan. Band-tailed Pigeons have moved into the center of Los Angeles. House Finches, Great-tailed Grackles, Inca Doves, Allen's Hummingbirds, and American Robins thrive in the altered nature of urban centers. Urban birds can be the hooks that get large numbers of people interested in the conservation issues of birds.

RED-MASKED PARAKEET
IN SAN FRANCISCO

Red-billed Queleas form a tumult in Kruger National Park in South Africa. The world's most abundant birds fly in huge flocks that can take hours to pass a point. Estimates of their population have been as high as ten billion.

efforts, with upward of 180 million killed annually in South Africa alone. Clearly, their overall numbers are astonishing. Massive breeding colonies, tens of millions strong, appear where seed crops are abundant and water is available, but these may suddenly be abandoned if food or water fails.

North America's premier nomad is the Red Crossbill, a conifer-seed specialist that can wander widely seeking good cone crops. These crossbills, which also occur across Eurasia, are quite variable in body size and bill size. Both the species' bill structure and the details of the ridges of the palate represent adaptations for extracting and manipulating particular kinds of conifer seeds. About a dozen morphologically distinct crossbill groups have been identified in North America (with more in Eurasia).

Some of these specialize on relatively localized conifers and do relatively little wandering. But others wander widely, seeking one or a few types of conifer seeds that they are most adept at handling. When the right crops are found in abundance, the exploiting crossbills will settle in and breed, only to move on when the crops begin to fail. Ornithologists have found that each of the morphological groups of crossbills has a unique and identifiable call that they give in flight, so field workers armed with recording equipment are well positioned to help sort out the wanderings of the various crossbill types.

Peacock Gate in Jaipur City Palace (built between 1729 and 1732), Rajasthan, India

CHAPTER FOUR

SCIENCE DISCOVERS THE BIRD

Catherine Herbert Howell

◇◆◇◆◇

Reptilian pterosaurs (bottom) became the first vertebrates to evolve powered flight; 60 million years later, the feathered Archaeopteryx (top) lived alongside the still-thriving pterosaurs.

Dinosaurs & Descendants

EVIDENCE OF PREHISTORIC PRECURSORS

As people of a certain age will recall from the cartoons of their youth, the Flintstones had a bird-activated record player and Ptrans-Pterodactyl Airlines flew out of nearby Bedrock Airport. That said, since the cartoon series had humans, dinosaurs, and saber-toothed cats living at the same time, it may be prudent to look elsewhere for information on the relationships among dinosaurs, other prehistoric reptiles, and birds. These relationships are complex, that much is known, and not all scientists agree on many of the key points.

FIRST IN FLIGHT

To begin with, there is the difficulty with the fossil record. When it comes to early birds and birdlike creatures, the findings are often meager. Their bones are thin and hollow and very fragile, and feathers—if present—seldom are preserved. It usually takes a

A flightless bird named Hesperornis *was an important early find in 19th-century paleontology. The aquatic creature lived some 80 million years ago and was more than five feet long. It had small wings but swam after fish with powerful hind legs.*

certain set of conditions for these delicate remains to be turned into useful fossils, such as a gentle enfolding in the ooze of a calm, shallow seafloor.

For the flying reptiles known as pterosaurs, including the well-known genus *Pterodactylus*, what is known about a current group of 120 named species rests on a total of a thousand fossil specimens worldwide. But there is enough variety among these to determine the basic types and relative sizes of pterosaurs, and some specimens are so well preserved that they provide clues to ecological niches and feeding strategies. Neither dinosaurs nor birds, pterosaurs experienced full flight, propelled by wings formed by a leathery membrane extending from an elongated fourth finger on the front limb.

Pterosaurs flapped and soared their way from their appearance in the Triassic period, 215 million years ago, to the end of the Cretaceous, 150 million years later. They ranged from sparrow size to wider than an F-16 fighter, with a wingspan of nearly 40 feet, and their remains are found on every continent. They met the same fate that befell the dinosaurs: a mass extinction likely caused by a large meteorite or asteroid that made the Earth uninhabitable for about three-fourths of all animal species.

Though not birds, pterosaurs appear neither to be the cold-blooded creatures that earlier paleontologists believed them to be. Specimens found in Kazakhstan in the 1960s displayed hairlike fibers, suggesting a need to keep an elevated body temperature and a warm-blooded physiology, like modern birds. But assertions based on meager evidence remain controversial. What is known is that by the

A fossil shows a Pterodactylus kochi, *a flying reptile that became extinct at the same time as the dinosaurs.*

end of their reign as the dominant vertebrate fliers, pterosaurs had maxed out in size, likely culminating in the behemoth *Quetzalcoatlus*, whose bill alone was as large as a man. Size and time were not on the pterosaurs' side, though, and they perished along with the dinosaurs some 65 million years ago.

Bird Brain

During the short Arctic summer, some shorebirds squeeze courtship, mating, nesting, and raising their young to independence into six hectic weeks. Then, their parental duties fulfilled, they begin their southbound "fall migration" as early as late June. The juveniles linger in the Arctic for an additional month or more before departing.

BIRDS IN THE MAKING

Dromaeosaurs are familiar to most people, just under a different name. This group of bipedal dinosaurs is from a line of theropods, or "beast-footed" dinosaurs, which includes *Jurassic Park* bad guys *Velociraptor* ("swift seizer") and *Deinonychus* ("terrible claw"). *Velociraptor*'s name confuses matters, as raptor is used for the whole group of carnivorous dinosaurs with seizing forelimbs—the maniraptors. These speedy and agile dinosaurs with the killer claws are obviously different from the modern predatory birds also called raptors.

Found in China in fossil form in 1999, the non-flying dinosaur named Sinornithosaurus *may have had a venomous bite.*

Many paleontologists believe theropods are the dinosaur ancestors of birds ancient and modern. They were fast and flexible, and their skeletal structures have many birdlike components, especially in the toes

> *Pterosaurs were just the coolest things that were ever in the air. They were the first vertebrates to fly. They did it long before birds and bats [and] pushed the envelope as far as it could go for a flying animal.*
>
> KEVIN PADIAN (PALEONTOLOGIST), *NATIONAL GEOGRAPHIC*, 2001

and forelimbs. But much has changed since Michael Crichton's book came out in 1990 and Steven Spielberg's film debuted in 1993. In fact, the whole understanding of dromaeosaurs and other theropods took off in the 1990s, with fossil discoveries in ultrafine limestone in northeastern China.

A big breakthrough came in 1999, when Chinese paleontologists uncovered *Sinosauropteryx*, a dromaeosaur with feathers, in volcanic ash deposits dating to the Cretaceous period. Additional specimens suggest that feathered theropods, not scaly ones, might have been the norm all along. Though feathers

Bird Brain

Like stealth bombers, owls are equipped with deadly tools. The edges of their wing feathers have soft fringes for silent flight, their night-vision eyes are large and forward-facing, their radar-dish heads can swivel through 270 degrees, and their large ear openings are set asymmetrically to give them three-dimensional hearing.

This skull of a Velociraptor *from 70 million years ago was found in Mongolia in the 1920s. Feathered but flightless, the six-foot Dromaeosaurid dinosaur stood on two feet.*

can be used for insulation, camouflage, or attracting mates, there is evidence that feathered theropod arms developed the capacity to fly, either from the ground up or perhaps also from the tree down, as a gliding motion. Discovery of a four-winged feathered theropod adds additional intrigue to the fossil picture, though it appeared to be a glider at best.

Not all paleontologists buy into the birds-as-dinosaurs premise. Some believe that birds and dinosaurs evolved along separate paths from a common ancestor, or even that some established ancient birds became flightless and evolved into theropod dinosaurs, turning the dino-into-bird theory on its head. The fossil record seems to create more questions than it answers, and keeps the origin-of-birds debate primed for re-examination with each new discovery.

THE MISSING REPTILE-BIRD LINK

In paleontology there are aha! moments when certain fossil specimens appear and provide a developmental bridge between a more ancient organism and its descendant. Often the presence of an intermediate phase is suspected and anticipated—the search for the missing link. By the time the first specimen of *Archaeopteryx lithographica* came to light in a limestone quarry in southern Germany in 1861, two years after publication of *On the Origin of Species,* it had been anticipated by Darwin and other scientists of the time who were already making a reptile-bird connection, based on such commonalities as scaly lower legs and feet.

The crow-size Solnhofen *Archaeopteryx* specimen was beautifully preserved and complete—except for missing a head. Very reptilian, as one would expect a late Jurassic fossil to be, it also revealed features that were unmistakably avian. Its wings were not formed of elongated fingers like a pterosaur's, but were instead supported by arm bones. The creature, which lived about 150 million years ago, had a reptilian tail,

ART & THE *ARCHAEOPTERYX*

In 1796, a Bavarian printer named Alois Senefelder discovered that images could be printed using slabs of limestone in a process known as lithography, literally "writing on stone." Lithography relies on the repulsion between oil and water, so that a stone prepared with an image rendered in a waxy or oily substance can be wetted and then inked, and only the image will take up the ink for printing.

In lithography, the stone must be hard, yet fine-grained and smooth-surfaced, and should split easily into thin plates. Limestone fits the bill, but not all limestone is lithograph worthy. The stone at the Solnhofen quarry in southern Germany formed some 150 million years ago, probably in an area where widespread flooding from shallow seas alternated with drier periods. High salt content and low oxygen kept out mats of microbes and other microfossil-creating organisms that would create imperfections in the stone. Quiet waters kept ripples out of the stone. Solnhofen's blemish-free limestone slabs quickly became the gold standard for lithography. And as for the *Archaeopteryx?* The texture that produced exquisite prints also made for exquisite fossils when Jurassic creatures washed into the Solnhofen sediments.

TWO BIRDS OF THE *ARCHAEOPTERYX* GENUS

An Archaeopteryx, *believed by many to be the oldest known bird, pursues a dragonfly in this painting. Claws can be seen on the leading edges of its wings.* Archaeopteryx *lived about 150 million years ago on islands close to the Equator.*

but it also had a well-developed, keeled breastbone where flight muscles would attach and a clearly present birdlike wishbone to strengthen the chest region. It also had feathered wings with real flight feathers.

Later fossil specimens showed that *Archaeopteryx* had teeth, a reptile trait that wasn't a deal breaker. It seemed to many that the first true prehistoric bird specimen had made its appearance. German paleontologists, counted among the doubters, had no objection to the sale of the Solnhofen fossil to London's Natural History Museum, where it is now universally known as the London *Archaeopteryx.*

 ◆ FLAMINGO ◆

Latin *flamma* and the later Provençal *flamenco* for "flame" describe the bird's bright red plumage. The English flamingo derives from the 16th-century Portuguese and Spanish *flamengo* for "flame-colored."

Nearly dwarfing a resting male, a Southern Cassowary chick stands on powerful legs in Australia. Males, smaller than females, raise the young. The largest bird in Asia weighs up to 190 pounds and is just over six feet tall.

THE ULTIMATE SURVIVORS

By the Cretaceous period, true birds patrolled the skies and seas. They included *Hesperornis regalis* ("regal western bird)," which seems to be the most truly marine bird that ever existed. *Hesperornis* measured seven feet long and had a body shaped like an enormous penguin, but in place of flippers it had giant feet that it apparently held out to the side for propulsion. It lived almost entirely at sea and preyed on fish with a long, sharp toothed bill. *Hesperornis* shared the Cretaceous with *Ichthyornis* ("fish bird"), a flier with teeth.

Then catastrophe struck in the form of an asteroid or meteorite impact that caused worldwide climate change, with reduced sunlight, colder temperatures, and greatly depleted food sources. In a short time, about three-fourths of all land species became extinct, including all the dinosaurs and most of the early birds. Only a few groups at most survived, and these went on to engender all the orders of modern birds in an explosive example of the evolutionary mechanism called adaptive radiation. Some paleontologists argue

Bird Brain

As a symbol of Judeo-Christian peace, the dove carrying an olive branch in its mouth originated in the biblical story of Noah and the flood, then it became secularized in Renaissance Europe. The dove as a specific anti-war symbol is associated with Pablo Picasso's lithograph, "La Colombe," adopted as the logo of the World Peace Congress of 1949.

Cape Gannet

that this was possible only because the basis of the modern bird existed in the Cretaceous. Others say there may have been only one survivor species and that modern birds evolved from that lineage. Sparse fossil evidence stalls the debate.

Recent fossil finds suggest birds that survived the Cretaceous-Tertiary mass extinction may have had brain power on their side. British scientists created virtual casts of the brain cases of two species of large fossil seabirds found in clay deposits on an island off southeastern England. Results showed the brains of these 55-million-year-old birds were remarkably like those of living birds in size and structure, with expansion in the regions controlling sight, flight, and high-level functions. Big-brained birds may have held a competitive edge in being able to adapt to the environmental changes that followed the cataclysmic event that caused worldwide climate change.

THE TAR PITS OF LA BREA

Los Angeles, the capital of the entertainment industry, has produced a mother lode of Pleistocene fossils. They emerged at the La Brea tar pits, currently in the middle of a park along Wilshire Boulevard, where slow evaporation of an ancient crude oil seep formed thick tar pits. Native Americans used the tar as glue and waterproofing, while European settlers tapped it for roofing and later drilled the site for oil production. Miners found bones of trapped animals and attributed them to ill-fated stray cattle.

In 1901, scientists from the University of California at Berkeley began systematic excavations, eventually uncovering hundreds of thousands of fossilized remains that were exceptionally well preserved by the asphalt. A large proportion of them represented birds of more than 135 different species from groups ranging from birds of prey to waterfowl to songbirds. The list of fossil birds, which lived between 40,000 and 8,000 years ago, shows species that still appear today, such as Bald and Golden Eagles, as well as ancestors of modern species of condors, vultures, and turkeys. Standing out among the La Brea bird booty is the predatory bird known as Merriam's Teratorn ("wonder bird"), a ground stalker that stood more than two feet tall, weighed about 30 pounds, and had a wingspan greater than 10 feet.

A COLUMBIAN MAMMOTH IN THE LA BREA TAR PITS

FOLLOW THAT BIRD

HOW BIRDS HAVE SHAPED MODERN SCIENCE

Birds played significant roles in the advancement of science that marked the last half of the second millennium. A bird component formed a portion of nearly every undertaking in the great wave of global exploration and scientific expeditions that gained momentum with each passing century. Explorers located and collected birds and sent back word of their discoveries and often the birds themselves to their home countries, inspiring delight and demand.

The constant identification of new bird species expanded international scientific inquiry and discourse exponentially. New birds led to new questions, new answers, and new ways of thinking about birds and everything else: geography and geology, environment, life-forms, and time.

Artist Sydney Parkinson painted this Banded Woodpecker, an Asian bird, on the first of three voyages by Captain James Cook in the mid-18th century. The British Navy instructed Cook to record flora and fauna on the voyages.

EXPLORING FOR BIRDS

The three voyages of Captain James Cook in the mid-18th century contributed greatly to this scientific endeavor. Each expedition had a natural history component. The first voyage included a team led by botanist Joseph Banks that was bent on documenting all the flora and fauna they encountered on land and sea. Among its members were two artists, Sydney Parkinson and Alexander Buchan, as well as Daniel Solander, a student of taxonomist Carolus Linnaeus, who was charged with promoting the new Linnaean system of classification. Before he died of fever on the return voyage, Parkinson made some 1,000 paintings and sketches, including 35 bird paintings—birds being quite overshadowed by botany on this voyage. The second voyage had the services of the grumpy but incomparable naturalist Johann Reinhold Forster and his son Johann Georg. They made many remarkable discoveries, but a number of their specimens deteriorated, and they were slow in publishing their reports.

By the third voyage (1776–1780), it was left to the ship's surgeon, William Anderson, to serve as naturalist. He had been trained under the Forsters and actually made a magnificent haul of at least 120 different bird species. He also took detailed notes that were passed on to Joseph Banks, who served for many years as president of the Royal Society of London and a trustee of the British Museum. Many of the bird specimens also made their way into the private cabinets of Banks and other prominent men, making them the envy of natural historians—and enthusiastic amateurs—everywhere.

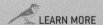 LEARN MORE

LINNAEUS NAMES THE BIRDS

When scientific inquiry took off with the great explorations and expeditions of the 17th century on, discoveries of organisms posed a problem to those who wanted to describe them to others. If a naturalist in the field found something new and exciting, he couldn't shoot off photos from his cell phone to his colleagues back home and then call to discuss its minutiae the moment he got a decent signal. It was a real challenge to describe an organism in the detail needed to nail its characteristics and give it an identity. This was true especially in botany and the study of insects, but it also applied to ornithology. Discovering birds, describing them, and naming them was fraught with obstacles.

In 1728, Swedish physician, botanist, and zoologist Carolus Linnaeus revolutionized scientific classification when he published the first version of *Systema naturae (System of Nature)*, which established a framework of hierarchical classification for the natural world. It also standardized naming by imposing a system of binomial nomenclature—genus and species. Binomial nomenclature helped to clear up confusion surrounding common names for the same species in different languages.

Consider the challenge to Prince Frederick von Hohenstaufen, Holy Roman Emperor, who compiled the 13th-century masterwork of falconry called *De arte venandi cum avibus (The Art of Hunting with Birds)*. He wrestled with a Latin description of a bird he saw in Africa, coming up with what translates as "a kind of bustard found in the desert that has a high crest on its head extending to the back, like a mane." Five centuries later, under Linnaeus's scheme, this was *Sagittarius serpentarius*, the Secretary-bird.

WALLACE & DARWIN: UNITED BY BIRDS

Without a doubt, the most important scientific development of the 19th century was the publication of *On the Origin of Species* in 1859 by Charles Darwin. It posited the basic mechanisms of evolution, including the most central—natural selection, a process by which organisms best adapted to their environment enjoy more successful reproduction and the ability to influence future generations. The modern discussion of Darwin and evolution sometimes overlooks the contribution of his contemporary, fellow naturalist Alfred Russel Wallace. The two arrived at similar conclusions about evolution in tandem but separately: They were separated by a

A male Wallace's Standardwing displays it finery. The Indonesian bird of paradise was named for Alfred Russel Wallace.

Bird Brain

Until 2007, when the French government began enforcing a long-standing ban, the greatest guilty pleasure of gourmands was eating Ortolan Buntings. Captured live, force fed, then drowned in Armagnac before roasting, the tiny birds were eaten whole, bones and innards included, by diners whose faces were covered by black linen hoods.

distance of some 10,000 miles at the time this realization hit.

As a young man, Darwin made a number of attempts to get his academic bearings. Medical school in Edinburgh was a wash, as was a stint studying for ordination at Cambridge. Always he reverted to his real love, nature, and to accruing the skills that would make him a bona fide field naturalist. John Edmonstone, a freed Guyanese slave, taught Darwin and other medical students the practice of taxidermy, a skill that soon came in very handy.

Among the books that inspired Darwin was Gilbert White's *A Natural History of Selborne* (1789). A minister, White observed and recorded the natural world surrounding his country parsonage in England's Hampshire. Darwin applied White's example, beginning with a journal of bird observations. By the time he signed on as naturalist at age 22 to a survey expedition on the H.M.S. *Beagle,* Darwin had great credentials.

Wallace, born 14 years after Darwin, did not have the luxury to experiment with academic majors. Reduced family circumstances required him to train for and take on a number of practical jobs, and he became skilled at surveying, joining his brother's business at several points. At 20, he set sail for years of exploration along the Amazon and later spent the bulk of his thirties doing the same in the Malay Archipelago.

Birds played a central part in the evolutionary thinking of both Wallace and Darwin. A detailed H.M.S. *Beagle* survey of the Galápagos gave Darwin the opportunity to study and collect bird species on all the islands. His later realizations about the differences among various species of birds commonly called ground finches helped bring adaptation into clear focus for him. Wallace, who spent a good part of his eight years in the Malay Archipelago tracking down every bird of paradise species he could find, drew similar conclusions on his own.

In 1858, he sent an article to Darwin for review, causing Darwin to realize immediately that both had arrived at the same path-breaking discovery. A consultation with prominent scientists Charles Lyell and Joseph Dalton Hooker led to a decision to present together Wallace's article and similar writings by Darwin at a meeting of the Linnean Society in London. Wallace learned of the event after the fact, but he was not dismayed and appeared content for Darwin to take most of the credit for natural selection. When Wallace returned from his travels in 1862 he called on Darwin and soon became his champion in the matter of explaining and defending evolution. Darwin spent his later years in the routines of scholarship and family life. He died at the age of 83 in 1882 and received a funeral

Charles Darwin, famous for his study of finches published in On the Origin of Species, *was photographed in 1881.*

worthy of a monarch or statesman. Among his pallbearers were two dukes, an earl, the American ambassador to Britain, and Wallace. Wallace's golden years played out in similar fashion. With Darwin gone, his status rose—he pioneered the field of biogeography—and he lectured and toured widely. He remained active until his death at 90 in 1913. It was suggested that he be buried next to Darwin in Westminster Abbey, but Wallace's family declined, and he was laid to rest in a small cemetery near his home in Dorset.

◆ CRANE ◆

In Greek *geranos* and in Latin *grus*, the name for "crane" probably comes from the Indo-European *gar* or *ker*, "calling" or "crying out." By about A.D. 1000, the bird was called *cran* in Old English. The word also refers to a tall lifting machine, and, as a verb, means to twist into a long-necked, birdlike position.

Spoon-billed Sandpiper

DARWIN'S FINCHES

Slightly more than a dozen species of drab, small perching birds played an immense role in the shaping of evolutionary theory. These were the so-called ground finches collected by Charles Darwin during the H.M.S. *Beagle's* sojourn on the Galápagos Islands, some 600 miles off the coast of Ecuador, beginning in September 1835. Once back in England, Darwin took his specimens to ornithologist John Gould for identification. Gould declared them a unique group of ground-finches new to science with an obvious origin in the Americas. Darwin then settled in to ponder their individual and aggregate significance.

These finches, it turned out, displayed a continuum of bill size and shape, from the tiny,

A land iguana, which grows to 25 pounds, allows a Small Ground-Finch to remove parasites from its skin in the Galápagos. Both species were known to naturalist Charles Darwin.

needle-like bill of the Warbler Finch to the large, seed-crushing bill of the Large Ground-Finch. In time, Darwin came to realize that the different species represented one ancestral species and that their differing bill structures reflected adaptations to the ecological conditions of each Galápagos island. The different ecological niches created a selection pressure to develop the appropriate bill size and shape to exploit different food sources, such as seeds, flowers, leaves, and insects.

It is now thought that the ancestor of these birds likely arrived in the archipelago two to three million years ago and that the differentiation Darwin saw occurred over that long period of time. But recent research shows that natural selection can operate on a much shorter schedule. Changing conditions can trigger recognizable bill changes in as few as two decades. This is what researchers from Princeton University discovered when the Large Ground-Finch arrived on a new-to-it island. The resident Medium Ground-Finches developed even smaller bills to avoid competition with the larger birds. The Medium Ground-Finches with their now-smaller bills could exploit smaller seeds that the larger birds tended to ignore. The work of Harvard researchers suggests a mechanism for this change: They isolated a protein regulating enzymes that can turn the genes responsible for bill sculpturing on and off.

A subspecies of one of Darwin's finches—the variety of Sharp-beaked Ground-Finch known as the Vampire Finch—carried adaptive specialization to the extreme: It obtains much of its nourishment by opening the

A group of Darwin's finches endemic to the Galápagos and key to his evolutionary theory rest atop his research journal.

feather veins of seabirds to drink their blood. Adult birds can tolerate these assaults, but chicks often succumb to the process, especially if mobbed by a group of the blood-hungry finches.

Bird Brain

Roger Tory Peterson is often credited with "inventing" the field guide in 1934, with publication of his bestselling *A Field Guide to the Birds.* Although Peterson set the standard for years to come, earlier books by Frank Chapman, Florence Merriam, Chester Reed, and Ralph Hoffmann were the foundation of Peterson's work.

DARWIN'S PIGEONS

Some of Darwin's most profound insights into the mechanisms of natural selection occurred much closer to his home than the Galápagos Islands. He found inspiration and answers among pigeon fanciers of Victorian London and the objects of their affection—birds that they bred and exhibited competitively.

Darwin began his experiments in pigeon breeding in March 1855 as he did every other pursuit—with

> *The pigeon is, if not actually sacred, at least highly respected in Venice. You will never be offered him roasted in a Venetian restaurant.*
>
> JAN MORRIS, *A VENETIAN BESTIARY*, 1982

the thoroughness of his ingrained scientific methods. In *On the Origin of Species* he offered this rationale: "Believing that it is always best to study some special group, I have, under deliberation, taken up domestic pigeons. I have kept every breed which I could purchase or obtain, and have been most kindly favoured with skins from several quarters of the world." He set up a dovecote at his home in Kent and got to work.

On forays into London he connected with pigeon fancier clubs, called columbarium societies, which were divided by social class, of course, and joined at least two. Society meetings combined pub-based

Charles Darwin bred ornamental pigeons to prove scientifically his theories about natural selection.

camaraderie with opportunities for the members to show their birds and have them judged. Darwin's new compatriots were more than happy to share their expertise, as were folks both in and out of Britain who sent to Darwin skins, skeletons, and information on an almost daily basis.

Despite his intention to keep this investigation a scientific endeavor, offering "no amusement," Charles Darwin lost his resolve before the year was out, writing to his friend, the geologist Charles Lyall: "I will show you my pigeons! Which are the greatest treat, in my

◆ EAGLE ◆

Derived from Latin *aquilus* for "dark-colored" (bird) and *aquilo* for "the dark north wind," becoming *egle* in Old French and then "eagle" in English by the 1300s. The golf term was in use by 1908, perhaps because an eagle soars higher than a birdie.

opinion, which can be offered to any human being."

Pigeon breeding allowed Darwin to observe variation and how selected traits are transmitted to succeeding generations in real time. Though these were not the naturally occurring, environmentally adaptive traits that changed the structure and appearance of the Galápagos birds, they still were traits under selective reinforcement that demonstrated a great capacity for variation. It also proved, as Darwin had suspected, that all these fancy pigeon breeds were descended from one species, *Columba livia,* the Rock Pigeon, and could be bred back to ancestral type. This is what happens over time with feral pigeons—domestic escapees. No matter how fancy they start out, before long the offspring look just like your basic pigeon on the street.

Bird Brain

Woodpeckers have exceptionally long tongues to extract insect larvae from deep within their burrows. The hyoid apparatus, which extends and retracts the barb-tipped tongue, wraps completely around the back of the skull, over the top of the head, and attaches to bone near the base of the upper bill.

POSITIVELY REINFORCING PIGEONS

By the mid-20th century, pigeons became the means for testing and establishing theories in the behavioral sciences. Harvard-educated behavioral psychologist B. F. Skinner, noting the pigeons roosting on his office windowsill at the University of Minnesota, decided to enlist the services of the species to explore the mechanisms of conditioning. His background working in an experimental biologist's rat lab and his passion for tinkering served Skinner well in his work. Amassing a large number of subjects who waited their turns in small, adjoining wall cages that looked like pigeon post boxes, Skinner and his assistants put them through a number of different experiments.

In many, pigeons were placed in an isolated box, now known as a Skinner box, that presented some kind of test and a reward outlet that turned up a food treat when the correct behavior was performed. The task varied: The pigeons might peck at a colored light or distinguish between two terms such as "peck" and "turn" by performing the requested action. They also underwent trials in which actions that approximated the desired final outcome were rewarded until small increments of a task, such as turning in a circle

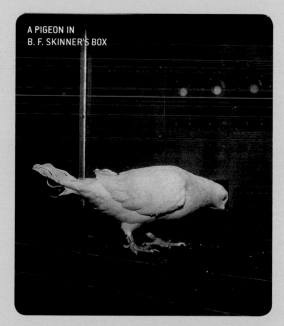

A PIGEON IN
B. F. SKINNER'S BOX

to the left, built up into the whole action. Skinner maintained that the results of his experiments clearly demonstrated that behavior is motivated by external factors and not by internal motivations.

Chimborazo Hillstar. Hand-colored print by John Gould (published 1861)

Sombre Hummingbird. Hand-colored print by John Gould and Henry C. Richter (published 1861)

Art as Science

BIRD ILLUSTRATION IN NATURAL HISTORY

Birds had been mythological, aesthetic, and symbolic subjects in art for millennia, but it was not until the 16th century or so that they began to be depicted for the sake of representing recognizable species. Accurate illustrations greatly enhanced even the most detailed descriptions of birds.

> *If we might call Catesby the "founder" of American ornithology, and Wilson the "father," then surely Audubon is the "patron saint."*
>
> ROGER TORY PETERSON

Aesthetics were not pushed aside, though. The development of representational bird art and ornithology proceeded hand in hand; progress in one sphere inevitably led to progress in another. Efforts originally centered in Europe, but the scientific and popular push to know more about the flora and fauna of the Americas created a species of explorer-artist that could get the job done on all fronts: travel, see, collect, and illustrate the birds. The first wave of these pioneers included the Englishman Mark Catesby in the early 18th century and the Scotsman Alexander Wilson, who immigrated to Philadelphia at its close.

AMERICA'S FIRST BIRD ARTISTS

Naturalist Mark Catesby embarked on the first of his two visits to North America in 1712, making

Mark Catesby's birds included the Pileated Woodpecker, which he called "the large red-crested Woodpecker."

Williamsburg, Virginia, where his married sister lived, his first stop. He explored and collected east of the Appalachians and in the West Indies before returning to England. His second trip was more focused, beginning in Carolina and its environs and going deep into Florida before visiting the West Indies again. On his return home in 1726, Catesby gathered up the specimens that preceded him and began the enormous task he would complete 17 years later, his two-volume folio edition of *The Natural History of Carolina, Florida, and the Bahama Islands.*

It came complete with descriptions of the species he depicted and other facets of North American natural history. Short on funds during production, he prepared the copper plates for etching himself. Birds figured in 109 of his 220 plates. He usually included vegetation in his compositions, although the plants depicted were not always actually associated with a particular bird and were not always to scale. Catesby's style now seems primitive and whimsical, but it set American ornithology on a glorious course.

Alexander Wilson, born in Paisley, Scotland, left his home country in 1794 and ended up in Philadelphia, where he found work as a teacher. He'd had a varied career back home, as a weaver-cum-poet-cum-peddler, but he also had some artistic talent. An immediate connection to North American birds defined the rest of his life's work, setting him on a

Bird Brain

Unlike most other scavengers and vultures, the diet of the Lammergeier, or Bearded Vulture, of the Eurasian and African mountains consists primarily of bones and marrow. Dropping large bones onto rocks below to shatter them, it ingests the pieces. An extra strong esophagus allows it to swallow sharp bone fragments without injury.

Mark Catesby depicted a male Red-winged Blackbird, perhaps the most-studied bird species in North America, perched on myrtle. His illustrations were not always to scale, but his artwork spurred interest in American ornithology.

Alexander Wilson's bird paintings show at left a male and female Red Crossbill (top), White-winged Crossbill (lower left), White-crowned Sparrow (center), and Vesper Sparrow. At right is a male (top) and female Common Nighthawk.

path of study, observation, and illustration that led to his producing a comprehensive book about American birds. Wilson's nine-volume *American Ornithology,* completed by a friend a year after Wilson's death, covered more than 250 species. He sold his work as a subscription series, as Audubon would do later, and counted presidents Jefferson and Madison among those who signed up. Wilson's art didn't match up to Mark Catesby's, although his bird descriptions are considered more valuable. But Wilson's work was an all-American production: conceived and executed by a naturalized American and printed in America.

On the whole, early explorer-artists such as Catesby and Wilson—and Audubon soon after—described what is now lost forever: species and abundances we will never see in North America again. Their determination was so great and their endurance so steadfast under such *Survivor*-like

◆ **HAWK** ◆

The name is probably of Germanic origin, related to the root word *hab,* "to seize or grasp, to have." The Anglo-Saxon *hafoc* evolved into the Middle English *hauk.*

conditions that their accomplishments are absolutely staggering in retrospect.

The Lewis and Clark expedition of 1804–1806 also fell into this category of accomplishment, and it proved the vanguard of a wave of western U.S. bird discoveries that was carried along by ornithologically inclined members of military expeditions.

Bird Brain

Pro sports teams love bird names. The National Football League has Cardinals, Eagles, Falcons, Ravens, and Seahawks. The National Hockey League has Mighty Ducks, Penguins, and Thrashers (the Blackhawks, Flyers, and Red Wings aren't named for birds), and Major League Baseball has Blue Jays, Cardinals, and Orioles. Bird-crazy Atlanta has three pro teams named for birds: the Falcons, Hawks, and Thrashers.

Cornus mas &c.

Turdus minor &c.
The Mock-bird.

The "Mock-bird" (Northern Mockingbird) was well known to Mark Catesby for its great variety of songs and its ability to mimic other species. The bird is shown here perched on a flowering dogwood, a tree native to eastern North America.

AUDUBON: BIGGER & BETTER

There was nothing about John James Audubon's early life to suggest that he would become the toast of several continents by the middle of his life, or that an original edition of his masterwork, *The Birds of America,* would fetch more than $11 million in the 21st century. He started life as Jean Rabin in 1785, the son of a French plantation owner in what is now Haiti and a Creole French maid. Raised largely in France, he came to the United States at 18 to avoid conscription in the Napoleonic Wars.

I wish the bald eagle had not been chosen as the representative of our country; he is a bird of bad moral character; he does not get his living honestly . . . The turkey is in comparison a much more respectable bird, and withal a true original native of America.

BENJAMIN FRANKLIN, IN A LETTER TO HIS DAUGHTER, 1784

Audubon seemed inept or unlucky at his many initial pursuits, whether it was managing the estate his father owned outside Philadelphia, trading on the frontier, or running his own general store. His lifelong passion for nature—especially birds—and his artistic talent kept taking him farther and farther afield to document American birds. He definitely had a clear

Audubon's elephant folio edition of bird prints included this Wood Stork.

plan: He wanted to paint all American species and to improve on, even surpass, the work of Alexander Wilson, whom he had met briefly in 1810. His wife, Lucy, held things together while he followed this quest. He collected his own specimens, prepared them, and arranged them in lifelike poses for sketching and painting. He preferred working in watercolor with touches of chalk, pastel, and gouache (opaque watercolor) for

◆ PLOVER ◆

For unknown reasons these birds were associated with rain, Latin *pluvia* for "rain" and then *pluvarius* for "rain-bird." The Old French for these birds *(plovier)* entered the English language as "plover" in about the 12th century.

BIRDS GO INTO PRINT

·······························

In the age of digital photography, it is easy to lose track of the painstaking efforts
that went into preparing and printing ornithological art.

Bird artists in the early centuries of book printing often had to rely on the craftsmanship of other artisans to prepare their work for the page. The woodcut, the earliest technique, involved cutting away the non-image areas on the side grain of a block of wood, leaving the image in relief to be inked and printed. The result was often crude and lacked detail. But the process of wood engraving, accomplished on the end grain of wood such as boxwood using tools similar to those involved in metal engraving, produced finer images.

Copperplate etching, an innovation of the late 16th century, involved scratching an image onto a sheet of copper coated with wax or resin and then submerging it into an acid bath. The acid etched lines on the plate that held the ink, which was squeezed out in the printing process. Artists would often create their own etchings, but the more advanced technique of copperplate engraving required a different set of tools and skills.

Audubon was the last of the great bird artists to rely primarily on copperplate etching to print his life-size folios of *The Birds of America*. He turned production of the plates over to renowned British printer Robert Havell. Havell excelled in the etching process known as aquatint, which gives a result similar to watercolor when the prints are hand tinted.

Lithography, image reproduction using stone, greatly changed the look and the abundance of bird illustrations. It began to flourish in the mid-1800s and allowed artists to regain control of the printed image by drawing directly with greasy crayon or ink on a smooth limestone slab. To prepare for printing, the limestone was wetted; greasy ink adhered only to the image to be printed.

Employees of Sotheby's auction house turn pages of three volumes of John James Audubon's Birds of America
before their sale. The four-volume illustrated work sold for more than $11 million in 2010.

emphasis. When he had amassed several hundred drawings, he traveled overseas to peddle printed subscription folios at the cost of about a thousand dollars each.

Despite earlier setbacks in his entrepreneurial activities, Audubon approached the marketing of *The Birds of America* with confidence. He created a modern prospectus to pitch his work, complete with a list of potential subscribers. The list began with "His Most Gracious Majesty"—George IV in 1828, an ironic phrasing for a naturalized American to use—and included 123 additional names of prominent early 19th-century movers and shakers, both individuals and institutions. He explained that the superiority of his work "consists in every specimen being of the full size of life, portrayed with a degree of accuracy as to

Audubon's artwork included the Tricolored Heron. The artist observed and painted this bird in southern Florida, but the landscape was added later by his assistant, George Lehman. Audubon's goal was to depict every species of bird in America.

proportion and outline" and touted "the great interest which has been excited by the exhibition of these drawings." Subscribers were told to contact Audubon or Robert Havell, his engraver, in London, or any one of six booksellers in different parts of England.

Audubon's decision to concentrate on sales in Britain and Europe followed an initial lukewarm response to the folio subscription in the United States. But after he was received enthusiastically overseas, where he often dressed in backwoods buckskin to give the Old World audience a taste of the New World frontier atmosphere they craved, American subscribers signed up. He got enough subscriptions to begin production—although no more than 200 complete sets of his 435 plates were ever made. Rendering birds at life-size often required some contortion on Audubon's part to get larger birds on a single plate. They were printed on the largest paper, known as double elephant, which measured 39.5 by 26.5 inches. He issued five plates at a time, in no particular order, with the idea that subscribers would have them bound upon receipt of the last folio, which arrived 12 years later in 1839. Audubon started the series with his signature bird, the Wild Turkey. The reproductions were exquisite, with the birds shown at a size and in natural postures and settings that set a new standard for ornithological art.

This edition of *The Birds of America* did not make Audubon rich, nor did the later octavo (one-eighth size) edition. He created *The Viviparous Quadrupeds of North America* with clergyman-naturalist John Bachman, a book that was completed by his sons. Audubon spent the end of his life trying to amass an estate to leave his family. Upon Audubon's death in 1851, how-

The Viviparous Quadrupeds of North America, *started by Audubon in 1845, included these Eastern Gray Squirrels.*

ever, his wife sold all his *Birds of America* watercolors to the New-York Historical Society for $4,000 and most of the copper plates to a scrap dealer. A few copies of the original edition are now held by institutions, including Philadelphia's Academy of Sciences, where each weekday at 3:15 p.m. a page is turned to display the complete masterpiece over time.

Bird Brain

Asia is a mecca for international birders, hosting more than 2,600 species of birds. As for Asian birders, the numbers are rising in Japan and India, but remain low overall. China, with a population of 1.3 billion, has an estimated 2,000 to 10,000 bird-watchers, and in Malaysia, a local bird tour leader estimated the number in his country at 300.

ART AFTER AUDUBON

Englishman John Gould wore many hats in the field of 19th-century bird art. Artist was one of them, although his output was small. The son of one of King George III's gardeners, Gould's success lay in his role as impresario to the publication of ornithological art. He managed other artists, located specimens—dead and alive—in museums and public and private zoos, oversaw the production of plates, wrote text, and marketed his publications to the proverbial crowned heads of Europe. He would give his own sketches to artists who took over the process from there, including drawing on the lithograph stones. Gould often neglected to acknowledge his collaborators, among them his wife, Elizabeth, happy to take credit for the nearly 3,000 lithographs that came out under this name. One of the most gifted artists in Gould's stable was Edward Lear, known better for his nonsense rhymes than for his colorful, detailed portraits of parrots and toucans. Lear's work was perfect advertising for lithography as a reproduction technique, and though failing eyesight drove him from bird illustration, he remains one of Europe's finest early 19th-century illustrators.

Dutch artist Johannes G. Keulemans was a multi-

John Gould was an artist, but his greatest talent was in publishing illustrated books and managing other artists. This depiction of a Common Tern feeding its chicks is from The Birds of Great Britain *and is attributed to both Gould and H. C. Richter.*

BEYOND THE OWL & THE PUSSYCAT

There was an Old Man with a beard, who said, "It is just as I feared!—
Two Owls and a Hen, four Larks and a Wren,
Have all built their nests in my beard!"

Edward Lear was born in London in 1812. At 18, Lear learned the relatively new printing technique of lithography and set out to create a folio series devoted to the family Psittacidae, the parrots. He abandoned the project two years later, after completing his 12th folio.

Within a few years Lear left Britain to spend decades roaming Europe, the Middle East, and India. He turned to landscapes and illustrations that accompanied the limericks he composed. Lear's best known work, "The Owl and the Pussycat," appeared in 1867.

tasker, working on a number of projects at once, which contributed to his prolific output—2,500 plates in books alone. Keulemans is perhaps best known for his illustrations for a monograph on hornbills, despite the fact that his lithographers often just summarized the detailed vegetation that he had lovingly rendered.

Great change marked the trajectory of bird art in the early 20th century. Sumptuous volumes filled with hand-tinted lithographs gave way to more modest publications produced in the marriage of photography and printing, and they allowed artists to reproduce works in diverse media. Black-and-white work was reinvigorated by accommodating different media such as pencil, charcoal, and pen and ink. These developments combined to usher in a new style not only in bird art but in wildlife art in general. Enter Bruno Liljefors, a Swedish painter born in 1860, who brought to his art a sportsman's unsentimental eye, with compositions that placed birds and other animals in the proper scale and scope of nature. Liljefors broke with tradition for wildlife artists by painting large canvases *en plein air*, in the manner of the Impressionists.

A NEW AGE IN AMERICAN BIRD ART

As the art of portraying birds was being freed of many of the conventions and constraints of the 19th century, it took off in many different directions. Much of the innovation and risk-taking was found in the Americas, with no one perhaps as wrapped up in his own vision (and some might say "visions") as the outspoken Abbott Handerson Thayer. Born in Boston, Thayer spent a large portion of his childhood freely exploring nature in the New England woods. He studied art in New York and in Paris at the École des Beaux-Arts, returning to New York to work as a successful portraitist. By his mid-thirties, Thayer spent his summers in a small New Hampshire town, where he created a kind of utopian community with his family and the students he drew to his atelier.

Blue Jays blend into blue snow shadows in this painting by naturalist Abbott Handerson Thayer.

> *At last, when they were about to leave the nest, I fixed a light silver thread to the leg of each, loose enough not to hurt the part, but fastened so that no exertion of theirs could remove it.*
>
> JOHN JAMES AUDUBON, THE FIRST TO BAND BIRDS FOR SCIENCE, ON HOW HE MARKED EASTERN PHOEBES IN PENNSYLVANIA, 1804

He expounded controversial views on the concealing coloration—camouflage—of birds and other animals. He applied his theories to his art, famously painting out the upper blue of a pair of blue jays against a snowy background. He maintained that even brightly colored birds have concealing coloration. In the jays' case, Thayer insisted, shadows thrown by spruce trees helped them blend with shadows on the ground. His mesmerizing showmanship convinced many people but brought scorn from those, including Theodore Roosevelt, who objected to Thayer's one-size-fits-all approach. Thayer left a radical legacy and also many students who became bright lights in bird illustration, trained in the rigorous Beaux-Arts methods of Thayer's Paris days.

Named for the great Swiss-born geologist, paleontologist, and natural historian, Louis Agassiz Fuertes was destined for the career that he fashioned for himself, despite his Cornell degree in architecture. As a young man and already an established painter, he drew Thayer's attention at a meeting of the American Ornithological Union and was invited to join the summer atelier free of charge. To balance Thayer's iconoclasm, Fuertes had as mentors Cornell's Elliott Coues, the most renowned ornithologist of his day, and Frank M. Chapman, curator of birds at New York's American Museum of Natural History. He also had the opportunity to amass priceless knowledge on many field expeditions, including the 1899 Harriman Expedition to Alaska. Fuertes combined his amazing skill at bird portraiture—his portrait heads became a trademark—with a deep understanding of bird attitude and behavior and an eye for habitat. He created illustrations for many publications, including *National Geographic* magazine, where, among many other contributions, his exquisite series of wood-warblers graced an article in the April 1917 issue (pages 236–237). His celebrated career ended abruptly in 1927, when a train hit his car in upstate New York.

Bird Brain

Eagle nests are called aeries; a pair of Bald Eagles usually builds its aerie atop a tall tree. Some pairs return annually to the same nest, adding more sticks, twigs, and grass. One nest in Florida eventually grew to 20 feet tall and 9 feet wide, and was estimated to weigh more than 4,000 pounds.

Although a trained architect, Louis Agassiz Fuertes devoted his life to painting birds like these Montezuma Quail of the Southwest. His illustrations appeared in numerous books and magazines.

Sabine's Gull

FIELD GUIDE ART & MORE

Not long into the 20th century, scientific precision and the influence of photography began to influence the direction of American bird art. This shift was in the style of the illustrations featured in modern bird field guides. There were exceptions to this trend, though, such as the work of Francis Lee Jacques (pronounced JAY-queeze), who mastered the painting of birds in flight against nuanced, light-rich skies.

George Miksch Sutton represented a bit of both worlds. His ornithological credentials were impeccable: He was the first bird artist to earn a Ph.D. in ornithology at Cornell. His field credentials spoke of broad experience in the Arctic, Texas, and Mexico. Much of his professional life was spent at the University of Oklahoma, but he balanced academic ornithology with the needs of amateurs. In his bird illustrations he largely dropped out setting, which was reduced to a few foreground details. He excelled at painting the fluffy natal down of baby birds and the more challenging down-plus-feathers combo of the developing adolescent.

Sutton also sought recognition as a fine artist, especially through publication of a volume on his travels and studies in Iceland. Near the end of his life, in 1979, Sutton published his inspiring correspondence with

A painting by Francis Lee Jacques shows Fuegian Oystercatchers in Falkland Sound around 1935. The painting is found in the Peabody Museum of Natural History in New Haven, Connecticut.

early mentor Louis Agassiz Fuertes in a volume called *To a Young Bird Artist,* which captures the spirit of mentorship that carried American bird art from one generation to the next.

Roger Tory Peterson's career had a familiar trajectory for a naturalist–bird artist of the time. As a precocious child in Jamestown in western New York, birds took over his life and shaped his talents. The tagline by his entry in his 1925 high school yearbook was prescient: "Woods! Birds! Flowers! Here are the makings of a great naturalist." After graduation from high school, he worked for a while painting in a furniture factory before taking off for New York City, where he studied at the Art Students League and the National Academy of Design. He joined in with the city's expanding birding and ornithological communities, getting to know the staff at the American Museum of Natural History.

Peterson's name will forever be associated with the field guides he pioneered and produced; these focused at first on birds and eventually on just about every topic in the natural world. In the decades since the first 2,000 copies of *A Field Guide to the Birds* were published in 1934, more than 7 million copies of the guide in all its editions and revisions have been sold. Peterson gave amateur birders the tool they needed in the field—a portable guide with illustrations that pointed to a bird's distinctive features, grouping species by similarities rather than by evolutionary relationships.

The debut of the field guide thrust Peterson into the limelight and into combined roles as naturalist, artist, educator—he served for a time as the education director at the National Audubon Society—and

American Roger Tory Peterson, famous for his bird guides, examines an Osprey too young to fly from its nest.

ardent conservationist. In the later years of his career, he devoted time to his photography and to art of a more painterly style, working to perfect the portrayal of landscape and lighting with his renderings of birds. Peterson died in 1996 in Old Lyme, Connecticut. Despite his death, the Peterson name remains a brand synonymous with birds and all things nature.

Bird Brain

The Tawny Frogmouth of Australasia may have the biggest mouth-to-size-of-bird ratio of all, about two inches wide and deep, enabling it to swallow a variety of insect and animal prey. It often sits for long periods with its mouth agape, then suddenly snaps it shut. Some observers speculate that the frogmouth has smelly saliva, which it uses to attract insects.

Vultures and eagles from below. Gouache painting by Roger Tory Peterson (unpublished, date unknown)

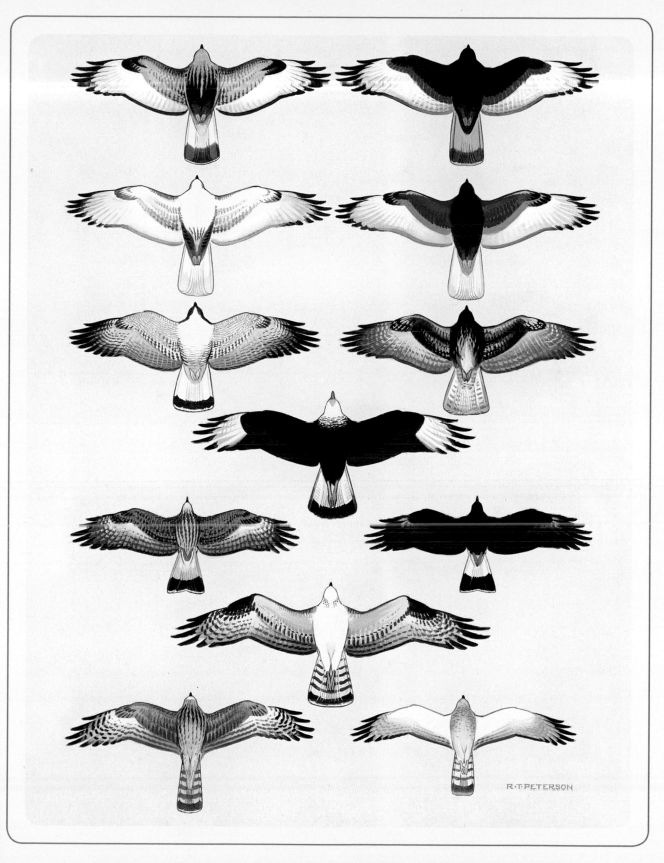

Various raptors from below. Gouache painting by Roger Tory Peterson (unpublished, date unknown)

BIRD MANIA

FASHIONABLE BIRDS & THEIR FOLLOWERS

Highly conversant about evolution and other scientific matters and avid followers of the breaking flora and fauna news from exciting expeditions, Victorians and Edwardians often became accomplished amateur naturalists. This was the case on both sides of the Atlantic, although Britain, as a clearinghouse for the treasures of its empire, held greater resources.

While the wealthy had more of a direct link to

Bird plumage became high fashion in the early 20th century as shown by this young woman as she models a feathered hat.

these desirable objects, there was definitely a trickle-down effect. Those who couldn't obtain them at least aspired to, jumping at any small chance to add to their collections.

THE RISE OF AMATEUR NATURALISTS

But it wasn't all about collecting objects. Both fine art and the burgeoning art of photography continued to capture the imagination. The development of motion pictures took the enthusiasm of amateur natural historians to another level entirely. When first shown to the London public, the gorgeous still photos and moving pictures of penguins taken by Herbert Ponting, the photographer and cinematographer of Captain Scott's

> *If I keep a green bough in my heart, the singing bird will come.*
> TRADITIONAL CHINESE PROVERB

1911 Terra Nova Expedition to the South Pole, created a frenzy for all things penguin.

A cherished hobby of the rich and famous involved the curiosity cabinet, a trend that flourished from at least the 16th century onward. Originally, a cabinet was a room filled with exotic artifacts and natural treasures—whether animal, vegetable, or mineral—and the more unusual and eccentric, the better. As it cost a great deal to amass, house, and maintain the contents of a cabinet, it was a hobby only kings or the

Sacred Kingfisher

spectacularly wealthy could afford. A cabinet usually contained actual cabinets (and shelves) stuffed with comprehensive collections in many categories, including, of course, birds. It was the ultimate, upscale, man cave of the era. Over time, the curiosity cabinet devolved to an actual cabinet and was adopted by individuals of more modest means. Popping around to see and hear about a friend's latest acquisition became a favorite pastime. The most treasured object in a cabinet often was kept in a secret compartment, to be shared only with one's closest friends.

Specimen acquisition was also a hobby across the pond, but some interested parties were more like Henry David Thoreau, a naturalist who became satisfied to observe, not collect. With regard to birds, he was a reformed practitioner of the "shoot-to-study" method espoused by ornithologists such as Alexander Wilson and Audubon. A creature of very entrenched habits, Thoreau took daily nature walks around his property in Concord, Massachusetts, and recorded his observations, in as much detail as he cared to, in nightly updates of his journal.

As an amateur botanist, Thoreau was more into classification and precise record-keeping; as a bird-watcher, he generally preferred to celebrate birds for their birdness and their connection with the rest of nature rather than their nomenclature. He also deplored the collecting mania that left nothing in its natural place as well as the practice of farmers who shot hawks to protect their chickens. "I would rather never taste chicken's meat or hens' eggs," he wrote, "than never to see a hawk sailing through the upper

Snowy Egrets display the filamentous plumes, or aigrettes, sought by hunters in this painting by Walter A. Weber.

air again." Thoreau's sentiments formed the stirrings of a nature conservation movement, but at the time they often were drowned out by the guns of the collectors.

Bird Brain

Red-eyed Vireos are known to be the most prodigious singers in North America. On one day in May 1952, naturalist Louise de Kiriline Lawrence counted a single Red-eyed Vireo vocalizing 22,197 times with 40 song variations during 10 out of the 14 hours of daylight. When it wasn't singing, the bird was preening and feeding.

SHOOT IT & STUFF IT

Nineteenth-century amateur naturalists of all walks of life loved the exotics, but they did not neglect the avian fauna of their home countries. Local birds and their parts, including skulls and skeletons, as well as their "ephemera"—eggs, nests, and shed feathers—were eagerly sought. Anything that could be arranged artfully on a shelf or in a case or frame was highly prized and gone after. This was as true for butterflies and beetles as it was for birds.

Whether for study or for show, the usual method of obtaining birds was to shoot them—artfully, of course, with fine bird shot and as little damage as

possible. There was little use for a mangled dead bird. Live birds were difficult to capture and cumbersome to transport, and if you were trying to collect a lot of specimens at one time, shooting was usually the only way. Even someone like Audubon, whose time spent observing bird behavior paid off in the natural rendition of the birds in his art, had no choice but to "shoot to study." Shooters usually prepared specimens by gutting the bird and perhaps stuffing cotton wool in the cavity. The fancier work came later. Many collectors felt it worth the effort to learn basic taxidermy, but others left preparation and mounting to the professionals.

If you were looking for a growth field in the 19th century on either side of the Atlantic, taxidermy might have been your ticket. At any one time there were hundreds of thousands of specimens in preparation in Britain alone, and storefront taxidermists were a common sight in towns large and small. Practitioners varied in skill, and the best ones created the most lifelike mounts. Both individuals and museums clamored for artistic taxidermy. Museums wanted specimens for their study collections, but they also wanted the elaborate dioramas of lifelike mounted animals that thrilled the public.

Taxidermy was largely a man's world, but Martha

The extinct Huia of New Zealand exists only in museums. Short-billed males differed radically from females.

Bird Brain

The Bible, in the Book of Leviticus, declares it an abomination to eat the following birds: eagle, ossifrage, osprey, vulture, kite, raven owl, night hawk, cuckoo, hawk, little owl, cormorant, great owl, swan, pelican, gier eagle, stork, heron, and lapwing—and also the bat.

A specimen of the last Dusky Seaside Sparrow lies in a jar. This Florida subspecies of the Seaside Sparrow became extinct in 1987 because of DDT used to control mosquitoes and the destruction of its marsh habitat for highway construction.

Maxwell, a petite American woman, made a huge statement with her skillfully mounted specimens and breathtaking habitat displays. A well-educated amateur naturalist, Maxwell got her start stuffing animals for a Wisconsin professor; but she really honed her skills and made her mark in Colorado, collecting her own specimens and mounting them. She wowed visitors to the Denver Agricultural Society fair in 1868 and soon won the attention of Spencer Fullerton Baird of the Smithsonian's National Museum of Natural History. Representing Colorado at the 1876 Centennial Exposition in Philadelphia, she created an amazing habitat display in which, as written by Scott Weidensaul in *Of a Feather,* "cougars leapt from cliffs of fake rock onto the backs of running deer, heavy-antlered elk stood among trees full of birds, and turtles lay next to a flowing stream."

Her next stop was Washington, where Smithsonian ornithologist Robert Ridgway named for her a subspecies of Eastern Screech-Owl *(Otis asio maxwelliae)* from her collection, making her the first woman to receive that taxonomic honor.

Sora

ALL BIRDS, ALL THE TIME

Twenty-first century birders and bird fans of all ages are never more than a click or a few keystrokes away from a bird connection. Every major birding organization from the American Birding Association to the Western Atlantic Shorebird Association has a site, with links to sightings, field trips and tours, education programs, and blogs. These groups can also be followed on Facebook and—most appropriately, perhaps—on Twitter. Many have special pages with activities and contests for young birders and welcome input from individual birders, giving them the opportunity to report or post their sightings or to share photographs and videos. Local birding organizations, as well as nature centers and parks, also share their resources and information on the Web. (Search your location with the word "birding" to find the sites that will point you to local birding hot spots and other possibilities.)

Northern Wheatear

HAWKS IN THE CITY: PALE MALE & COMPANY

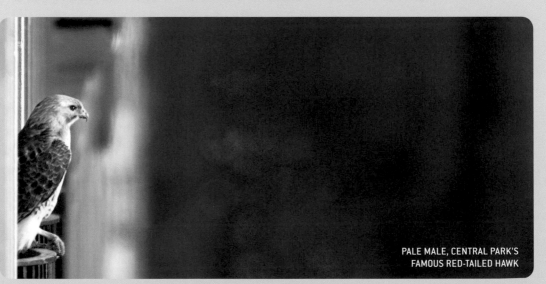

PALE MALE, CENTRAL PARK'S
FAMOUS RED-TAILED HAWK

On any given day in Central Park, you can see a small army of paparazzi training their lenses on the upper reaches of upscale Fifth Avenue high rises. The object of their stakeout is a Red-tailed Hawk and his mate. Pale Male first showed up on the Upper East Side in the early 1990s and took a succession of mates, raising broods of chicks in a nest perched on ornamental stonework. He stayed with Lola, his most enduring mate, for about eight years. They used Central Park as a hunting ground and place for their fledglings to practice flight skills. Pale Male and Lola were evicted from their nest for their messy ways, and when the nest was reinstated, the two tried unsuccessfully to raise chicks. Then Lola disappeared, leaving Pale Male to find other mates going forward. Throughout all this, neither rain, snow, nor blistering sun has kept the Pale Male devotees from their vigils in this Red-tailed soap opera.

Every topic under the sun has its bloggers, and birding is no exception. Although many birding experts blog, the field is not limited to those with recognized credentials. Bird blogging attracts some of the most passionate amateur birders and they live everywhere, from the Arctic to the tropics, in the country and in the city. Some bloggers blog every spare moment and some are very interactive, answering comments late into the night. You can follow a noted national birder, a local blogger tuned in to birding in your area, or one on the other side of the world in a location you'd like to visit some day.

Along the way in Internet birding, you'll invariably run into heated debates, as birding and bird interest in general stirs strong passions. Birding, like politics, runs an ideological gamut that can polarize opinion, whether it involves animal rights and protection or the superiority of a field guide or a pair of binoculars. It's certainly not free of contention, but on the whole, the Internet birding community is fairly tame and respectful. And, as if there were not enough real-life birding action to be had, there are stirrings of interest in fantasy birding, à la fantasy football and baseball leagues. A version exists in Britain that operates more like a pool: Individuals submit a list of possible bird

TOP 10 MOST COMMON BIRD BLOGS

You can get your bird fix 24/7 on any one of these sites.

10,000 BIRDS
10000birds.com

AMERICAN BIRDING ASSOCIATION BLOG
blog.aba.org

LEE'S BIRD-WATCHING ADVENTURES PLUS
leesbird.com

BIRDINGBLOGS.COM
birdingblogs.com

BIRDCHICK BLOG
birdchick.com/blog.htm

NEMESIS BIRD
nemesisbird.com

BILL OF THE BIRDS
billofthebirds.blogspot.com

BIRDING IS FUN
birdingisfun.com

URBAN HAWKS
urbanhawks.blogs.com

BIRD ECOLOGY STUDY GROUP
besgroup.org

Bird Brain

According to early American folklore, a backache could be cured if the sufferer heard the song of a Whip-poor-will and turned somersaults in time with the bird's calls. This mode of treatment was later replaced by chiropractic, anti-inflammatory medications, and memory foam mattresses, which proved more effective.

sightings from different categories of rareness, and the one with the highest number of verified species sightings at the end of a calendar year wins. There is virtually no end to the possibilities of Internet birding involvement.

THE ATTENBOROUGH EFFECT

It is probably safe to say that at any given moment, a nature documentary or other nature-based programming is currently airing on at least one of the hundreds of television channels now available. What used to be a once-a-week special, at best, is now part of the daily television experience. And people now expect this to be so. Evidence shows that people watch some episodes of their favorite nature programs over and over.

Wood Duck chicks get ready to jump from their nest hole.

Take the case of David Attenborough's series *Planet Earth,* a favorite of college students everywhere, which features a global overview of Earth's habitats. Many can describe in loving detail their favorite parts, which often have to do with birds—such as when the baby Mandarin Ducks first jump out of their nest high up in a tree (little fluff balls going airborne on mom's calls and instinct) or the amazing, deep-diving shearwaters that work cooperatively with dolphins to catch mackerel. And don't even get them started about the wild mating dances of the male birds of paradise.

More than five decades in nature programming has made the avuncular, globe-trotting David Attenborough synonymous with nature; his career began in Britain, where he was also known for producing the Queen's annual Christmas message to her people for a number of years. His quietly excited, breathy voice is now heard in collaborations with National Geographic, such as the thrilling 3-D film *Flying Monsters,* in which Attenborough pilots a glider while a star of the movie, the pterosaur *Quetzalcoatlus,* flies above him—all thanks to computer-generated special effects, of course.

National Geographic's *March of the Penguins* scored a documentary film Academy Award in 2005 and has been thrilling penguin fanatics ever since.

Bird Brain

The Parasitic Jaeger pirates food from other birds more often than it obtains it on its own, though it is a capable hunter. In the North Atlantic, these jaegers time their nesting to coincide with the nesting of Atlantic Puffins, so they can steal the fish the puffins have gathered for their own chicks.

An Emperor Penguin with a camera attached to its back prepares to dive into Antarctic waters. Crittercams have brought important information to scientists and great footage to filmmakers. The device was invented by Greg Marshall in 1986.

It follows a breeding season in the lives of Antarctic Emperor Penguins as they march hundreds of miles in blizzards and gale force winds to their breeding grounds; here, females lay eggs and leave them with the males to incubate and hatch, while they trek back to the sea to feed. When they return, bringing essential nourishment to the chicks, the starving males take their turn going to feed.

National Geographic brought decades of nature production experience to the project, including footage and information from Crittercam. National Geographic controls development of this remote-imaging device, first developed by marine biologist Greg Marshall and used initially with marine mammals. Emperor Penguins casually wear their Crittercams like backpacks and capture breathtaking footage when they hit the seas for a meal. The units are programmed for a timed release from the animal's back. In water, they float to the surface and are located by tracking signals.

◆ JAEGER ◆

The name for these piratic seabirds comes from the German *jager* for "hunter" and the earlier Old Norse *jaga*, "to hunt." British birders know these birds as skuas, a Faroe Islands name, possibly echoic of the bird's cry.

BREAKING NEWS

NEW IDEAS & CURRENT RESEARCH IN THE WORLD OF BIRDS

We often take birds' abilities for granted. Birds have lulled us into thinking of their calls and songs as routine and predictable—and identifiable, if we take the time to learn them. But learning to identify common tweets and trills is the proverbial tip of the iceberg when it comes to understanding the exceedingly complex vocal production of birds, as science reminds us on a regular basis.

AVIAN IDOLS

If you're a male bird, having a larger playlist with which to serenade the ladies is definitely an advantage. And enhanced song repertoires apparently are linked not merely to brain size, but also to the relative size of different regions of the avian brain. In a study of 49 species of common songbirds from the United States, Europe, and South Africa, researchers from Cornell University, found that the greater the difference in size

Constant calls keep Long-tailed Tits together, like this trio occupying a snow-covered berry bush in Japan. The calls become faster and longer if an individual becomes separated from the group. The tiny Eurasian bird gathers in flocks in winter.

between upper brain region (equivalent to the cerebral cortex in humans) and the lower areas (regions responsible for motor functions), the greater the ability to learn notes and expand a song repertoire. Over time, female songbirds choose these gifted singers as mates again and again, greatly reducing the chances of the mediocre contestants. Try as they may, those males don't get past the audition stage, which means they don't get a ticket to the next round, so to speak.

The Marsh Warbler is easily confused with other species because of its use of the songs of other species.

The best way is the simplest. Begin with the commonest birds, and train your ears and eyes by pigeon-holding every bird you see and every song you hear.

FLORENCE MERRIAM, *BIRDS THROUGH AN OPERA GLASS*, 1889

It's long been known that the male hormone testosterone supports singing abilities; in fact, it is crucial to courtship song production. Castrated male birds do not sing, even if they were singers before their surgery. But males do not necessarily have a monopoly on courtship songs. Female birds can be induced to sing like males through a few injections of testosterone. In a classic experiment conducted in Germany, researchers injected female canaries with testosterone. As the testosterone started to kick in, all the females stopped gathering materials for nest building. Then all but one of them started to sing like a male after receiving two to four injections of the hormone. These transgender songsters continued to sing for a number of days after receiving their final injections. The female who did not

sing full out nevertheless started to act like a male: She strutted on the perch with an enlarged throat while singing garbled song fragments. She was walking the walk while desperately trying to talk the talk.

Bird Brain

KFC, the world's most popular chicken restaurant chain, serves more than 12 million people a day and cooks about 750 million chickens annually. There is no truth to the urban myth that KFC had to change its name from Kentucky Fried Chicken because its scientists developed a strain of genetically engineered birds that hardly resemble chickens.

Alex, the Bird With the Big Vocabulary

If ever a bird looked intelligent, it was Alex. The African Gray Parrot possessed piercing black eyes widely circled with snowy white. His body was feathered in crisp banker's gray. His wings were clipped, but lack of flight did not diminish him. When he acquired the right words, he could be commanding.

Over the course of three decades as the protégé of research psychologist Irene Pepperberg, Alex surpassed all benchmarks of avian language use and learning. He knew more than 150 words, numbers up to six and how to count with them, seven shapes, and five colors. He put words together in novel ways and made specific requests that he expected to be honored to the letter; if they weren't, he stonewalled his trainer until he got his way. He also showed that he had a notion of the concept of zero by responding "none" when asked a question about a particular attribute that did not occur among his choices or when there was no difference in attribute among a group of objects. All this put Alex on a par with a human child of about four years old.

When led through his paces in a variety of tasks, Alex responded correctly about 80 percent of the time. Sometimes he gave incorrect answers on purpose, seeming to like to mix it up to counter boredom. When he wanted a break, he said, "Wanna go now."

At his untimely death at 31 in 2007, about half of an African Gray's average lifespan in captivity, Alex was celebrity enough to be eulogized on the nightly news.

BIRDS AS TOOLMAKERS

When it comes to the talent of toolmaking, crows and their relatives seem to be right up there with humans, surpassing even chimpanzees in this activity. Studies even single out a crow species from the remote South Pacific islands of New Caledonia (*Corvus moneduloises*) as master tool craftsbirds that apparently go so far as to share with others of their kind some of the many different tools and manufacturing techniques and refinements they have devised over time. Researchers Gavin R. Hunt and Russell D. Gray of the University of Auckland in New Zealand set out

White Stork

to survey crow toolmaking behavior on the isolated French territory. The birds there fashioned tools from twigs and also from the long, stiff barbed leaves of the pandanus tree, or screw pine. The crows use these tools to probe crevices and to pry out the various species of insects that they eat.

Using their bills to rip and snip, New Caledonian Crows manufacture three basic types of tools to fit their various probing needs: They make narrow strips, wide strips, and strips that taper from wide to narrow by means of steps that the crows snip and tear into the leaf edges. Each tool requires a number of steps to make and is fashioned in a completely separate

A New Caledonian Crow is the only non-primate known to make new tools by modifying existing ones.

Bird Brain
The Harpy Eagle, a huge monkey-eating raptor from Central and South America, has five-inch talons and a crushing grip of 530 pounds per square inch. That checks in at almost nine times the force of a human grip, which averages about 60 pounds per square inch.

process. The intention to make a specific type of tool seems firm from the beginning of the process. Hunt and Gray realized that chances were slim that they could observe a useful number of crows at work, so they looked at the trees themselves to find evidence of toolmaking. They sought out mirror images of the various tools on leaves still attached to the pandanus trees.

Examination of more than 5,000 tool imprints at more than 20 different sites throughout the islands showed patterns of distribution and suggested that each type of tool represented a unique origin—not a discovery made multiple times. It also became apparent that both the narrow and stepped tools represented more advanced versions of the wide tool. In other words, tools manufactured by New Caledonian Crows showed evolution and refinement over time, much as human-made tools do.

Additional observations and experiments further lionize crow intelligence. Viral video of a captive New Caledonian Crow called Betty shows the bird bending straight wire into a hook to pull up a bucket of meat from a glass cylinder. Betty uses the curve of glass to shape the hook, a solution she came up with entirely on her own. As toolmakers, New Caledonian Crows and other corvids so far seem to trump chimpanzees, with their individualized, hit-and-miss techniques.

CHANGING WITH CLIMATE

As the planet warms at an accelerating pace, birds struggle to find ways to survive: to locate suitable habitats, ample food, and conditions ripe for successful breeding. This is a tall order for many birds, especially the abundance of species that make the tropics their home. Heading somewhat northward does not much improve conditions, as it might for birds of temperate regions, due to the general uniformity of temperatures in the wide tropic zone. And as flora reacts relatively more slowly to the warming trend, it does not serve birds well to relocate ahead of their habitat or especially of their food sources.

It seems as if Nature had taken precautions that these her choicest treasures should not be made too common, and thus be undervalued.

A. R. WALLACE, *THE MALAY ARCHIPELAGO*, 1869

A strategy available to tropical birds in the midst of global warming is to head up, not out. Increasing altitude allows birds to find cooler temperatures and suitable habitat—up to a point. Eventually, habitat runs out in that situation, as well. However, scientists are finding that many tropical species, especially those in more specialized niche habitats, are slow to head higher and escape the heat. They are lingering at the lower altitudes at rates greater than expected, and that may bode poorly for the future.

Ongoing bird research in the area at the northern end of San Francisco Bay is changing the way we think about rules of thumb related to biology and temperature as they apply to birds. Nearly 40 years of data involving almost 15,000 individual birds collected at Point Reyes National Seashore demonstrate that, contrary to the biological axiom known as Bergmann's rule, bird size as measured by mass and wingspan has been increasing as the climate warms. Usually, birds of the same species grow larger in colder climates, perhaps to be better equipped to conserve body heat. But the Point Reyes birds—

TOP 10 BIRD MOVIES

Here are the films featuring birds that grossed the most money, listed in alphabetical order.

The Birds (1963)

Chicken Run (2000)

Fly Away Home (1996)

Happy Feet (2000)

Happy Feet 2 (2011)

Legend of the Guardians (2010)

March of the Penguins (2005)

Paulie (1998)

Rescuers Down Under (1990)

Winged Migration (2001)

A male Ruby-crowned Kinglet bares its red crown, usually hidden unless the bird is displaying or agitated. The North American migratory bird arrives earlier at breeding grounds in northern woods and leaves later because of climate change.

which included migrants and residents and among both groups individuals that had been captured and banded multiple times—grew an average of 2 percent larger over the span of 40 years as temperatures trended upward in the area.

What could be the reason for this game-changing, contrarian biological shift? Perhaps, scientists suggest, the birds over time are laying on greater mass as a result of changes in the plants that provide their food supply. Or they could be bulking up to better withstand the challenges posed by severe weather events.

Bird Brain

Some of the world's smallest birds have the longest English names: Northern Beardless-Tyrannulet, Yellow-capped Pygmy-Parrot, Sapphire-vented Puffleg, Southern Chestnut-tailed Antbird, Greater Double-collared Sunbird, Cinnamon-breasted Tody-Tyrant, and Javan Gray-throated White-eye—to name a few of the tongue-twisting tiny avians.

The Goat-sucker. Hand-colored print by Mark Catesby (published 1754)

TO BE A BIRDER

◇◇◇◇◇

A hand-colored print by John Gould (published 1869) depicts Collared Inca hummingbirds.

A BIRDING LIFE

HOW-TO HELP FOR THE BEGINNING BIRD-WATCHER

Of all the animals in nature, birds are the most visible, and they are among the most favored of Earth's creatures to study and enjoy. They coexist with us in a variety of shapes and colors—from common birds to the exotic—and animate the landscape we live in. There are 10,000 or so species recognized in the world, and almost 1,000 have been found in North America, north of Mexico. Birding, the act of looking for and identifying birds, sharpens your perceptions and intensifies your outdoor experience. You find that you see everything more acutely—the terrain, the season, weather, plant life, and other animals.

BECOME A BIRDER

Most of us enjoy the challenges of putting names to the birds we see. The abundance of species and their variety can keep it interesting for a lifetime. Some birds are easy to identify: male Northern Cardinals, for example. Other species, such as dowitchers, are more difficult. A few species remain nearly impossible to identify in the field with 100 percent certainty.

There is also the excitement of the "hunt": What will you find today? Especially as winter winds down in the Northern Hemisphere, birders anticipate the arrival of the first spring migrants from the south. Every outing offers the chance of identifying a rare

A vagrant bird is watched by a crowd of twitchers, a British term for avid pursuers of a previously located rare bird. Bird-watching, or birding, became popular in the late 19th century with the call for the protection of birds.

bird, a species unusual for your area. As you become more involved in birding, you'll discover that you are part of a large fellowship of birders, many of whom enjoy participating in field trips and gatherings of

> *I certainly do not think that the blackbird has received justice in the books. I knew that he was a singer, but I really had no idea how fine a singer he was.*
>
> THEODORE ROOSEVELT, *AN AUTOBIOGRAPHY*, 1913

birding clubs. It is a community bound by a love of nature, and of birds in particular.

Birding doesn't require sojourns into wilderness areas. It can be enjoyed virtually anywhere—a city park, a local marsh, or even your own backyard. For instance, New York City's 843-acre Central Park is one of the most renowned birding spots in North America during migration. Many birders enjoy keeping a yard list, noting the number of species seen in or from your yard. How many different kinds of birds come to your yard depends on where you live. If you make your yard attractive by landscaping and add feeders, nest boxes, or a birdbath, you will see more birds than you ever thought possible.

Once you've moved past your backyard and local parks, new horizons will open up. The maps in your field guide make it clear that an Elegant Trogon is not going to visit your yard in Massachusetts, nor will a Sooty Shearwater be coming near your apartment in Denver. Visiting places with special birds—such as southeast Arizona (home of that Elegant Trogon) and

The Northern Hawk Owl, a resident of northern forests, has a falconlike appearance and sometimes hunts during the day.

the lower Rio Grande Valley of Texas—is one of the joys of birding. Beginners will find that birding is easy, relatively inexpensive, and full of discovery. All you need is a mid-priced pair of binoculars, a field guide, and a desire to learn about the birds around you.

Bird Brain

Some Native Americans revered California Condors as thunderbirds, believing that they controlled rainfall and carried messages from the Great Spirit. In the 20th century, Thunderbird was co-opted as the name of a model of Ford car, a model of Triumph motorcycle, and a cheap fortified wine made by the E & J Gallo Winery.

KEY STEPS IN LEARNING TO BIRD

Developing as a birder is a personal quest. For every birder, though, three kinds of learning are essential: observing birds in the field, learning from others, and studying books and other references.

◆ Look at Birds

Get outdoors, find a bird, hoist your binoculars, and you've become a birder with field experience. That bird has entered your memory bank, even if you don't know its name. Over time, these mental images become linked with a bird's name and other details of its life history. The effect is cumulative: The more you

A painting depicts a Swainson's Thrush, Gray-cheeked Thrush, Wood Thrush, Hermit Thrush, and Veery.

go birding, the faster you'll progress, the more you'll learn, and the more enthusiastic you'll become.

◆ Go Birding With Other Birders

To jump-start your skills, join a group field trip or go on an outing with a birding friend; both of these are opportunities to check up on how your skills are developing. Talking with someone about a bird that both of you are watching will help focus your attention, and you'll be less likely to give up on an identification. Many groups, such as your local Audubon Society chapter, offer field trips.

Fieldcraft—how to move, where to look, how to use your equipment—is another skill best learned by birding alongside someone experienced. Feel free to ask questions during a break on a field trip. Most veteran birders are delighted to share their knowledge.

◆ Study Your Field Guide at Home

When you're out birding, concentrate on the birds you see, not on the information in your field guide. Experience the living bird in front of you. Look at its behavior, study its shape, describe its patterns and plumage details; keep looking as long as it remains nearby. If you have time, make some notes or a sketch.

On occasion, leave your field guide at home. Not having it with you will force you to look critically and work at remembering what you've seen. The end result? You'll learn faster. When you return home, check your guide against your observations. That said, your field guide is your primary reference and an essential piece of birding equipment. To use it effectively, you need to become familiar with how it is organized.

You, Too, Can Have an Eagle Eye

....

Binoculars come in all shapes and sizes and can be a great tool for watching birds.
Here is a quick guide of what to look for when deciding what works well for you.

To see birds well, to identify them with any certainty, and to enjoy them in all their stunning detail, you need good birding binoculars. Here is a quick guide to what to look for when deciding what kind of binoculars works best for you.

Binoculars come in all shapes and sizes. A piece of advice for those new to birding: The old ones that have been lying around the house for years will probably not do. Most will be of low quality, out of alignment, and unsuitable for birding. Take the time to compare them to entry-level birding binoculars (starting at about $100), and you will be convinced. Birding doesn't require a big outlay of cash, but this is the place to spend what you can for quality. With good birding binoculars, you will see more detail with less eyestrain and identify birds faster. Once you know that birding interests you, you'll likely want to upgrade.

Listed below are some important features to become familiar with so that you can make an informed decision that's within your budget.

EYECUP
Should be adjustable; usually eyecups fold down for eyeglass wearers.

EYEPIECE
Provides magnification so that birds appear larger than with the naked eye. Most birding binoculars magnify an image from seven to ten times (7x to 10x).

ARMORING
Rubber or synthetic coating that protects binoculars and makes them easier to hold.

FOCUS KNOB
Achieves and maintains precise focus of an object.

DIOPTER RING
Allows eyepieces to be set to match visual acuity of each eye.

OBJECTIVE LENS
Collects light, enabling high-resolution observation of distant objects.

A Guide to the Guide

These two pages show a sample spread from the National Geographic *Field Guide to the Birds of North America*, sixth edition. The various features are annotated around the periphery. Many field guides have similar layouts.

SCIENTIFIC FAMILY NAME

FAMILY ACCOUNT
Very brief text on features shared by all species in the family, followed by worldwide number of species found in North America.

SCIENTIFIC NAME
Genus and species together (binomial) form a species' unique name.

RANGE MAP
The different colors delineate breeding (red), winter (blue), year-round (purple), and migration (yellow) ranges.

LENGTH
Given in inches and centimeters (most useful for comparison to other species). Wingspan is given for species often seen in flight.

SPECIES ACCOUNT
The text describes the important field marks and notes age-related and seasonal differences.

RANGE DESCRIPTION
The text often includes a brief habitat description and mentions the abundance level.

GREBES Family Podicipedidae
A worldwide family of aquatic diving birds. Lobed toes make them strong swimmers. Grebes are infrequently seen on land or in flight. SPECIES: 22 WORLD, 7 N.A.

Least Grebe *Tachybaptus dominicus* L 9¾" (25 cm)
A small, grebe with golden yellow eyes, a slim, dark bill, and purplish gray face and foreneck. **Breeding adult** has blackish crown, hindneck, throat, and back. **Winter** birds have white throat, paler bill, less black on crown. In flight, shows large white wing patch.
VOICE: Gives nasal *beep;* in display, a descending, rapid, buzzy trill.
RANGE: Rather uncommon and local; may hide in vegetation near shores of ponds, sloughs, and ditches. May nest at any season on any quiet, inland water. Casual straggler to southern AZ, southeastern CA, south FL, and upper TX coast.

Pied-billed Grebe *Podilymbus podiceps* L 13½" (34 cm)
Breeding adult is brown overall, with black ring around stout, whitish bill; black chin and throat; pale belly. **Winter** birds lose bill ring; chin is white, throat tinged with pale rufous. **Juvenile** resembles winter adult but throat is much redder, eye ring absent, head streaked with brown and white. In flight, shows almost no white on wing.
VOICE: On breeding grounds, delivers a loud series of gulping notes.
RANGE: Nests around marshy ponds and sloughs; sometimes hides from intruders by sinking until only its head shows. Common but not gregarious. Winters on fresh or salt water. Casual to AK.

Horned Grebe *Podiceps auritus* L 13½" (34 cm)
Breeding adult has chestnut foreneck and golden "horns." In **winter** plumage, white cheeks and throat contrast with dark crown and nape; some are dusky on lower foreneck. Black on nape narrows to a thin stripe. All birds show a pale spot in front of eye. In flight (page 74), white secondaries show as patch on trailing edge of wing. Bill is short and straight, thicker than Eared Grebe; neck is thicker too, crown flatter. Smaller size and shorter, dark bill most readily separate winter Horned from Red-necked Grebe (page 74).
VOICE: Mostly silent, except on nesting grounds.
RANGE: Breeds on lakes and ponds. Winters on salt water but also on ice-free lakes of eastern North America; a few winter inland in West.

Eared Grebe *Podiceps nigricollis* L 12½" (32 cm)
Breeding adult has blackish neck, golden "ears" fan out behind eye. In **winter** plumage, throat is variably dusky, cheek dark; whitish on chin extends up as a crescent behind eye; compare with Horned Grebe. Note also Eared Grebe's longer, thinner bill; thinner neck; more peaked crown. Lacks pale spot in front of eye. Generally rides higher in the water than Horned Grebe, exposing fluffy white undertail coverts. In flight, white secondaries show as white patch on trailing edge of wing.
VOICE: Most vocal on breeding grounds; most frequent call is a rising, whistled note.
RANGE: Usually nests in large colonies on freshwater lakes. Rare in eastern North America. Casual to AK.

ENGLISH NAME

GREBES

Least Grebe
brachypterus

juvenile
golden-colored iris
slender bill
purplish gray neck
breeding adult
winter
white throat

SUBSPECIES NAME
Usually given if the illustration depicts a known subspecies or subspecies group.

white rear end
dark eye
ring on thick, whitish bill
striped head
Pied-billed Grebe
podiceps
breeding adult
black chin
juvenile
winter
white throat
tawny brown neck
downy young

ILLUSTRATIONS
All markedly different plumages are depicted. For Pied-billed Grebe, breeding adult, winter, juvenile, and downy young are shown.

"horns" raised
Horned Grebe
cornutus
adult in spring molt
molting birds in spring can be confused with Red-necked Grebe
flat crown
small pale lore spot
breeding adult
golden "horns"
breeding adult
chestnut neck
darker winter
white cheeks
pale tip to straight bill
winter

THUMBTABS
For quick access to major bird families.

REDUCED-SCALE FIGURES
These show variation, additional plumages, specific behaviors, or comparisons to other species.

puffier cheeks, and white almost meets on back of head
winter
Horned
Eared
Eared Grebe
californicus
1st fall
buffy wash to neck
some quite pale-necked like Horned
paler winter
peaked or rounded head
golden "ears"
often raises and fluffs out rear end
upturned all-dark bill
dark cheek
dusky neck
downy young
breeding adult
black neck
winter

MAIN FIGURES
The main figures on the same page are all shown at the same scale.

HERE, THERE, & EVERYWHERE

Accomplished birders are in tune with the regular unfolding of the seasons and the birds that accompany them—known as the patterns of distribution—and have become familiar with a species' population and habitat requirements. These birders know what to expect and what to be surprised by, or they know where to get more information. Their learning is inspired by field experience, but they also have a foundation of knowledge that underpins their experience.

◆ From Abundant to Rare

Status refers to the numerical abundance of a particular species. Some of the more frequently used terms are abundant, common, fairly common, uncommon, rare, casual, and accidental. It is important to keep in mind that when a source identifies a species as common or fairly common in a certain area, this is true only in the right habitat and at the right time of year. This same species is likely to be much more uncommon, rare, or even nonexistent in a different habitat or time of year. Some species are local—numerous in one area but absent in another—even when the habitat seems to be appropriate. Still other species are irregular (or sporadic): This means they are common or even abundant in some years yet strangely absent in others.

A Red-breasted Nuthatch with a sunflower seed in its bill perches on a sprig of bittersweet. The nuthatch is named for its habit of wedging a seed in a crevice and knocking it open, or hatching it, with its bill.

THE CURIOUS CASE OF THE CONNECTICUT WARBLER

Many birders agree that warblers are the most compelling birds migrating through North America, and the Connecticut Warbler may be the most sought-after species among them. Scarce and secretive, this bird has a poorly documented winter range.

In fall, much of its migration is over water on its return to South America. The Connecticut Warbler probably winters south of the Amazon. Its arrival in early May in south Florida establishes it as our latest arriving wood warbler. It typically migrates west of the Appalachians in spring, arriving in the upper Ohio and Mississippi river valleys after May 10 and in the southern Great Lakes after May 15. Yet many purported sightings occur in late April and early May in the upper Midwest and upstate New York. Are these early sightings incorrect identifications? Probably so. All are undocumented, and considering April 27 is the earliest record for south Florida, earlier records for upstate New York are unlikely. Female Mourning Warblers and Nashville Warblers are the probable culprits; they are similar enough to cause confusion.

CONNECTICUT WARBLER

Red breasted Nuthatches and Bohemian Waxwings are two examples of species that wander much farther south some years than others.

The birding community has made an effort to standardize the terminology for rarities. The American Birding Association and the Committee on Classification and Nomenclature of the American Ornithologists' Union have jointly embraced the following terminology: *Rare* species are those that occur in very low numbers but that occur annually in North America. They include visitors and rare breeding residents. *Casual* species are those not recorded annually in North America but for which there are six or more total records—including three or more in the past 30 years. *Accidental* species are those that are have been recorded in North America five or fewer times, or fewer than three times in the past 30 years. Of course, such terminology can also be applied to smaller areas, such as a state or province.

Bird Brain

In the spring, the Northern Cardinal establishes its nesting territory and defends it from others of its own species. Unfortunately, evolution has not taught the bird about reflections. No matter how relentlessly it attacks an apparent rival seen in a window or car's mirror, it can't drive it away. Only when hormones subside does the behavior stop.

A Eurasian Collared-Dove takes a drink from sun-splashed waters in Spain. Named for the black ring around its neck, the colonizer spread from Asia across Europe in the 19th century and to North America in the 20th.

◆ Species Range

Distribution refers to the range of a species—where it is regularly found. Most field guides, regional distribution works, and guides to specific bird families include range maps. Using different colors or patterns, a range map depicts the general breeding and winter ranges of each species.

Range maps vary greatly in their accuracy and in the level of detail they show, and they may evolve over time. For example, it's hard to find an accurate map for the Eurasian Collared-Dove, a species that is rapidly expanding northward and westward. Often, changes in distribution represent not a sudden change in a species' status, but rather our increased understanding of its distribution. Without question, the most significant contributions toward fine-tuning our knowledge of bird distribution are breeding bird atlases, which have been completed for most states and provinces, and in some instances for counties. Some species are known to have become more numerous and widespread; others, unfortunately, have declined. This knowledge enables us to raise the alert and develop conservation strategies for imperiled species.

◆ Seasonal Patterns

The excitement of local birding is greatly enhanced by watching for new arrivals and departures through the seasons and by keeping track of the permanent and seasonal residents. It's best to start with an area you know well—for example, your own backyard.

Keep notes of what you see and record numbers. By making daily recordings, you will begin to learn which species are always at hand, which are present only in summer or winter, and which are present only during migration times. The surprise of recording a new species for your yard or a surprisingly early or late date of a species' arrival is part of the fun. You will find that some birds are a resident, or present year-round, such as the Northern Cardinal over much of the East or the Western Scrub-Jay in the West. In reality, many resident species move around locally and, more rarely, disperse over large distances.

◆ **Nesting Niches**

In addition to learning the ranges and distributional timing for a species, it is also important to learn its habitat. Knowing the precise habitat is essential for finding local species during the breeding season. Even during the winter and migration periods, most species frequent particular types of habitats. For example, along the Atlantic coast during winter, one's search for the Purple Sandpiper will be confined to rocky coastlines rather than sandy beaches. In the West, Le Conte's Thrashers favor open desert with sparse, low vegetation, whereas the related Crissal Thrasher prefers more heavily vegetated sites—especially those near water and in stands of mesquite or piñon juniper.

TOP 10 MOST COMMON STATE BIRDS

Popular birds to look for, depending on where you live

 1. NORTHERN CARDINAL, 7 States
Illinois, Indiana, Kentucky, North Carolina, Ohio, Virginia, West Virginia

 2. WESTERN MEADOWLARK, 6 States
Kansas, Montana, Nebraska, North Dakota, Oregon, Wyoming

 3. NORTHERN MOCKINGBIRD, 5 States
Arkansas, Florida, Mississippi, Tennessee, Texas

 4. AMERICAN ROBIN, 3 States
Connecticut, Michigan, Wisconsin

 5. EASTERN BLUEBIRD, 2 States
Missouri, New York

 6. BLACK-CAPPED CHICKADEE, 2 States
Maine, Massachusetts

 7. AMERICAN GOLDFINCH, 2 States
Iowa, New Jersey

 8. MOUNTAIN BLUEBIRD, 2 States
Idaho, Nevada

 9. COMMON LOON, 1 State
Minnesota

10. CHICKEN, 2 States
Delaware, Rhode Island

North American wood-warblers. Watercolor painting by Louis Agassiz Fuertes (1917)

see note on back for this image

North American wood-warblers. Watercolor painting by Louis Agassiz Fuertes (1917)

Through the Lenses

LITTLE DETAILS MAKE ALL THE DIFFERENCE

Many beginning birders find bird identification a challenging subject. After you've had a few experiences birding, you'll discover it's not all that difficult. Many birds are actually distinctive and easy to identify. Our brains are geared to latch onto distinctive patterns, colors, and behaviors: Consider how good you are at recognizing a friend's face. You may not have memorized a bird's name yet, but you can train yourself to remember what you saw long enough to flip through a field guide.

FIELD MARKS

Feather details are important. You need to know your way around the various feather groups of a bird, since that's where you'll find most field marks—multiple distinctive features that are unique to a species. That's why a basic understanding of bird topography should be part of your birding knowledge.

Seeing a suite of field marks is the best approach to identifying a bird. A common pitfall for beginners is latching onto a single field mark. For example, in summer, the adult male Indigo Bunting and Blue Grosbeak

Subspecies variation can complicate identification. The birds in this painting by Louis Agassiz Fuertes are all Spruce Grouse, but the two males facing each other are different subspecies—with differences in the tail tip and white spotting just above.

Blue Jay vs. Western Scrub-Jay vs. Steller's Jay

WHAT IS THE DIFFERENCE? Three birds, all with blue markings, are called jays but each is a different species. Most common over eastern and midwestern North America is the garrulous Blue Jay (left). Closely related is the Steller's Jay (right), which is found in western North America and has a more prominent crest and more solid-blue plumage. The Western Scrub-Jay (center) lacks a crest, although it shares some of the behavior characteristics of the others.

are both blue birds. However, you cannot rely on the blue color to identify the males of either species. In addition to plumage field marks, Blue Grosbeaks often pump and partially spread their tails, especially when landing, and they give loud, explosive calls. Taken together, these features add up to a breeding adult male Blue Grosbeak. Seeing just one of these features leaves the identification inconclusive.

SIZE & STRUCTURE

Size is a rather vague term when used alone. What we're really referring to is overall size. Take your time and try to observe the bird from various angles and distances. Even with something for comparison—a nearby bird is best—accurate size assessment is best

viewed as approximate. The comparison of Hairy and Downy Woodpeckers makes a good example. These widespread species overlap in range and have nearly identical plumage. But they are quite different in size. Since they are rarely seen next to each other, direct size comparisons are uncommon. You'll probably need something more to seal the identification. Structural differences—in this case the proportional differences between bill length and head length—are more reliable. The term structure refers to the parts of a bird and their proportions. Many structural features are related to the bird's underlying skeletal framework. An important caveat is that a bird's overall shape can be dramatically altered by whether or not its feathers are fluffed out.

The male Baikal Teal is a stunning bird from Asia. Its beautiful colors, ornamental feathers, and striking patterns also make it easy to identify. It is a great rarity in North America that draws hordes of birders when one is found.

PLUMAGE

Plumage colors can be startling in their intensity or intriguing in their complexity. Even the coal black of the American Crow has subtle variations of iridescence that change with the intensity and angle of the light.

Colors are so central to the identification of birds that they are reflected in many bird names: "Blue This" and "Black That," or "Red-breasted This" and "White-tailed That." Some colors define our memory of a species, such as the cinnamon of a male Cinnamon Teal or the sky blue of a male Mountain Bluebird. Other colors come in unique combinations, like the steely blue and rust of a male American Kestrel and the metallic blues and greens of an adult Purple Gallinule.

◆ Color Descriptions

Problems sometimes arise with descriptions of colors. One person's blackish brown is another's brownish black. As a starting point, decide what the overall color is, make that the noun, and then modify it in whatever color direction you want. If the brown color leans toward black, it's blackish brown; if it leans toward red, it's reddish brown. When a color appears to be an equal mix

Golden-winged Warbler

of two colors, use both colors with a hyphen between them, as in blue-black or yellow-orange. Color descriptions crop up in birding that are rarely used in other situations: *Rufous* is the bright reddish orange-brown color found on the tail of the Great Crested Flycatcher, and *roseate* describes any bird with a pinkish tinge on some part of its plumage, like the pink of Roseate Spoonbill.

◆ Color & Lighting

Our perception of colors is affected by the type of lighting present, although the brain automatically compensates for minor differences in lighting and alters our perceptions to moderate the effect. In the bright green light of a spring forest, the yellow of many warblers takes on a strong greenish cast, but the brain filters out the effect and sends the message that the color is

In the proper light, the iridescent plumage of a Common Grackle glows with purple, blue, and bronzy highlights.

clear yellow. Some light effects are so strong they override the compensation. The warm light of late afternoon or sunset is especially potent. Colors take on a strong orange tinge, sometimes obliterating color differences that are important to identification.

◆ Plumage Patterns

Human eyes and brains are attuned to patterns, such as strong light and dark or color contrasts. The black-and-white pattern of an adult Black-throated Sparrow is immediately memorable and easy to identify. As happens with many species, one plumage is very distinctive, whereas the plumage of other sexes, ages, or times of year are different. The juvenile Black-throated Sparrow lacks the adult's black throat patch, which results in a much less distinctive pattern.

Few species are quite as boldly patterned as an adult Black-throated Sparrow, but many plumage patterns are obvious and important, such as wing bars, head stripes, streaking, and barring. Patterns can be as distinctive as the black-and-orange of an adult male American Redstart or as subtle as the vermiculated patterns on the Eastern Whip-poor-will. Always look for any patterns when you're birding. Often times, they are most useful at getting you to the right group of birds. Once you've narrowed the field, an exact identification is easier to make.

Your field guide will point out many patterns, but be open to discovering new ones. Common birds make good test cases, and sometimes field guides gloss over their identification.

WATCH & LISTEN

For some species, distinctive behavioral traits such as flight, movement, and voice can be as important as structure and plumage when making an identification.

◆ Flight

Flight style can help with identifications. Watch a known species until it flies, and then concentrate on the frequency of wingbeats and glides. Note whether the flight line is straight or undulating, whether the wingbeats are jerky or smooth, and whether the wings are open or closed during any glides. Some species are usually seen in flocks; others give distinctive flight calls. Farther afield, the flight styles of raptors and seabirds can clinch an identification.

◆ Movements

A species' habitual movements can also be extremely useful clues to identification. For example, tail bobbing is a consistent feature of the two waterthrushes, similar-looking warblers. As you get familiar with these two species, you'll notice that there are noticeable differences in how they bob their tails. The Northern Waterthrush bobs its tail almost continuously in an up-and-down motion; in contrast, the Louisiana Waterthrush has a slower, more deliberate action that

A birder glasses the activity at sunset in New York as an unidentified gull and a Black Skimmer fly by.
Flight silhouettes, wing patterns, and flight style can all be important clues to a bird's identity.

involves more of its body, and its tail moves in a side-to-side, circular direction.

Birds' feeding activities are often associated with distinctive movements, from general behaviors (most woodpeckers cling vertically to tree trunks as they feed) to species-specific behavior (American Dippers forage underwater).

◆ **Voice**

Bird vocalization is often the first clue to a species' presence and a directional clue to its location. Nearly half of the world's species are popularly known as songbirds (technically called oscine passerines), which in North America include all the passerines except the flycatchers. Songbirds have developed more complex songs than all other bird groups, and they produce the music that humans appreciate.

For most songbirds, the male is the singer and his primary song serves as a territorial declaration. Some species change songs: The song used for establishing territory and attracting a mate becomes a slightly different song once the pair is established. Other species have slightly different songs depending on whether they are in the center of their territory or on the edge. Calls are short, standardized vocalizations produced by all birds. Calls are innate and given year-round by both sexes, which make them reliable identification aids. Among the variety of call types, the most commonly heard are contact calls—calls are used to maintain contact not only with a mate but also with flocks of the same or different species. For example, the mixed flocks of songbirds common in winter and during migration keep together using contact calls. Even though calls are brief, they can be distinctive and important to identification. Fish and American Crows look almost identical. Fortunately, the *caw, caw, caw* of the American Crow is different from the *uh-uh* call of the Fish Crow.

LEARN MORE

HOW TO DESCRIBE BIRD CALLS

Like any music, birdsongs and calls can be discussed with reference to tempo, pitch, and loudness. Generalizations such as high-pitched and fast tempo are useful for describing the basics of a specific song. If possible, compare the song or call to a similar one with which you are familiar. As you listen to songs, pay close attention to the pattern of the notes and the length of the pauses between phrases.

The description of the quality of a song is often useful. A field guide might say that a song "is composed of liquid, flutelike notes that spiral downward in pitch." Liquid, flutelike notes are a signature sound of the brown thrushes in the genus *Catharus*. Another approach is to use visual annotations for taking written notes. One system uses long and short dashes to denote time; placement of the dashes at higher or lower positions denotes pitch.

◆ OSTRICH ◆

The Greek *strouthion* and Latin *struthio* both refer to the Ostrich, which was common in North Africa and the Middle East. Spoken Latin added *avis* (bird) to *struthio;* then followed the Old French *ostruce* and the English "ostrich."

TALKING LIKE A BIRDER

BASIC FIELD GUIDE VOCABULARY

Knowing the parts of a bird—the names and locations of feather groups and bare parts, also called bird topography—is important to the identification process. They will help you understand how a bird's body is organized and why it is shaped the way it is. Bird topography is an element of the "language" of birding, and most field guides assume you already have a basic understanding of it.

All the names and details may seem overwhelming when you're just starting out. Don't worry, though—you can still enjoy going birding and you can identify many birds even if you don't know all of the terminology. You don't have to learn everything

A pair of Woodland Kingfishers display to each other with outstretched wings in Zimbabwe. Notice how the wing feathers are arranged in neat overlapping rows—the ten outermost blue-and-black wing feathers are called the primaries.

before you start. Over time and with experience, you will become fluent in this new language.

FACTS ON FEATHERS

The evolutionary development of the feather is shrouded in time and mystery. What we do know is that feathers brilliantly solve a number of survival issues, such as flight, insulation, camouflage, and communication. Overlapping feathers cover almost entirely the exposed areas of a bird's body. The unfeathered parts are referred to as the bare parts.

Different types of feathers have different functions, but most feathers are built around a basic plan. The central feather shaft has two flat webs (or vanes) of barbs along its upper length that are knit together by barbules featuring Velcro like hooks and edges. If a feather becomes disheveled, the interlocking quality of the barbules allows the feather to be preened and the barbules reknit, something most of us have experienced by stroking a feather between our fingers from its base to its tip.

The Yellow-billed Magpie is a California bird that is easy to identify due to its flashy pattern.

TOP 10 WORDS FOR BIRD CONGREGATIONS

The English language offers an amazing assortment of poetical terms for groups of specific birds.

A MURDER OF CROWS

A PITEOUSNESS OF DOVES

A CHARM OF FINCHES

A SIEGE OF HERONS

AN EXALTATION OF LARKS

TIDINGS OF MAGPIES

A PARLIAMENT OF OWLS

A MUSTER OF PEACOCKS

AN UNKINDNESS OF RAVENS

A MURMURATION OF STARLINGS

Unlike a mammal's fur, a bird's feathers do not cover its body uniformly. They grow in symmetrical groups that have a precise arrangement, often visible as overlapping rows. Most feather groups are found in all families of birds, and the names used to describe them are the same for all species. Birds as different as condors and chickadees each have scapulars, primaries, and uppertail coverts. They may have different shapes, sizes, and colors, but typically the same feather groups are found in the same relative positions.

Parts of a Songbird

Knowing the parts of a bird—the names and locations of feather groups and bare parts—is important to the identification process. Passerines are a large order of birds that includes all our songbirds. Since their body plan and feather organization are uncomplicated, they are good examples to feature bird topography.

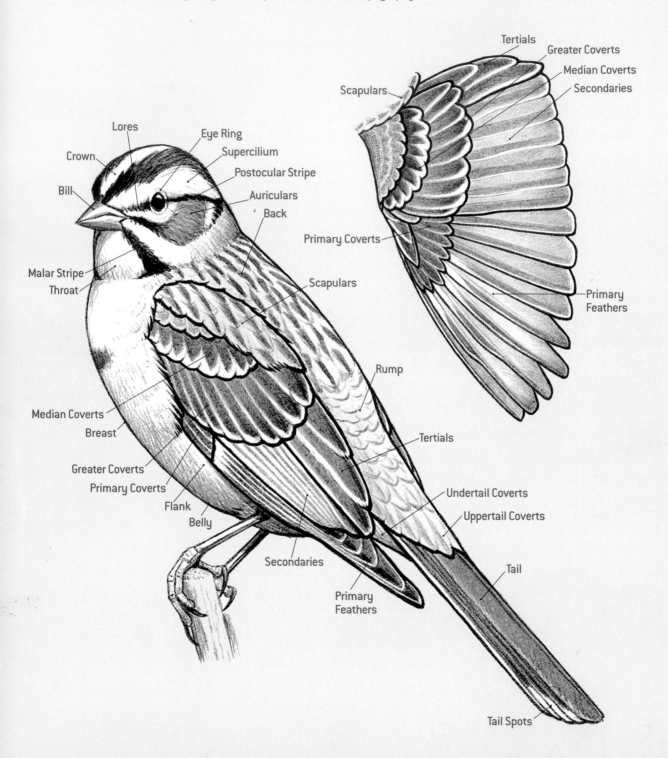

Tertials

Greater Coverts

Median Coverts

Secondaries

Scapulars

Lores

Crown

Eye Ring

Supercilium

Postocular Stripe

Bill

Auriculars

Back

Primary Coverts

Malar Stripe

Throat

Scapulars

Primary Feathers

Median Coverts

Rump

Breast

Tertials

Greater Coverts

Primary Coverts

Undertail Coverts

Flank

Uppertail Coverts

Belly

Secondaries

Tail

Primary Feathers

Tail Spots

THE HEAD

Crown	Top of the head, from the bill to the back of the skull.
Supercilium	Feathering below the crown that extends from the bill to behind the eye.
Lores	Located between the eye and the bill.
Auriculars	Feathers below and behind the eye (also called ear coverts).
Postocular stripe	Facial stripe that extends behind the eye just above the auriculars.
Malar Stripe	A dark line of feathers on either side of the throat.
Eye ring	Tiny feathers that grow in a ring around the eye, contrasting with surrounding feathers.
Bill	Made up of two parts—top is the upper mandible; bottom is the lower mandible.

THE OUTER WING

Primary feathers	Large flight feathers of the outer wing.
Primary coverts	Small feathers that overlay the bases of the primaries.

THE INNER WING

Secondaries	Long flight feathers of the inner wing or arm.
Tertials	Innermost secondaries.
Greater coverts	Row of coverts that overlay the secondaries and tertials.
Median coverts	Row of shorter coverts that overlay the greater coverts.

THE TAIL

Tail	Seen from above as it closes, two central tail feathers overlay pairs of outer tail feathers.
Tail spots	Pale tips on the outer tail feathers.

THE UPPERPARTS

Scapulars	Feathers that originate from the area of skin where the wing attaches to the body.
Back	Below the nape and between the left and right scapulars.
Rump	Between the back and the uppertail coverts.
Uppertail coverts	Neatly arranged rows of feathers that cover the base of the tail.

THE UNDERPARTS

Throat	Below the chin and framed by the malar feathers on either side.
Breast	Group of feathers occupying the area directly below the throat.
Flanks	Elongated feathers that cover the body area below the wings.
Belly	Below the flanks and breast, extend down to the undertail coverts.
Undertail coverts	Cover the underside of the tail.

PAST THE PASSERINES

The following sections delve into the specialized feather groups and terminology of a few nonpasserine families: waterfowl, herons and egrets, raptors, shorebirds, and gulls. The birds within each of these groups may have the same basic body features and feather groups as songbirds, but their body proportions and feather shapes are very different.

◆ Waterfowl

The feather locations on a swimming duck are often puzzling to beginning birders. When a duck lands, its wings seem to disappear. Where did they go? The answer lies with the length of certain feathers and how the wings fold.

On a flying Mallard, the feathers of the wing appear to be organized much as they are on a songbird—primaries, secondaries, and coverts in neat rows. The black-and-white tips of the greater coverts form a wing bar in the center of the wing. The prominent secondaries on ducks often display a patch of iridescent color known as the speculum. Notice the pale crescent above the orange legs that is formed by the rearmost flank feathers. The flank feathers will play an important role as the wing folds.

Upon landing, the lower edge of the folded wing is quickly tucked behind the flank feathers and hidden from view. On a swimming Mallard, the only wing feathers visible are the big gray-and-brown tertials, the tip of the primaries, and a few white tips of the greater coverts. This feather arrangement gives the bird a sleek shape that helps protect it from the elements.

Three Mallard drakes with their distinctive green heads fly near Montgomery, Alabama. The iridescent blue bar on the inner wing is called the speculum, a plumage feature of many ducks. Mallards are the ancestor of most domestic ducks.

◆ Herons & Egrets

Most species in this family of wading birds have long legs, long necks, and long bills for stalking food in shallow water. Long, graceful plumes called aigrettes grow from the scapular region and adorn egrets in breeding season. Commercial plume hunters in the pursuit of aigrettes decimated the populations of Great, Snowy, and Reddish Egrets around the turn of the 20th century, when these feathers were in great demand for ladies' fashion. Concerned women in Boston organized in opposition to the slaughter of these birds, and their efforts led to some of the United States' first conservation laws—and the rise of the Audubon movement.

◆ Raptors

Raptors are birds of prey, including hawks, eagles, falcons, and their relatives. The unrelated owls are also considered to be raptors.

On the head, check for patterns around the bird's eye and bill, looking especially at the facial stripes on various falcons and the presence or absence of a pale supercilium. The cere is the fleshy covering at the base of the upper mandible that surrounds the nostrils. The color of the cere and the orbital ring are useful for determining the age of some species. On large falcons, these areas are bluish gray on juveniles and yellow on adults.

Wing shapes are often distinctive on flying raptors and help to identify them. Important areas to study are the shape of the wing tip, the length and width of the wing, and the shape of the trailing edge. The patagium is the leading edge of the inner wing; a dark patagial bar is found on most Red-tailed Hawks. A window is a pale translucent area at the base of the primaries: For instance, you can see crescent-shaped windows on a soaring Red-shouldered Hawk.

Many raptor species have distinctive patterns of light and dark bands on the tail. A terminal band is a band located on the tip of the tail, and a subterminal band is located just in from the tip.

Raptors, like this Red-tailed Hawk, have large, forward-facing eyes that allow them to spot prey from great distances.

◆ PENGUIN ◆

Originally the Welsh word for the extinct Great Auk of the North Atlantic, a combination of *pen* (white) and *gwyn* (head)—the Great Auk had a large white patch on its head. By the late 1500s, sailors were using "penguin" to describe the similar-looking but unrelated birds of the Southern Hemisphere.

A migrating flock of Western Sandpipers makes a rest stop on a Washington mudflat before continuing north. In spring, the rusty-edged scapulars (located above the wings) and the rusty cap and ear coverts are good field marks.

◆ Shorebirds

Shorebirds have a reputation for being difficult to identify. If you're just starting out, get familiar with the features of the most common species in your area. Then you'll know to take a closer look at something with a different shape or behavior.

Scapulars on the upper parts of standing shorebirds dominate—plus the coverts and tertials of the folded wings that are located below them. The scapulars grow like a graduated bunch of flowers from the small area where the wing attaches to the body. The upper scapulars consist of three rows of smaller feathers, and below them are two rows of larger lower scapulars.

Tertials are just forward from the folded primaries; three or four are usually visible. The primary projection past the longest tertial is an important feature on some species. Leg length and color help identify shorebirds. Length is extremely variable, allowing different species to forage in different water depths. Color can be obscured when birds feed in muddy areas.

◆ Gulls

Our next group, gulls, are often found near shorebirds. There are 30 species of gulls recorded from North

America, but this number, large as it is, belies the bewildering array of plumages available for study. The larger gulls take about four years to attain adult plumage and have especially complex and varied plumages. Your field guide will help you sort them out, but identifying gulls—especially immatures—is tough. As a first step, it often helps to sort a gull flock into small (Bonaparte Gull size), medium (Ring-billed Gull size), and large (Herring Gull size and larger) birds, or into dark-mantled and light-mantled birds.

Bill size and structure are fairly constant in gulls, but color and pattern change with age on many species. To judge the shape of the bill, consider the depth of the gonydeal angle (the angle on the lower margin of the bill as it slopes up to the bill tip) and the shape of the culmen (the bill's ridge line).

Mantle is an all-inclusive term describing the feathers of the back, scapulars, wing coverts, and tertials visible on a standing gull. On adult gulls, these feathers are all the same color—from light gray to blackish gray. The terms dark-mantled (blackish gray mantle) and light-mantled (all the rest) separate the various species into two easier-to-manage groups; a few species are intermediate. On wingtips, look for any black-and-white patterns. A mirror is a small white spot just in from the tip of an outer primary.

An adult Black-legged Kittiwake soars on gray wings with neat black tips. There are lots of species of gulls and most of them look confusingly different in winter and summer and at different ages.

Brown Pelican. Hand-colored print by John James Audubon (published 1827–1838)

Yellow-crowned Night-Herons. Hand-colored print by John James Audubon (published 1827–1838)

Doing Your Fieldwork

BIRD-WATCHING SUCCESS AT HOME OR AFAR

As birders, we make a conscious effort to connect with nature and to the movements and instincts of wild animals. Some part of our minds is always ready to engage when bird events present themselves. Although several variables and the accessibility of sites affect your birding success, there are ways to optimize your chances of finding birds.

TUNE YOUR SENSES

◆ First Steps

When you arrive at a new birding spot, put yourself into position to see and hear any bird activity before you move around. Birds of interest might be hiding from you, or they may be secretive by nature. Give them a few minutes to return to their natural activity level before you start moving. When you do move, move slowly.

◆ Using Your Ears

Wherever you are birding, make a conscious effort to listen for bird sounds. Beginning birders often focus on the sounds of songbirds and ignore the equally distinctive calls of hawks, shorebirds, gulls, and other species. Often a sound will be your first clue to where a bird is. Many vocalizations are soft, so you need to be as quiet as possible and listen carefully. Take your clothing into account: Avoid noisy synthetics. Wind and traffic noise also obscure bird sounds; under those circumstances, alter your search tactics or location. Cup your ears with both hands and slowly swivel your head to pull

The Winter Wren sings a long exuberant song on its northern breeding grounds, but is much quieter and secretive in winter.

in distant sounds. If a bird is a persistent vocalizer, walk toward the sound and scan for movement. The singer might be behind a branch.

Other types of audible clues include the alarm calls of nearby birds, often used to signal the presence of a predator. When you hear this behavior, check for a raptor. The rustling of leaves is another clue, often revealing the presence of ground-foraging birds such as towhees and thrashers.

◆ Using Your Eyes

Before you reach for your binoculars, find birds with the naked eye. The binoculars' field of view is too restricted for general scanning. In open habitat, scanning with binoculars is sometimes useful—to check pond edges, a distant ridgeline, or the ocean's horizon—but the technique rarely yields results in forests and fields.

Looking for movement is an effective way of finding birds. Movement in a natural setting often means the presence of a bird. To look for movement, you need to stand still. Take in the wide picture rather than concentrating on a specific area, and move your head slowly.

Unless the day is overcast, most birders prefer to wear a hat. Strong light and glare cause the pupils to contract, reducing the ability to see subtle details.

◆ Getting Close

You don't need to get close to birds to identify them, but it helps. Move slowly and quietly. Birds have become habituated to people in some locations, and some juvenile shorebirds are approachable. But in most situations, birds avoid people.

If a bird you're approaching seems ready to take flight, wait until it relaxes. The closest distance at which you can approach a bird before it takes flight is known as the flush point. You will learn how close you can approach different species. If birding with a group, it is bad form to overstep the limit and flush the bird that's garnering everyone's attention.

Birders in a Pennsylvania rhododendron thicket train their glasses on a bird. In most situations, it's much more productive to look for movement with the naked eye and then—without looking away—raise your binoculars to your eyes.

ATTRACTING BIRDS

What can you do if you suspect that the movement in the bushes is made by a bird hidden from view? You can give the bird some time to emerge on its own—this being the least intrusive and often best option. If the bird doesn't work its way into view, you can move to a new position, though you risk flushing it. A third option is to stay where you are and entice the bird into the open with sounds *you* produce.

◆ Pishing

Birds often respond to intrusion by investigating and even scolding and mobbing, so birders have learned to attract birds by making rhythmic hissing or shushing sounds (known as pishing) that imitate the scolding or alarm calls made by small songbirds when they sense danger. Hissing sounds are hisses broken into a series by opening and closing your lips; shushing sounds are made by pushing out sound between your puckered lips. Chickadees, titmice, and many sparrows and warblers are likely to react to these sounds, and if you're near the center of all this attention, you can get stunning views. When birds react and make their own scolding sounds, distant and unseen birds are sometimes drawn in as well. When pishing, start out softly and get louder. A minute or two of pishing will either get a reaction or not. Don't overdo it, especially in heavily birded areas or among other birders. Keep in mind that sometimes pishing can have the opposite effect of driving birds away.

◆ Owl Calls

The calls of small owls—the ones that prey on song-

The Black-capped Chickadee can be hand-tamed, but it usually takes a period of weeks working patiently with the same bird.

birds—elicit a strong response during daylight hours from the very songbirds at risk. Eastern or Western Screech-Owls, Northern Pygmy-Owl, and Northern Saw-whet Owl are all good candidates for imitation. Listen to recordings and seek advice from fellow birders. If you intersperse an occasional owl call with pishing sounds, the songbirds' reaction is sometimes intensified.

◆ Recordings

Many lightweight options for carrying prerecorded bird sounds into the field are available these days. For example, you can buy small players (iPods and the like) with preloaded recordings and add tiny speakers for playback in the field. Birding apps for smart phones are more popular than ever. Enticing birds with recordings is intrusive, more so than pishing or imitating owl calls, because you are entering a bird's territory and creating the illusion that a rival bird is challenging him. So if recordings are employed at all, use should be minimal.

FOUR STEPS TO A GREAT FIELD SKETCH

Here is a demonstration of how to draw a Carolina Chickadee. The same basic principles apply to any bird. Consider taking out a sheet of paper and making your own pencil sketch.

1. DRAW THE BASIC SHAPES Start with two ovals—a large one for the body and smaller one for the head. Concentrate on getting the relative sizes correct. At the rear end, a wedge shape—for the uppertail and undertail coverts—connects the tail to the body. Keep your drawing loose and sketchy, and don't hesitate to erase.

2. REFINE THE SHAPES Start to refine the outside shape with transitional lines at the throat and back of the head, and make your first indication of the bill and eye. In most species, the eyes usually fall close to the bill, not in the center of the head. Indicate where the legs come out of the body. Add another elongated oval shape for the folded wing, and erase any extra lines.

3. ADD DETAIL Keep refining your shapes and start to add feather details. A basic understanding of topography is helpful to have. Particularly important is the relationship of the various feather groups of the wing. Notice how the various feathers overlap.

4. ADD PATTERNS & ANNOTATIONS After you're happy with the basic structure of the bird, add patterns by shading. Write any annotations on color and any other features you noticed. Add watercolor washes to your sketch later, if you like.

eye blends into black cap

nost bib

worn wings w/ grayish edging

white

gray-butt flanks

Carolina Chickadee
9 June 2007
Washington, D.C.

X MARKS THE SPOT

Another valuable field skill is being able to communicate the location of a bird you're watching to others. The dilemma is that if you take your binoculars off a bird, you'll probably lose track of it; yet it is almost impossible to describe a bird's location without lowering your binoculars. If you choose to stay focused on the bird, the best instruction you can probably offer is, "Try to look where I'm aiming," and then describe any larger landmarks you might see.

◆ Perched Birds

If a bird is perched, begin by describing the location of an object near the bird or the object on which the bird sits. Note anything distinctive about it, such as "It's on the ground near the fifth fencepost left of the shed." Give the distance if you can estimate it. Some birders use the binocular field (the diameter of your field of view) as a measure of distance: for example, "The tree is two binocular fields to the left of the water tower."

◆ The Clock System

Having verbally guided your birding partner onto the right object—say, a tree—you now need to use the clock system to describe where the bird is on that tree. Visualize the tree as an upright clock: Halfway up the tree trunk is the center of the clock, where the hands start. The top is twelve o'clock, the bottom is six o'clock, and so on. You might say something like, "It's at two

A male American Kestrel (left), the continent's smallest falcon, offers food to its mate.

o'clock, about three feet in from the outside edge, but moving down."

◆ Flying Birds

Describing the location of flying birds is much trickier. First, communicate whether the bird is above or below the horizon as well as the direction in which it's flying. Indicate any distant landmarks—buildings, distinctive variations in the horizon line, lone trees—and then add how far above or below the horizon it is. You'll need different methods, such as using distinctively

◆ ALBATROSS ◆

Arabic *al-qudus,* "a bucket on a water wheel," was borrowed by Spanish and Portuguese as *arcaduz* and *alcatraz* and became the word for pelican, referring to the pelican's bucket-size pouch. By the 1700s, English sailors were using "albatross," possibly combining the Portuguese word with the Latin *alba* for "white."

shaped clouds for orientation, to describe high-flying birds. If a bird is high overhead in a blue sky, your best option is to simply point.

◆ **At Sea**

On a boat at sea, your reference points change—for the boat and the horizon are the only constants. In this case, the boat becomes the clock: The bow of the boat is twelve o'clock, the stern is six o'clock, starboard (right side) is three o'clock, and port (left side) is nine o'clock. The other two essential directions are the distance above or below the horizon and the direction (left or right) in which the bird is flying. You might say, "It's at two o'clock, just above the horizon, flying left."

READY, AIM, DIGISCOPE!

The term "digiscoping" refers to using a compact digital camera to take pictures through a birding scope. The practice has become popular in the birding community and offers a low-cost method for documenting your birding discoveries. Many birders are casual digiscopers: They carry a small digital camera in case they run into something interesting. Camera phones can also work, with the benefit that you can share your photos while you're in the field.

At the most basic level, all you do is hold your camera's lens up to the eyepiece of your scope and press the shutter release. In a pinch, you can even hold your camera up to your binoculars. Handheld results can be quite good. Use the lowest magnification on your scope, and zoom the lens on your camera a little to reduce vignetting. Practice holding and aligning the camera, and take lots of images. Adapters that hold your camera in perfect alignment with the scope are available. Some do-it-yourselfers fashion heavy paper or flexible plastic sheeting into a tube.

WHERE TO GO BIRDING

You can bird anywhere and everywhere, but some places are much better than others. The following general situations apply to most parts of the continent.

◆ Habitat Edges

Boundaries between forest and field, hedgerows, watery edges, and coastlines are attractive to many species because they tend to offer a greater variety of food items as well as nearby cover.

◆ Sheltered Area

Birds seek shelter from strong winds when possible. In open situations, they shelter by getting on the lee side of any ground structure. In vegetated areas, the lee side of a windbreak of trees offers shelter and stays warmer.

A Northern Mockingbird splashes as it takes a bath in a Texas pond. Water draws birds, especially in arid areas.

◆ Water

Water is a magnet for many birds. Any water feature or damp spot, natural or artificial, is worth investigating. The more arid the surrounding countryside, the more attractive any available water is to residents and migrants alike.

Hudsonian Godwit

◆ Desert Oases

These habitat islands of the West are also bird magnets during migration. Some species are nesters or year-round residents, but oases can be overflowing with migrants for a few weeks in spring and fall.

◆ Sewage Ponds

It's a bit hardcore, but sewage ponds can be great places to bird. Check that the facility is open to birders and that it's the right type of facility: You want a two-stage sewage treatment plant, which has settling and aeration ponds.

◆ Landfills

Similarly, landfills not only draw gulls and dump trucks. Sometimes adventurous birders can be spotted there, too. Contact local officials to see which landfill sites welcome birders.

Bird Brain

Every year on March 19, crowds gather to celebrate the traditional day that the Cliff Swallows return to Mission San Juan Capistrano. The problem: Swallows rarely visit the mission anymore and those few that do often arrive weeks earlier. Locals have tried in vain to lure more swallows back, but the festival goes on nonetheless.

◆ Your Local Patch

Many birders adopt a nearby bird habitat to check on regularly. The study of local birds and your knowledge of their occurrence become your baseline of information when you go farther afield.

WHEN TO GO BIRDING

Knowing when to visit these locations is crucial, too. Dedicated birders try to make smart decisions about when to bird. Timing visits to coastal locations depends on knowing the local tides; timing a search for migrants is affected by large-scale weather patterns.

◆ First Light

Birders are, or become, morning people. Land bird activity usually peaks during the hour or two just after sunrise. Songbirds have high metabolisms and need to feed in the morning. Most migrate at night, which can further deplete their energy stores.

◆ Tidal Rhythms

Feeding opportunities also determine viewing times. Many coastal species synchronize their feeding activity with the tide. Some of the best shorebirding is done during an incoming tide, when rising water pushes flocks closer to dry land. Low tide is prime feeding time, and birds tend to spread out over a large area.

◆ Weather Fronts and Migration

Weather affects the movements of migratory birds profoundly. Whether there are any birds to see in your area has more to do with the weather that day and the few previous days than the season.

 LEARN MORE

KEEPING LISTS AND FIELD NOTES

Bird-watchers of all skill levels enjoy keeping track of their birding experiences. Usually this involves keeping a list or multiple lists—life lists, year lists, yard lists, state lists, county lists, and so on—that form a personal history of your birding experiences. Your lists bring back fond memories and remind you of what you still want to find. And by keeping a journal of your sightings, the process becomes a true learning experience.

The simplest form of note taking, which is also more informative than keeping a checklist, is writing a list of species with the number (or an estimate) of individuals seen at a specific location and the date. Add a line or two describing the time you spent, who you were with, the weather, and type of habitat, and you have a basic journal entry. Keep entries in a notebook and turn the page when you move to new location.

Write a description (not just a number) when you see a new species, a species you don't see very often, or a common species doing something unusual or in an unusual plumage. For those sightings, try to note all the details you can. It's best to do this while you are looking at the bird and before you consult a field guide. Describe what you actually see. Sometimes you will only see enough to write a partial description. That's OK. Describing your impression of a bird's behavior or shape can be as important as describing the color or pattern of its plumage. These are field marks, too, even though describing them with precision can be difficult. Adding a sketch to your description, with lines pointing out the bird's features, is effective. A digital camera, even a point-and-shoot, can capture habitat information.

Following Birds to Far Horizons

TRAVEL TIPS FOR AVID BIRD-WATCHERS

The farther you travel from home, the greater the changes in birdlife you'll notice. Distance is just one variable. Habitat and time of year can be equally important. Avid birders soon long to bird in new places with new birds. It's natural to start near home and gradually broaden your reach—from county, to state or province, to country. If you're lucky enough to have the time and money to search for birds overseas, the birds can be spectacular and almost endlessly varied.

TRAVELING IN SEARCH OF BIRDS

The American Birding Association's official checklist for North American birds of continental North America, north of Mexico, lists 970 species of birds as of November 2011. Many of them are rare, casual, or even accidental. California (644 species) and Texas (636 species) have the largest state lists—and no wonder, since both are very large states that border Mexico and have a variety of elevations, climates, and habitats, including seacoasts. How can

Bird-watchers train their scopes on Snow Geese taking off at dawn at Bosque del Apache National Wildlife Refuge in New Mexico. Traveling to prime birding locations is a great way to see the country . . . and build a long life list.

a state like Ohio compete? It can't. Its state list currently stands at 425 species. Sure, rare birds show up in Ohio, but to have a chance of seeing a large percentage of the continent's birdlife, you're going to have to hit the road.

Remember that the most beautiful things in the world are the most useless; peacocks and lilies for instance.

JOHN RUSKIN, *THE STONES OF VENICE*, 1851

You can get a good idea of where various species live by picking up a North American field guide and studying the range maps in it. The maps are a goldmine of information. Most range maps indicate year-round, summer (breeding), winter (nonbreeding), and migration ranges (spring and fall). At a glance, you can see that Eastern Bluebirds can be found year-round in Ohio, but Mountain and Western Bluebirds don't normally occur west of the Mississippi River. If you live in Ohio, you'll have to head west to see the other two bluebirds.

◆ Birding Hot Spots & Festivals

Hot spots, the most notable birding locations, offer visiting birders the best chances of seeing regional specialties, avian rarities, or concentrations of migrants. These places are no secret. You'll hear about them from other birders and by surfing online birding sites. Fortunately for traveling birders, excellent site guides exist for many of these locations and are important resources for planning a trip. Some

TOP 10 SPOTS TO SEE RARE BIRDS

Birding hotlines light up with sightings of rare birds. Here are North America's best spots.

1. ATTU, ALEUTIAN ISLANDS, ALASKA

2. GAMBELL, ST. LAWRENCE ISLAND, ALASKA

3. MONTEREY BAY, CALIFORNIA

4. SOUTHEAST ARIZONA

5. LOWER RIO GRANDE VALLEY, TEXAS

6. COASTAL BEND OF TEXAS

7. FLORIDA KEYS

8. GULF STREAM, OFF CAPE HATTERAS, NORTH CAROLINA

9. CAPE MAY, NEW JERSEY

10. NEWFOUNDLAND

guide books cover an entire state or province, some feature a special location or habitat, and others detail the birds of a particular national park or wildlife refuge. The American Birding Association (ABA) publishes a highly regarded series of bird-finding guides to most of the premier birding locations in North America. They cover such places as southeast Arizona, Florida, the Rio Grande Valley, and southern California. In fact, the ABA even publishes *Birdfinder: A Birder's Guide to Planning North American Trips,* which suggests birding trips across the continent, and *A Birder's Guide to Metropolitan Areas of*

Getting his feet wet for art, a bird photographer focuses on a Great Egret in Fort Myers, Florida. Sharing digital photographs over the Internet has become very popular; even images of rare birds often get posted the day they are seen.

North America—a reminder that business trips don't have to be birdless.

Many of these famous locations hold festivals during their best birding seasons. Festivals feature birding-related exhibitors, programs, and demonstrations, but it's the organized field trips that draw the crowds. These trips are a great way to see an area's special birds and learn about new birding locations. The ABA website lists nearly 40 birding festivals, from Maine to Alaska.

Among the most outstanding and longest running are the Rio Grande Birding Festival in Harlingen, Texas (early November), and the Space Coast Birding and Wildlife Festival in Titusville, Florida (late January).

◆ On the Bounding Main

Sometimes you have to go farther than your feet and car will carry you. Special offshore birding trips—pelagic trips—are the only way to see a good selection of open-ocean birds. Many pelagic birds rarely come within sight of land, except when breeding, so you have to go to them. Such species include the tubenoses—albatrosses, petrels, shearwaters, and storm-petrels—as well as the phalaropes, skuas, jaegers, alcids, and pelagic gulls and terns. Some of these occur in both oceans, but many are restricted to one ocean or the other. To see a wide selection of species, you'll have to take trips to a variety of locations during a variety of seasons.

Local birding clubs often arrange pelagic trips, but you'll also find regularly scheduled commercial trips available in the best locations. Monterey Bay, California, and Cape Hatteras, North Carolina, are two prime locations. The ABA publishes a near-comprehensive list of scheduled trips. The standard trip is a daylong outing and costs about $150. Pelagic trips always have experts onboard. Whale-watching trips and longer ferry trips sometimes offer views of pelagic birds, but they are not as rewarding if your focus is birds.

◆ Into the Night

To see most owl species, you'll have to make a nocturnal outing—known as owling—when these birds are actively hunting and vocalizing. While birding during the day, you may occasionally flush a roosting owl, but usually the bird flees before you get a good look at it. A few owl species are active during the day, and some nocturnal species occasionally call during daylight hours.

Vocalizations are the primary clue to the presence of an owl. Stormy or windy nights make it difficult to hear anything, and most birders think that your chances are better on nights with less moonlight. Since owls are thinly distributed, it's wise to cover as much ground as possible. If you're walking trails, keep your light turned off until you need it and talk only in whispers. When you do encounter an owl, use your light sparingly and don't shine it directly at the bird. If you hear an owl calling, approach slowly and try to visualize where the owl is before turning on your light. Owl calls can have a ventriloquial quality, so if you're with companions, separate from one another and try to triangulate the location of the sound by pointing in its direction. During the nesting season, you should listen for the begging calls of young owls.

Eastern Screech-Owl fledglings glare at the camera in Florida. Owling requires nighttime work.

PASSPORT BIRDING

Once you've journeyed down North America's birding highways and become familiar with this continent's birdlife, you'll discover that many of the most amazing avian treasures can only be sampled abroad. The fact is, North America's 970 bird species represent less than 10 percent of the world's approximately 10,000 species. Sure, North America is home to some striking species: a multitude of ducks, a wonderful variety of raptors, some beautiful thrushes, and an abundance of wood warblers. But if you like our bluebirds, wait until you catch sight of Brazil's violet-blue Hyacinth Macaw. Our Scarlet Tanager certainly has a tropical brilliance about it, but tiny Ecuador has more than one hundred tanager species dressed in an astonishing array of colors and patterns. Colombia, a country smaller than Alaska, has more than 1,800 bird species, about twice as many as the continental United States and Canada combined. And that's just a sample from our neighbors to the south. Compare the number of breeding species

Three Emperor Penguins appear to make use of a tourist's camera gear. Adding these largest of the penguins to one's life list can be a challenge since they live only in Antarctica.

A Blue and yellow Macaw comes in for a landing. This parrot is found in northern South America.

 LEARN MORE

WHERE TO SPOT THE MOST SPECIES

An endemic species is one that occurs in a certain geographic area and nowhere else. When birders travel the world, the search for locally endemic species is often the focus of their pursuits.

For example, if you're in Australia, look for an Emu because that's the only place in the world it occurs. When a species is endemic to a very small area, it is referred to as highly endemic. Due to their small population sizes, highly endemic species are often the ones most threatened with extinction.

Here is a list of the countries with the largest numbers of endemic species.

375 Indonesia
313 Australia
202 Brazil
192 Philippines
113 Peru
98 Madagascar
90 Mexico
76 Papua New Guinea
68 Solomon Islands
67 Colombia
59 New Zealand
50 China
45 Venezuela
40 India
35 Ecuador/Galápagos
28 Jamaica
25 Fiji
25 São Tomé & Principe
24 Sri Lanka
22 Tanzania

found in the various continents: South America has 3,100, Asia has 2,400, Africa has 2,000, North America has 670, Australia has 600, and Europe has 500.

Some travelers will opt for the safety and reliability of a professional birding tour; others will strike out on their own with just a field guide, binoculars, and a plan. Fortunately for international birders, we live in a time when birding field guides are available for almost every nook and cranny of the world. And site guides have been published for many areas. National Geographic's *Global Birding* by Les Beletsky is a great introduction to all the best birds and birding regions.

Australian Brush-Turkey. Hand-colored print by John Gould (published 1869)

FLIGHT & MIGRATION

Scott Weidensaul

Flamingos wade in shallow waters off Andros Island, the Bahamas, in this painting by Allan Brooks.

DEFYING THE LAW OF GRAVITY

THE MARVEL OF BIRDS IN FLIGHT

Flight hinges on the physics of a simple curve—the curve of a single feather, the curve of a wingful of long, stiff feathers—and the way all those curves (which scientists call airfoils) generate lift and make possible the everyday miracle of flight.

THE MECHANICS OF FLIGHT

Consider a young Peregrine Falcon, leaping from its high aerie on the side of a cliff, a vertiginous abyss below it. For weeks the falcon has been exercising its wings, building strength in the massive pectoral muscles of its breast, pumping so hard its feet occasionally

A Peregrine Falcon in flight displays long, stiff feathers arranged in a curve, creating lift that allows the bird to fly. With folded wings, Peregrines dive at speeds of more than 200 miles an hour, making them the world's fastest animal.

leave the rocks for a giddy instant. But when its drive to fly finally overcomes its innate caution and the young bird launches itself into the void for the first time, the falcon clumsily but instinctively masters the forces that will make it the world's greatest aerialist.

Seen in cross-section, the falcon's wings have a curved, asymmetrical shape—the airfoil, which is echoed in the shape of each of its major flight feathers.

There is symbolic as well as actual beauty in the migration of the birds . . . There is something infinitely healing in these repeated refrains of nature, the assurance that after night, dawn comes, and spring after the winter.

RACHEL CARSON, 1952

The air rushing over their bulging upper surfaces has a longer distance to travel than that crossing the shorter gap across the underside of the wing. This forces the moving air down and creates a counterforce, or lift, which raises the bird.

But lift is just one of four forces that the young falcon, making its first clumsy flight, must balance if it is to stay in the air. Lift and gravity vie against each other as the awkward bird tumbles, but then the first down-strokes of the raptor's strong wings generate thrust to propel it forward, pushing against the viscosity of

Least Terns are streamlined, long of wing, and light in body. They rarely soar but are capable of long flights.

close-packed air molecules, which create drag. An aeronautical engineer can neatly diagram the forces of lift, gravity, thrust, and drag. But a falcon, without benefit of blackboards or equations and drawing only on a genetic legacy stretching back millions of years, senses the pressures and competing forces in the blink of an eye. Its wingbeats fall into a steady rhythm. It levels itself—and it flies.

◆ JAY ◆

Tracing back to Latin *gaius* and Old French *jai,* the name is probably echoic of the European bird's call. "Jaywalking" is an American word from the early 1900s, perhaps in reference to the jay's bold and impudent behavior.

A WING FOR EVERY PURPOSE

Anyone who has watched birds knows that flight comes in many forms, from the slashing speed of an attacking hawk to the gently wheeling circles of a vulture, from the explosive flush of a grouse to the frenetic blur that is a hummingbird. Just as each style of flight is different, so is the structure of the wings that makes it possible.

The most basic form of flight is flapping. Think about a robin flitting across a backyard or a duck racing across the gray dawn of a marsh. Each downstroke of the wings, sometimes at a rate of several a second, generates lift, while a pause in the flaps may cause the bird to stall and drop.

The most aerodynamic design for flapping flight is a long, narrowly tapered wing, of the sort seen in falcons, swallows, swifts, and many shorebirds. Flapping is an expensive way to fly, however. It burns up a lot of energy. Many birds have evolved to move more efficiently, as reflected in their wings.

Birds that habitually soar—including eagles, vultures, storks, and cranes—have wide, broad wings with widely separated primary feathers ("slotted" is the technical term) that add lift and stability at slow

A Roseate Spoonbill's broad pink wings are needed to lift its body, up to four pounds in weight, as it flies.

HOVERING HUMMERS

Hovering is so difficult and energetically expensive that few birds attempt it. None do it so well as the hummingbirds, which—alone among birds—can also fly backward. The secret to a hummingbird's aerial abilities lies in its internal framework. The bones of the wing are fused into a single, rigid structure that can withstand the tremendous force generated by up to 60 beats per second (200 beats in some courtship flights), while the shoulder girdle is unusually flexible, allowing the hummingbird to create shallow figure-eight wingbeats for hovering flight or to tilt its wings to generate reverse thrust for backward flight.

Powering such flight requires a metabolic furnace also unmatched among birds. An active hummingbird's heart races at 1,200 beats per minute, and it may take five breaths a second. To fuel this engine, a hummingbird has to consume one and a half times its weight in insects and nectar each day—the equivalent of up to 2,000 individual visits to a flower.

GREEN-CROWNED BRILLIANT

speeds. This design works well in a rising bubble of warm air, known as a thermal, which is what lifts a circling hawk until it is a dot in the blue. This also works well when the hawk reaches the top of the thermal, sets its wings, and begins a miles-long gliding descent to the next thermal. Gliding flight is used by raptors, too, as they migrate along mountain ridges, where winds are deflected upward by the hills, creating waves of lift on which the hawks can ride effortlessly.

Birds that depend on a rapid burst of speed—grouse and pheasants, or bird-eating raptors like Sharp-shinned Hawks that sprint after their prey in thick cover—have short, rounded wings. But perhaps the most extreme wing adaptation is that of the albatrosses, among which the wings are extraordinarily long and narrow. This design allows them to milk every bit of lift from the ceaseless winds of the open ocean in a style of flight known as "dynamic soaring." Their wings are so long they can barely flap, and they must take off by running into a stiff breeze or leaping from a cliff.

Sometimes the challenge is not getting into the air, but doing it quietly. Silent flight is essential for owls, so their feathers have a soft, velvety surface and downy trailing edges that deaden the rush of passing wind, so that sharp-eared mice don't hear them coming.

FLOCKS & FORMATIONS

Why, asks the old joke, is one side of a V-formation of geese always longer than the other? Because there are more geese in it, obviously. (Cue laugh track.) But humor aside, there are sound reasons why birds travel in flocks and why some of them habitually fly in V-formations—regardless of the length of the sides.

Flocks can provide security, serve as an information-sharing network, and ease the aerodynamic burden of flying. Some birds flock habitually, whereas others do so only under specific circumstances. Many birds, especially songbirds, never flock up at all. Raptors, for

example, tend to be solitary hunters, but a few migratory species like Swainson's Hawks in the West, and Broad-winged Hawks in the East, form immense aggregations known as kettles as they migrate through Mexico on their way to the tropics. A single flock in the rising air of a thermal bubble may comprise tens of thousands of birds, swirling like gnats—each one monitoring its neighbors' rate of rise, so it can stay near the center of the thermal for optimal lift.

The reason birds can fly and we can't is simply that they have perfect faith, for to have faith is to have wings.

J. M. BARRIE, *THE LITTLE WHITE BIRD*, 1902

The classic flock is a V of geese, swans, or cranes, and the shape—often just a diagonal line instead of a complete V—is not accidental. Each downstroke of a bird's wing creates vortices of air, which subtly reduce the drag for a bird flying just off its wing tips. Thus, the lead bird in a V must work a bit harder while those farther back get an easier ride—an energy savings of up to 14 percent, one study of Eurasian Great White Pelicans showed.

A Ross's Goose brakes for a landing amid a wintering flock at Merced National Wildlife Refuge in California.

Bird Brain

The Ostrich may be flightless, but it's far from helpless. This nine-foot-tall giant from Africa can weigh up to 350 pounds and run at speeds of 45 miles an hour. Its well-muscled legs are also formidable weapons, capable of delivering a kick of 2,000 pounds per square inch, enough to kill a lion.

A flock of starlings in Scotland flees an attacking Peregrine Falcon. Gregarious starlings usually move and roost in flocks of thousands. Their numbers may give individual birds safety from aerial predators.

To keep things fair, however, the bird in the lead position regularly drops back and is replaced by another member of the flock. For smaller birds, flocks provide security. A rapidly wheeling flock of Sanderlings, banking with split-second precision over a beach, may be enough to confuse and slow a pursuing Merlin. Mass roosts in the nonbreeding season may attract flocking birds by the millions, like the great mixed-species blackbird roosts in the South and the flocks of Red-billed Queleas in Africa, which may number in the tens of millions.

Yet no collection of living birds, however numerous, can compare with the immense migratory flocks of now-extinct Passenger Pigeons. In the early 1800s, Scottish-American ornithologist Alexander Wilson, observing one flock in Kentucky, estimated that each cubic yard of air contained three pigeons: Thus, the flock, which passed at the rate of a mile a minute for four hours, was made up of 1.2 *billion* birds.

Canada Goose

THE GREATEST JOURNEYS

THE WONDERS OF BIRD MIGRATION

Perhaps the biggest myth about bird migration is that migrants are fleeing winter's cold. Birds can tolerate exceptionally low temperatures—if they have enough to eat. It's not the cold weather driving northern birds south in autumn. It's the lack of seasonally abundant foods like insects, nectar, and fruit. Alternatively, it may be the loss of habitats like open water, which waterfowl and marsh birds need and which freeze solid in winter.

WHY BIRDS MIGRATE

There are insects in the northern forests even in

Crowding a Delaware beach, Dunlin, Semipalmated Sandpipers, and other birds create a blur of motion while migrating to Canada and Alaska. Moving in flocks of thousands, the restless shorebirds are dependent on stopovers such as Delaware Bay.

midwinter. That's how chickadees, kinglets, creepers, and other small, insectivorous birds survive; but there are not enough to sustain the hundreds of millions of insect-eating migrants that breed there in the summer. But to understand how migration evolved, it helps to reverse how you usually think about migratory birds: Imagine these not as northern species fleeing home for the tropics, but as tropical birds making a brief sojourn north to breed.

One swallow does not make a summer, but one skein of geese, cleaving the murk of a March thaw, is the spring.

ALDO LEOPOLD, *A SAND COUNTY ALMANAC*, 1949

Scientists have noted that most long-distance migrants belong to families that are most abundant and diverse in the tropics: vireos, flycatchers, thrushes, warblers, tanagers, and orioles, to name a few. Short-distance migration is common among tropical species, which make seasonal movements to follow the waves of ripening fruit or the mass emergence of edible insects.

It's not much of a stretch for those migration routes to gradually lengthen with time, as migrants

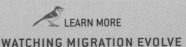

LEARN MORE

WATCHING MIGRATION EVOLVE

In two remarkable cases, scientists have been able to watch new migratory routes and wintering areas evolve right before their eyes.

The Blackcap, a small Old World warbler that nests in Eurasia, traditionally wintered in southern Europe or Africa. Starting around 1960, growing numbers of Blackcaps wound up each autumn in Great Britain, where warmer winters, an abundance of berry-producing shrubs, and backyard bird feeders made it an ideal spot for the species. Now the U.K. is prime Blackcap real estate in winter.

Similarly, several species of western North American hummingbirds, most notably the Rufous Hummingbird, have been showing up in rapidly increasing numbers in the East and Southeast, instead of at their traditional wintering grounds in Mexico. Like the Blackcaps, these hummingbirds are probably born with a genetic hiccup that causes them to orient in the "wrong" direction—a mistake that, thanks to a warmer climate, lush backyard gardens, and lots of carefully tended feeders, now pays them big dividends.

expand farther and farther north—especially during periods like the last 10,000 years, when most of the Northern Hemisphere has been free of glacial ice. All that ice-free land provides lots of elbow room, up to 24-hour-a-day sunlight in the highest latitudes, and an abundance of food. Come autumn, these once-tropical species simply reverse the path of colonization their ancestors pioneered and, following orientation cues embedded in their DNA, go back where they originally came from.

Bird Brain

Mistletoe plants growing high in the Peruvian Andes are dependent for their survival on the White-cheeked Cotinga, the only seed dispersing animal living at that elevation. The cotinga eats the mistletoe fruits and regurgitates the seeds onto branches, where they can germinate.

Fork-tailed Flycatcher

MANY MIGRANTS, MANY STRATEGIES

Just as there are thousands of species of migratory birds, there is also a kaleidoscope of approaches to their migration patterns.

It is not a simple north-to-south-and-back system, for one thing. Arctic Warblers and Northern Wheatears from Alaska migrate to Borneo and Africa to winter, while shearwaters from Tasmania migrate to the Bering Sea, feed through the northern summer, then return to Australia to nest. Tundra Swans from the North Slope in Alaska and Black Scoters from the Northwest Territories both cross the continent to the southeast to winter on the Atlantic coast.

And just as birds in the Northern Hemisphere fly south for the winter, many birds that nest in southern South America, like Fork-tailed Flycatchers, migrate north at the end of the austral summer, some wintering as far north as the Amazon Basin.

What most people think of as migration—a bird's

MIGRANTS IN SPITE OF THEMSELVES

The Boreal Owl is nonmigratory for most of its life, remaining summer and winter on its breeding territory in the conifer forests of the far north. But every so often this raptor's food supply—voles, mice, and other small rodents—undergoes a population crash. Faced with poor hunting, the Boreal Owl heads south, sometimes appearing as far from home as Ohio and Nebraska.

Such irregular movements are known as irruptive migration, and they add a lot of excitement to winter birding, in part because of their unpredictability. Along with northern raptors, which depend on cyclically abundant rodents, most irruptive migrants are seed-eating birds like Evening Grosbeaks, White-winged and Red Crossbills, Purple Finches, and Pine Siskins. When the conifers on which they depend periodically fail to produce a crop of cones, millions of these northern birds flood south, delighting feeder-watchers in more southerly regions. The flights sometimes take them clear across the continent, from Alaska to the Northeast and back again.

Irruptive flights do not always involve northern birds flying south. Pallas's Sandgrouse, a bird of the central Asian steppes and deserts, is a rare vagrant to western

BOREAL OWL

Europe, but it made a series of remarkable westward irruptions in the late 19th and early 20th centuries, reaching Great Britain and Scandinavia. No one knows exactly what triggered the great flights or why they haven't happened again.

Blackpoll Warbler vs. Common Yellowthroat

WHAT IS THE DIFFERENCE? Among closely related groups of birds, it's often possible to judge which species migrate the farthest by looking at their wings. Among wood-warblers, the wing of the Common Yellowthroat (right) is fairly blunt and rounded because its primary feathers are relatively short. Its stubby wings are sufficient for that species' short migration, which may only be a few hundred miles to the Southeast or Caribbean. The wings of a Blackpoll Warbler (left), on the other hand, are long and tapered—an adaptation for its extraordinary migration from Canada and Alaska to the jungles of South America.

flying long distances between its nesting and wintering grounds—is a strategy that scientists call complete migration. In complete migration the entire population leaves the breeding grounds for a separate wintering ground hundreds or thousands of miles away.

But many species have much more complex migration patterns: Some individuals or regional populations migrate long distances, some make much shorter journeys, and others may not migrate at all. This is known (somewhat confusingly) as partial migration. Blue Jays, Red-tailed Hawks, Western Bluebirds, and many other species are partial migrants.

And many birds avoid migration entirely. They are permanent residents, settling down in a single territory for their entire life—a strategy followed by Downy and Pileated Woodpeckers, Great Horned Owls, and most grouse and quail, to choose just a few examples.

A Wandering Albatross spreads its long wings as it readies for takeoff near South Georgia Island. Once airborne on a wingspan widest of any bird, the albatross uses its superb soaring ability to travel hundreds of miles a day.

NEAR & VERY, VERY FAR

With the exception of the central Antarctic landmass, bird migration is essentially universal on Earth: Birds move across virtually every square mile of the planet, from the driest deserts to the emptiest reaches of the Pacific Ocean.

As scientists learn more and more about bird migration, thanks to ever-smaller tracking devices, the mantle of champion migrant has been shifting. The Arctic Tern, which nests across the Northern Hemisphere and winters in sub-Antarctic waters, was traditionally credited with the longest migration, estimated at 22,000 to 25,000 miles a year.

But in 2006, scientists found that Sooty Shearwaters traveled nearly 40,000 miles a year between their nesting grounds in New Zealand and their foraging areas off Alaska, California, and Japan. The Arctic Tern was dethroned, but not for long. In 2010,

◆ AMERICAN CROW ◆

This bird's name derives from the sound it makes—in Old English *crawe* and in Middle English *crowe*. The modern word is also a verb that means "to make a loud noise" or "to exult."

scientists using newly miniaturized trackers found that terns nesting in Greenland and Iceland averaged nearly 44,000 miles a year, with some birds traveling nearly 50,000 miles.

No bird flies as far as albatrosses; although because their movements lack seasonal directionality, they are usually not considered true migration. Studies of Gray-headed Albatrosses nesting on South Georgia Island showed that some birds circumnavigated Antarctica, covering 16,000 miles in as little as 46 days.

Wandering Albatrosses, true to their name, have been tracked across more than 114,000 miles of meandering oceanic flight in the course of a single year.

Not every migrant travels immense distances. Dusky Grouse in the Rocky Mountains, for instance, migrate largely on foot, moving just a few miles—but up or down thousands of feet in elevation—from lower, warmer nesting areas in summer to high, snow-choked conifer forests in winter, where they feed almost exclusively on fir needles.

TOP 10 LONG-DISTANCE MIGRATION CHAMPS

Many of the world's long-distance migrants have never been tracked; especially for birds too small for tracking devices, the distance is based on the species' range.

1. ARCTIC TERN
49,000 miles round-trip
Greenland/Iceland to Antarctica

2. SOOTY SHEARWATER
40,000 miles round-trip
New Zealand to Alaska

3. SABINE'S GULL
24,000 miles round-trip
Greenland to Southwest Africa

4. PECTORAL SANDPIPER
20,000–22,000 miles round-trip (est.)
Greenland to Southwest Africa

5. BAR-TAILED GODWIT
18,600 miles round-trip (est.)
Alaska to New Zealand

6. TIE: AMUR FALCON (SHOWN)/SHORT-TAILED SHEARWATER 18,000 miles round-trip
eastern China to South Africa/Tasmania to Bering Sea

7. RED KNOT
16,600 miles round-trip
Canadian Arctic to Tierra del Fuego

8. NORTHERN WHEATEAR
16,000 miles round-trip
Alaska to East Africa

9. SWAINSON'S HAWK
15,800 miles round-trip
Western North America to Argentina

10. TIE: WILLOW WARBLER (SHOWN)/ BLACKPOLL WARBLER
13,000–14,000 miles round-trip
Siberia to southern Africa/Alaska to Amazon

GLOBE-TROTTING GODWITS

BAR-TAILED GODWITS ON A
SHELL BANK IN NEW ZEALAND

The longest *nonstop* migration in the world is the astounding flight of the Bar-tailed Godwit, a pigeon-size shorebird that nests in western Alaska. In 2007, scientists used a satellite transmitter to follow one godwit as it made a 7,200-mile nonstop flight across the widest part of the Pacific Ocean to its wintering grounds in New Zealand. Beginning in March, the godwits head north by way of the Yellow Sea in Asia, completing an 18,600-mile round-trip back to their nesting sites in Alaska.

FLYWAYS AREN'T HIGHWAYS

The notion that birds follow neatly ordered routes known as flyways had its basis in 20th century studies of waterfowl. North American ornithologists talked in general terms about the Atlantic flyway, the Mississippi, and Central and Pacific flyways; but to non-scientists, it sounded as though birds followed carefully demarcated lines north and south.

The reality is far more complex and messy. Birds ricochet across the globe, with each species—indeed, each individual—forging its own migratory path, one thread in an immeasurably complicated tapestry of movement that knits together the entire planet. But in some places, geography and weather combine to bring many smaller tributaries of flight into immense, migratory rivers—flyways in every sense of the word.

In the Western Hemisphere, there are major migratory routes down the Pacific coast and Mississippi Valley, along the Rocky and Appalachian mountains, and down the Atlantic coast. Millions of migrant raptors pass around the western Gulf of Mexico and through the Isthmus of Panama, while hundreds of millions of songbirds make a more direct, trans-Gulf flight between the southern United States and the Yucatán Peninsula. Some birds, like the Blackpoll Warbler, make a southbound flight from the Northeast coast

Ruby-throated Hummingbird

across the western Atlantic, flying some 90 hours nonstop to the northeastern coast of South America. The Blackpolls stop in the Amazon basin, while other migrants on this route, including American Golden-Plovers, continue all the way to Brazil or Argentina.

Migrants in the Old World have several notable barriers to cross. Among them are the Mediterranean Sea, Sahara, and Himalaya. Many flyways converge where it's possible to evade these barriers: across the Strait of Gibraltar, around the eastern Mediterranean, or through southeast Asia island-hopping all the way to the Philippines, Australia, and New Guinea. The route followed by a few species—stretching from Siberia and western Alaska to southern Africa—is one of the longest land-based flyways on Earth.

Bird Brain

During part of the 19th century, the Guanay Cormorant was considered the most important bird in the world because of the guano it produced. Nesting on arid islands off Peru, the droppings had accumulated for centuries and made a potent and valuable fertilizer. Conflict ensued, including a war with Spain, and overharvesting led to a guano crash by the end of the century.

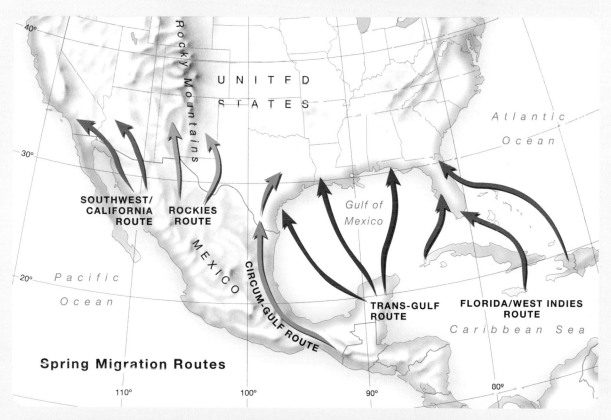

Spring Migration Routes

A map shows the major spring migration routes into North America from the Caribbean and Mexico. The route across the Gulf of Mexico saves on flight distance, but headwinds or a storm can be deadly to migrating birds.

961.

Martinet.

La grande Frégate, de Cayenne.

Magnificent Frigatebird. Hand-colored print by François N. Martinet (published 1765–1783)

916.

Martinet

La Grande Barge rousse.

Black-tailed Godwit. Hand-colored print by François N. Martinet (published 1765–1783)

READY, SET, GO

THE UPS & DOWNS OF BIRD MIGRATION AROUND THE GLOBE

It's not hunger that speeds a migrant south in the fall, nor temperature that propels it north with the spring—though food supplies and weather obviously play a role in migration. Instead, the timing of migration is driven by subtler environmental cues—some as universal as sunrise and sunset, some as individualistic as a bird's own internal clock.

HOW DO THEY KNOW?

The changing length of daylight and darkness, known as the photoperiod, is one of the most powerful drivers in biology, and birds are no exception. Longer days cause males' gonads to increase in size, for example, prompting them to sing and become territorial, and cause females to exhibit nesting

Ungainly on the ground but graceful in flight, Whooper Swans wing over Finland on their fall migration route. Shorter days and instinct prompt many birds that breed in the Northern Hemisphere to fly south to warmer climates.

WARNING: BAD WEATHER MAY FORCE FALLOUT

Every spring, hundreds of millions of migrant songbirds cross the Gulf of Mexico, making a nonstop flight from the Yucatán Peninsula to the southern coast of the United States. Usually this is a fairly easy 600-mile flight, but several times each spring, the migrants encounter bad weather partway across the Gulf that slows the travelers to a crawl. Under such conditions, the crossing may take up to 35 or 40 hours, and the exhausted survivors pile onto the first land they find—although they may also seek temporary shelter on offshore oil rigs or fishing boats.

OVENBIRD (LEFT) AND BLACKBURNIAN WARBLER

Such awful conditions for the birds can be a bonanza for birders, creating the phenomenon known as fallout. The trees and shrubs in coastal birding sites from High Island, Texas, east to Fort Morgan, Alabama, may be dripping with tired, hungry birds. After a few hours to rest, drink, and feed, most of the tired migrants will push on, leaving any birder lucky enough to witness the fallout stunned by the experience.

behavior. Photoperiod also signals the proper timing for molting feathers. But changes in the photoperiod—detected by a bird's pineal gland and acting in concert with its own internal circadian rhythms to set off a cascade of hormonal changes—also bring it into migratory condition, a process that may take weeks to fully develop. They feed voraciously, laying on precious fat that will fuel their flights. Their muscles begin to grow—in the absence of exercise, which intrigues human physiologists—and in some species the heart may enlarge substantially to better pump blood during the marathon to come.

Proof that migration is a genetically coded,

Thoughts pass in my mind like flocks of ducks in the sky. I hear the voice of their wings.

RABINDRANATH TAGORE, *STRAY BIRDS*, 1916

wholly instinctive process triggered by photoperiod came in the 1960s, when scientists raised Indigo Buntings in captive isolation, exposing them to artificial photoperiods. Regardless of the actual season outside, the researchers could manipulate the birds into acting as though it was spring or fall, and trying to migrate in the "correct" direction for the fake season.

◆ WREN ◆

Europe has only one species of wren and the derivations of the word are obscure. Early Germanic languages refer to the bird as *werna,* and the name may be related to Old Icelandic *rindill.*

FOOD, FAT, & FUEL

Among the most remarkable changes a bird makes in preparation for migration is altering its feeding behavior. It begins to feed incessantly, a process known as hyperphagia, laying on thick layers of fat beneath its skin and among its internal organs. The weight gain can be astonishing: In only a few weeks, a Bar-tailed Godwit preparing for its migration may more than double its weight, jiggling like a water balloon when

A Cape May Warbler perches on a branch. Named for their New Jersey habitat, most spend the winter in the Caribbean.

> And I say, "O that I had wings like a dove!
> I would fly away and be at rest."
>
> PSALMS 55:6

it walks. Having gained so much weight, the godwit's body will drastically shrink the size of its digestive tract, while its heart and flight muscles expand.

Fat is the fuel for migration, and birds are incredibly efficient at using it. A Blackpoll Warbler that usually weighs 11 grams may add 9 or 10 grams of fat, which will carry it from Nova Scotia to South America. This is the equivalent, scientists have calculated, of getting 720,000 miles to a gallon of gas. Plump with fat, many songbirds can fly 100 hours and more than 1,500 miles without refueling, while medium-size shorebirds like Dunlins have a potential range of up to 2,400 miles.

As the photoperiod signals the coming migration season, birds also experience what scientists call

zugunruhe—a German term referring to a premigratory restlessness that was noted in caged birds as far back as the Middle Ages. A wild bird experiencing zugunruhe may make nervous, false-start flights evening after evening for weeks before the compulsion to migrate finally becomes too strong to ignore, and it races aloft, the journey begun at last.

Many birds gather in large numbers in rich feeding grounds, before they begin their migration or at way stations along the route where they can rest and refuel, in what is known as "staging" behavior. Each March, for example, more than 600,000 Sandhill Cranes

◆ SPARROW ◆

The name derives from an ancient word from the Indo-European *sper,* to "flutter" or "quiver." Hence, the Anglo-Saxon *sperwa,* "flutterer"; the Middle English *sparowe* referred to any small bird.

gather along the Platte River in Nebraska. Here they spend several weeks gleaning waste corn and grain from farm fields, building fat reserves that will carry many of them to the Arctic—some as far as Siberia.

On the Atlantic coast, a million-plus shorebirds, some having flown there nonstop from South America, stage up in May on the shores of Delaware Bay. They are drawn by millions of horseshoe crabs, which clamber onto the beaches and lay their eggs—a perfect food for hungry migrants, which may double their weight in two weeks before making a fresh nonstop flight to the Arctic. It should be noted that, unfortunately, overfishing has caused the horseshoe crab population to collapse, and with it the populations of several shorebirds.

Bird Brain

The Capercaillie, a large grouse, feeds on young pine needles, which makes its meat taste like turpentine. This has not prevented it from being eaten, however. To get rid of the unpleasant taste the Swedes traditionally soak the bird in sour milk, and the Scots bury it for a while.

Members of the large family of sandpipers are seen together on a beach in this painting. Millions gather along the shores of Delaware Bay to feed on horseshoe crab eggs during spring migration before continuing north.

WEATHER & MIGRATION

The single greatest element that shapes bird migration is weather. Prevailing winds, storm fronts, thermal air currents, and many other meteorological forces play a critical role in where and how birds migrate. For a migrant on the wing, the weather can literally be a matter of life and death. For a birder in the field, knowing how to read the weather can make the difference between an excellent day and a dull one.

Although photoperiod sets the stage for migration, it's weather that determines exactly when and where a bird will travel—and for how long. Cold fronts in autumn and warm fronts in spring are the major migratory triggers, in large part because they produce tailwinds for the travelers: Northerly winds to push them south in fall, and southerly winds to nudge them north in spring. Changes in wind direction, speed, and temperature seem to be what the birds pay closest attention to.

A dead tree stump is the perch for a group of Great Tits during a snowstorm in Poland. The songbirds, common in Europe and Asia, don't generally migrate southward unless winters are especially severe.

THROUGH WIND, SNOW, SLEET, & HURRICANES

Even the planet's most potent weather does not stop some migrants. Recently, Whimbrels tagged with satellite transmitters and migrating across the western Atlantic were followed as they repeatedly flew into the most ferocious quadrants of tropical storms and hurricanes—and flew out the other side, safely. One of the Whimbrels pushing into violent headwinds averaged just 9 miles per hour for 27 hours. But when it finally came out the other side of the storm, those same winds, now at its back, helped rocket it along at more than 90 mph.

WHIMBREL IN RESURRECTION BAY, ALASKA

Weather and topography play a crucial role in migration. Along north-south mountain ranges like the Appalachians, prevailing northwest winds that strike the sides of the hills produce buoyant updrafts, along which migrant hawks can soar. Once the birds reach the western shores of the Gulf of Mexico, they

A robin redbreast in a cage
Puts all heaven in a rage.

WILLIAM BLAKE, "AUGURIES OF INNOCENCE," 1803

depend instead on rising thermal bubbles, which the tropical climate produces in abundance. Through such shifting means, a migrating raptor may travel thousands of miles while rarely having to flap its wings.

Especially after a long period of poor conditions for migration, a sharp change in the weather can bring about almost unbelievable numbers of migrants. Scientists using radar to track birds in northern Georgia have recorded as many as 200,000 southbound songbirds passing per mile, per hour, through the night—a rate of passage suggesting that tens of millions of birds were crossing the region.

The advantage of harnessing a strong tailwind explains some of the more inexplicable migration routes. Some songbirds like Blackpoll and Connecticut Warblers, as well as many shorebirds including American Golden-Plovers, make an extraordinary ocean crossing each fall from the northeastern coast of North America to northern South America. But instead of making a beeline from land to land, they follow a route that curves surprisingly far out into the Atlantic. By timing their departure with the passage of a strong cold front, they

◆ GULL ◆

The name may be related to early words meaning "to weep," referring to the wailing sounds made by some gulls, or may come from the earlier Latin *gula* ("throat") and refer to many gulls' willingness to eat almost anything that can be swallowed.

One of the longest migrations of any small bird is made by the Northern Wheatear, an Alaskan nester that flies to East Africa and back, a journey of some 16,000 miles.

ride the northwesterly winds well out into the ocean beyond Bermuda—where they eventually pick up the northeasterly trade winds, which arc them back toward landfall in Venezuela, Guyana, or Suriname. What looks like a detour actually saves them time and energy.

How fast a migrating bird flies also depends on the weather. Studies have shown that most migrants—from small songbirds to large raptors—generally travel between 20 and 45 miles an hour. Some—loons and some of the larger ducks are good examples—

may fly considerably faster. And all birds can be aided or held back by the wind.

Migratory birds are also responding to wider climate

Bird Brain

John James Audubon gave the Western Meadowlark the specific name *Sturnella neglecta* in 1844, as a rebuke to the explorers and settlers who traveled west of the Mississippi for overlooking the bird. It had first been described as different from eastern birds by Meriwether Lewis in 1805.

changes, as the planet warms and its weather patterns begin to shift. This has been most pronounced among short- and moderate-distance migrants, which may be more sensitive to local weather when fine-tuning the timing of their migrations; such migrants now arrive weeks earlier in the spring than they did just a few decades ago. Long-distance migrants, on the other hand, whose timing may depend more on photoperiod and circadian rhythms, have shown less flexibility in the face of climate change. Some, like the Pied Flycatcher of Europe, now arrive after their spring food supply peaks and have suffered catastrophic declines as a consequence.

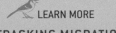 LEARN MORE

TRACKING MIGRATIONS

Although most bird migration takes place at night, there is one tool that can reveal it that is as close as your home computer: the nation's Doppler radar network. During spring and fall migrations, rising flocks of birds appear just after sunset, forming circular blobs—generally blue or green on the screen—that expand outward from the radar site. Searching the Internet for the phrase "radar ornithology" will produce a number of websites dedicated to tracking and interpreting birds on Doppler radar.

Caught in a blizzard, an Ortolan Bunting takes refuge under truck tires in Georgia's Caucasus Mountains. Native to Europe and western Asia, the bird migrates to tropical Africa in winter and sometimes returns too soon.

AND A STAR TO STEER BY

NEW FINDINGS IN MIGRATION SCIENCE

For centuries, the true nature of bird migration was cloaked in darkness. Most migrants—even those like songbirds that are normally active by day—travel largely at night, taking advantage of the cooler, moister air that prevents dehydration and overheating. The nighttime air is also less turbulent and relatively free of predators.

It is less safe than once assumed, however. Scientists in Spain have discovered that the Greater Noctule bat—a large, fast-flying hunter—regularly preys on migratory songbirds, which it apparently snatches out of the night sky.

INNER MAP AND COMPASS

It's little wonder that migration remained mysterious for so much of human history. And then, as science began to reveal the kinds of epic journeys birds were undertaking, little wonder that migration took on an ever-greater sheen of the miraculous. How could birds cross such distances, finding their way through the unmarked skies with such extraordinary precision?

At first, people assumed that migration was a learned behavior—that young birds would follow their elders south, learning the route and destination, like the mixed-age flocks of geese and cranes they saw traveling together each autumn. But research in the 20th century showed that migration was, for most birds, a largely instinctive process only polished by learning. With the discovery of genes and DNA, the mechanism by which a genetic map could be imprinted on a young bird while still in the egg became clear.

LEARN MORE

CATCHING UP ON SHUT-EYE

When a diurnal bird has to spend much of its time migrating at night, it pays a price: serious sleep deprivation. But unlike sleepy humans, migratory birds seem to have evolved ways around the problem.

After a night of flying, birds can't simply sleep all day. They still have to feed in order to rebuild their depleted fat reserves. But studies with Swainson's Thrushes show that they take "micro-naps," each about 30 seconds to a minute long, throughout the day. They also briefly rest alternate sides of their brain and the corresponding eye, a phenomenon known as unihemispheric sleep, which allows for some of the benefits of sleep without nodding off completely and risking a predator attack.

Furthermore, researchers have found that even when migratory birds are getting only two-thirds their usual amount of sleep, they continue to be able to learn new tasks and execute them as well as rested individuals—a feat tired humans can't match.

◆ BUZZARD ◆

Although there are no North American birds known officially as buzzards, the word was used by early colonists to describe the Turkey Vulture and is still in use in some areas. In Britain the larger soaring hawks (or buteos) are known as buzzards, which derives from the Old French *buisart* and originally traces back to the Latin *buteonem,* for "hawk."

While genetics lays out the route that a migrant must follow, the bird must still accomplish two difficult and complimentary tasks: orientation and navigation. Orientation is the ability to sense the cardinal points—north, south, east, and west—while navigation allows the flying bird to use that information to locate itself while moving across the landscape, all the while compensating for external forces like crosswinds. Genetics provides the map and orientation the compass, while navigation combines them both, allowing a migrant to follow its instincts to a destination it has never seen.

> *Did you ever chance to hear the midnight flight of birds passing through the air and darkness overhead, in countless armies, changing their early or late summer habitat? It is something not to be forgotten.*
>
> WALT WHITMAN, 1881

Yet despite all the discoveries of the past century in migration research, there is much scientists still do not know. Each breakthrough only deepens the awe that

Imprinted Graylag Geese follow an ultralight piloted by a person (not shown). Birds have migration built into their genes, but among a few groups like waterfowl, youngsters learn specific routes by following older birds.

Olive-sided Flycatcher

humans feel at what even the smallest migratory bird accomplishes when it crosses continents and oceans—the wider, richer sensory world through which it moves. Migratory birds use landmarks and topography like rivers, coasts, and mountains. They track the apparent movement of the sun across the sky and the wheeling stars at night; they tap into the Earth's magnetic field, listen to the ultra-low-frequency boom of ocean surf and keening winds; and they may even follow their sense of smell to find a single nesting burrow out of millions of others in a pitch-black night.

While scientists employ ever-more-sophisticated means to track bird migration, even in the dark, one of the oldest

Snow Geese may migrate by day or at night in flocks that can number in the thousands and include countless family groups. Most birds, however, migrate on their own or with others their own age.

methods is available to anyone with a pair of binoculars and a view of the night sky—moon-watching. Pick a night with a full (or nearly full) moon, just after dark during spring or fall migration. Focus on the face of the moon, and wait. You should see the crisp, momentary silhouettes of migrant birds passing across the white disk.

At one time, moon-watching was cutting-edge migration science. For five nights in October 1952, more than a thousand volunteers at hundreds of

~~~~~~~~~~~~~~~~~

Crows know the value of organization, and are as well drilled as soldiers—very much better than some soldiers, in fact, for crows are always on duty, always at war, and always dependent on each other for life and safety.

ERNEST THOMPSON SETON, *WILD ANIMALS I HAVE KNOWN*, 1898

~~~~~~~~~~~~~~~~~

sites from Maine to Florida and California watched the moon through telescopes and counted passing migrants, creating the first continental snapshot of bird migration. While science has moved on, moon-watching can still be a thrilling way to connect to one of the oldest and most dramatic natural dramas, played out every night during migration season.

Bird Brain

Extinct by 1680, the last existing moth-eaten specimen of a Dodo was set for destruction at the Oxford University Museum of Natural History in 1775. At the last moment, someone pulled the head and a foot from the fire. Those pieces and some skeletons are all that remains of the iconic Dodo, a flightless native of Mauritius.

TOP 10 HOT SPOTS TO SEE BIRD MIGRATION

Where are the most popular oases for avian migrations?

WESTERN HEMISPHERE

CAPE MAY, NEW JERSEY
(SPRING AND AUTUMN)

LAKE ERIE COAST—CRANE CREEK/ MAGEE MARSH, OHIO; POINT PELEE, ONTARIO
(SPRING)

FARALLON ISLANDS, CALIFORNIA
(SPRING AND AUTUMN)

POINT REYES, CALIFORNIA
(SPRING AND AUTUMN)

ATTU, ALEUTIAN ISLANDS, ALASKA
(SPRING AND AUTUMN)

VERACRUZ, MEXICO
(AUTUMN)

EASTERN HEMISPHERE

FALSTERBO, SWEDEN
(AUTUMN)

STRAIT OF GIBRALTAR
(SPRING AND AUTUMN)

EILAT, ISRAEL
(SPRING AND AUTUMN)

BEIDAIHE, CHINA
(SPRING AND AUTUMN)

Endangered young Whooping Cranes follow an ultralight to teach them migration in their first flight.

BURIED IN THEIR GENES

The idea of the wise veteran leading young birds south on their first migration is a deeply ingrained image—and where the vast majority of the world's migratory birds are concerned, a false one.

No migratory bird has to be taught to migrate; the instinct is preprogrammed at the genetic level. In a few groups, notably waterfowl and cranes, youngsters do learn specific travel routes and stopover sites by traveling with experienced adults.

But more typical is the case of shorebirds like the Sanderling, the common sandpiper that chases waves back and forth along most of the world's coastlines. Once Sanderling chicks—which are born in the Arctic of Canada, Greenland, Eurasia, or Scandinavia—are about three weeks old, and just after they've learned to fly, the adults abandon them, and soon leave the Arctic entirely on their southward migration. The young Sanderlings gather in flocks of a dozen or so and later follow their own genetically coded maps south as far as Chile or Australia.

The clearest evidence for the genetic basis of migration, orientation, and navigation comes from captive songbirds, raised in isolation and then tested in planetariums to see which way they instinctively orient. The Blackcap—the Old World warbler that appears to be evolving a new migratory path—is a favorite experimental species of European researchers. When Blackcaps that normally migrate to the southwest were paired with mates from populations that normally migrate to the southeast, their hybrid offspring neatly split the difference—half went southeast, half went southwest. Crosses between migratory Blackcaps from Europe, and nonmigratory populations in Africa, also produced chicks with an intermediate level of zugunruhe pre-migratory restlessness.

◆ BRANT ◆

This small, dark goose is known in Britain as the Brent Goose. "Brent" derives from the Anglo Saxon *bernan* (to kindle) and *beornan* (to burn), a reference to the dark (or scorched) color of the plumage. "Brent" was changed to "Brant" in Americanized English and the reference to "goose" was dropped.

It's usually a hiccup in the genetic software, rather than storms and bad weather, that accounts for most of the rare species that birders find far from their normal ranges. Most often these wayward birds are youngsters making their first migration.

But even a wholly instinctive migrant learns from experience, refining its route year after year, returning to the same breeding and wintering grounds with ever-increasing accuracy. As young ducks, geese, swans, and cranes travel south in mixed-generation flocks—propelled along by their instinct to migrate—they learn specific routes, resting sites, and wintering grounds that they will retrace in later years.

It is this combination of instinct and learning that conservationists have harnessed through projects like Operation Migration, which uses ultralight planes—piloted by humans dressed in crane costumes—to lead Whooping Crane chicks south from Wisconsin to Florida, establishing a new migratory population of this highly endangered bird. Having been led south once, the cranes return to their nesting area on their own and make subsequent migrations south without assistance.

Two Sandhill Cranes create a mirror image in Michigan. Their broad wings allow the cranes to soar easily on thermals while migrating. Their loud, rolling calls can be heard from far away.

WHICH WAY?

When a bird launches itself into the sky on its migration, it is alive to a world of sensory perception that we humans can barely comprehend but that helps steer the migrant through a vast and confounding world of winds and storms to its destination.

Birds depend on two major orientation systems—celestial and geomagnetic. The sky becomes imprinted on a young bird's consciousness within its first month of life—especially the apparent rotation of the stars around Polaris, the one fixed point amid the wheeling constellations. This anchors the bird among the cardinal points of the compass. Accordingly, if raised in a planetarium under an artificial sky that rotates around, say, the star Betelgeuse, the bird learns to orient on that "north" star instead.

Birds that migrate by day, like many raptors, depend not on the stars but on the position and apparent movement of the sun across the sky. Of course, the sun and stars are often obscured by clouds—but birds have other important strings to their bow. One is a band of polarized light, invisible to humans, which tracks the movement of the sun across the sky and which is visible to birds even through clouds.

Among the most important orientation cues, though, is the Earth's magnetic field. It is also the

An Arctic Tern flies in an Alaskan sky. The bird with one of the longest migrations—some 49,000 miles each year—can navigate even on cloudy days, able to sense the path of the sun across the sky.

most mysterious of a migratory bird's senses, the one least understood by science. Noting that many migratory birds have deposits of magnetite, a magnetic form of iron oxide, in their brains—as do many organisms that can sense natural magnetic fields—ornithologists assumed the crystals acted like a crude compass, pointing the way north.

But recent research with European Robins and Garden Warblers has shown that geomagnetic orientation is far more complex and weird. When light enters a bird's eye and strikes proteins called cryptochromes, the protein releases unstable free radicals, which respond differently depending on the strength and orientation of the surrounding magnetic field. Thus, in a strange but real way, migrating birds "see" the planet's magnetic field, keeping them on track even in darkness or bad weather.

Birds can also tap into other sensory realms to pinpoint their direction or location. Some birds, especially seabirds, depend on a keen sense of smell. Some species may also use ultra-low-frequency sound waves, generated by wind, tectonic activity, and ocean waves—and which may travel halfway around the world—to triangulate their location.

But how does a small bird, migrating alone for the first time, follow a zigzagging route from, say, eastern Labrador down to the Gulf of Mexico, around that body of water and into Central America? Scientists suspect they use a simple "time-distance program"—genetic instructions that prompt the bird to fly for a certain number of nights on one heading before a switch in the bird's brain flips and its orientation changes to a new heading for another

The European Robin, not closely related to the American Robin, migrates to northern Africa in especially cold winters.

predetermined number of night flights. Like a hiker following a set of instructions with a series of compass bearings and paced-off distances, the bird will be brought to its ancestral destination even though it doesn't know where it's going.

Bird Brain

Israel leads the world in the amount of turkey consumed per person: more than 34 pounds per year, more than twice the average amount consumed in the United States. The first turkeys were brought to Israel from the United States in the 1950s. In a country where red meat is expensive and pork isn't kosher, turkey consumption skyrocketed.

Gyrfalcons. Hand-colored print by John James Audubon (published 1827–1838)

Carolina Parakeets. Hand-colored print by John James Audubon (published 1827–1838)

FLYWAYS & REST STOPS

HOW GEOGRAPHY SHAPES MIGRATION

A glance at the maps of migration routes around the world shows the stark reality facing a migrant: the many barriers a bird must cross to get from one place to the other—oceans and gulfs, immense lakes, high mountains, wide deserts. Depending on a bird's needs and adaptations, these may be utterly hostile environments offering no opportunity for food, rest, or water.

Such barriers shape migratory pathways as much as do prevailing winds and weather systems—the way many Old World migrants squeeze through the Levant in Jordan and Israel into Africa, for instance, while others simply vault across the deadly expanse of the Sahara.

PATHWAYS, TRAPS, PIT STOPS, & HOT SPOTS

Geography concentrates migration—sometimes spectacularly so. Peninsulas like Falsterbo in Sweden, Point Reyes in California, and Cape May in New Jersey funnel millions of migrants into a limited area, creating a smorgasbord for birders, who may see tens of thou-

Lesser Yellowlegs squabble during a migration stop at Jamaica Bay Wildlife Refuge in New York City. The refuge provides a prime location for viewing birds such as these medium-size shorebirds during their annual migration.

A flock of White Storks migrates across Spain. A long-distance flier, it winters in sub-Saharan Africa and India before flying back to Europe and Asia. Many legends are attached to it, topped by the story that storks bring human babies.

sands of migrant raptors, shorebirds, seabirds, and songbirds in a single day.

And migrants crossing inhospitable terrain seek out oases, whether natural or man-made. Islands that lie below major migratory routes can be lifesavers for birds when the weather turns sour—and hot spots for ornithologists and birders, who make pilgrimages to places like Block Island off Rhode Island, the Farallon Islands off San Francisco, and Fair Island north of Scotland. Central Park in Manhattan is justly famous as a migratory hot spot, drawing hundreds of species every year to its rectangle of green amid the gray concrete of New York City, but urban parks worldwide serve a similar function for weary migrants.

◆ BIRD ◆

The everyday Old English word for bird was *fugol*, of Germanic origins, but *bridd* was sometimes used to describe a young bird or nestling. By about 1300, *bird* or *byrd* referred to various young animals and even human beings, particularly a young girl. The word's usage gradually narrowed to its present-day meaning.

FULL-SERVICE HOTELS & FIRE ESCAPES

Few birds complete their migration in a single, nonstop flight. Most break up the trip into shorter segments, with periods of rest and refueling in between—what scientists call migratory stopovers. A successful stopover depends on quality habitat, but not all stopover sites are the same. Conservationists have grouped them into three categories that any travel-weary human can understand: full-service hotels, convenience stores, and fire escapes.

"Full-service hotels" are the crème de la crème of stopover sites, places where a tired and hungry migrant finds everything it needs to rebuild its strength: abundant food, water, and safety from predators. Such a site may be a lush swamp woodland along a Gulf Coast river, an immense stretch of unbroken forest in the Appalachians or Cascades, or a fecund native

> *The flock seems to travel as a single bird, a single soul—as if in the intensity of flight, it had pierced a dimension of reality, of knowing in which all signals were superfluous.*
>
> PETER MATTHIESSEN, *THE WIND BIRDS*, 1994

prairie on the Great Plains. Full-service hotels are big enough to encompass many habitats, from wetlands and river edges to uplands and openings, and huge numbers of birds.

"Convenience stores" are a step down in quality. They are not as large or as rich in resources as the full-service hotels. They usually comprise scattered patches of habitat—a place where a bird can get some rest, a drink, and enough food to allow it to make a short flight to a better location. These may be the most common kind of stopover site in agricultural regions like the Midwest, or urbanized areas where parks, cemeteries, and backyards offer the only sanctuary.

Birders enjoy an observation stand at Higbee Beach on Cape May, a migratory stopover in New Jersey.

Bird Brain

Can you hear me now? City songbirds with low-frequency songs are having trouble communicating with mates and rivals in the urban jungle. As a consequence, some species appear to be narrowing the range of their songs, dropping out the lowest parts—developing a "city dialect" in order to be heard better.

A jumble of Wilson's Phalaropes passes over Blanca Wetlands in Colorado's San Luis Valley during migration. The sand-pipers winter in the central Andes of South America and summer in the western prairies of the United States and Canada.

"Fire escapes" are small, isolated pockets of critical habitat where birds need them the most—near migratory barriers like oceans, deserts, and large lakes. Barrier islands and peninsulas along the Gulf of Mexico are a prime example. These are often bypassed when the weather is good, but they provide a temporary refuge for millions of birds when storms strike. All three kinds of sites are important for migrant birds, yet as development and habitat loss eat away at the landscape, it's harder and harder for birds to find safe havens. That's why conservationists are trying to build a protected network of stopover habitats, so that no matter where a traveling bird may roam, a safe place to stay won't be far away.

◆ **INDIGO BUNTING** ◆

PASSERINA CYANEA: By 1300 the Middle English *bountyng* was the name given to a number of small larklike birds. "Indigo" refers to the blue color derived from the indigo plant, which the Greek called *indikon*, "blue dye from India." *Passerina* is a Latin word for "sparrowlike," and *cyanea* comes from the Greek *cyaneos*, "dark blue."

CONNECTING THE DOTS

PIECING TOGETHER THE STORY OF MIGRATION

I t took science a long time to figure out where all the birds went each winter, and why. As far back as the Bible, humans were remarking on the seasonal movements of birds. "Doth the hawk fly by Thy wisdom [and] stretch her wings toward the south?" the Book of Job asks.

SLEEPING WITH FISHES

Aristotle, writing about migration in the third century B.C., noted that "weakly birds"—those unable to face the cold—sometimes came "from places near at hand; in others they may be said to come from the ends of the world, as in the case of the crane; for these birds migrate from the steppes of Scythia to the marshlands south of Egypt where the Nile has its source." He also claimed that the legions of cranes did battle there with armies of pygmies on miniature horses—an image drawn from Homer's *Iliad* and perhaps even more from ancient Egyptian folktales.

But while it was obvious that the clangorous flocks of waterfowl and cranes were traveling, the nocturnal flights of most birds masked their comings and going. Aristotle believed that many birds "decline the trouble of migration and simply hide themselves where they are. Swallows, for instance, have been often found in holes, quite denuded of their feathers."

As proof, Aristotle made a challenge: "We would defy any one to assert that he had seen a turtle-dove

A fourth-century mosaic shows two birds perching on the edge of a birdbath. Birds have long figured in art but have been misunderstood. Migration historically puzzled people until they learned that some birds spend their winter elsewhere.

HÖLCHOKO, THE SLEEPING ONE

On a frigid morning in October 1804, Captain Meriwether Lewis found a Common Poorwill, a relative of the Common Nighthawk and Whip-poor-will, along the Missouri River. The bird was so sluggish that Lewis concluded "it appeared to be passing into the dormant state."

Scientists paid little attention to Lewis' observation. After all, the Aristotelian notion of hibernating birds had long been discredited. But in 1946, an ornithologist in California found a Common Poorwill jammed in a rock crevice in the Chuckwalla Mountains of southern California; another was found that same winter inside a rotten log. Like Lewis's bird, they were unresponsive. The next winter it (or another Poorwill) was back in the same spot. Ornithologists now realize that Poorwills are the only

COMMON POORWILL

bird known to regularly hibernate through much of the winter. It was a surprise to science, but not to the native people of the American Southwest, including the Pima and the Hopi. The latter call the Poorwill Hölchoko, the sleeping one.

---

in winter." (Which is true enough—but what Aristotle didn't know is that European Turtle-Doves all migrate to sub-Saharan Africa for the winter.) Barnacle Geese, he believed, began life as goose-necked barnacles, whose black-and-white pattern and fleshy "necks" resemble a goose, and he thought some species of birds transformed into others with the changing season—European Robins into Common Redstarts, for instance.

Because Aristotle's writings were the foundation of Western wisdom well into the Renaissance, his notions about migration, morphing, and hibernating birds took deep root. In 1555, the Bishop of Uppsala wrote about fishermen hauling up nets full of swallows hibernating underwater "among the canes and reeds."

No less an authority than Carolus Linnaeus, the founder of modern taxonomy in the 18th century,

continued to write about swallows passing the winter beneath lakes, even as colleagues tried to persuade him the idea was wrong. As late as 1878, the eminent American ornithologist Elliott Coues admitted, "I see no reason why a Swallow should not stay a while in the mud in a state of suspended animation . . . I have never seen anything of the sort . . . but I have no means of refuting the evidence, and consequently cannot refuse to recognize its validity."

Even by the 16th century, though, some Europeans with a scientific bent were piecing together the facts of migration, to replace the myths. By the early 1800s, Scottish-born ornithologist Alexander Wilson estimated that "at least one hundred million of birds enter Pennsylvania from the south" every year, and he noted that most of them traveled by night.

A RING & A PRAYER

The most basic and effective way to study migration is to place a numbered metal band on a bird's leg. But the first bird banding was accidental: A falcon owned by French King Henry IV, which was banded with a metal ring inscribed with the royal insignia, escaped and turned up a day later on the island of Malta, 1,350 miles away—a flight of about 56 miles per hour.

John James Audubon is often credited with the first scientific banding experiment in the early 1800s, but organized bird banding did not begin until 1899 in Europe. The trend crossed the Atlantic in 1902, when Paul Bartsch of the Smithsonian Institution put numbered, dated rings on Black-crowned Night-Herons

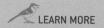 LEARN MORE

IF YOU FIND A BANDED BIRD

Anyone who finds a deceased banded wild bird is encouraged to report the event. In the United States, call the federal Bird Banding Lab at 1-800-327-BAND, or go to www.reportband.gov. You'll be asked for the date, place, species of bird (if you know it), and cause of death. You needn't return the band.

The finder receives a certificate of appreciation listing where, when, and by whom the bird was banded, its species, age, and sex. The bander also receives the information about the encounter.

An adult Graylag Goose wears identification rings on its legs in Scotland. Scientific bird banding began with Audubon in the early 1800s and remains a critical tool in studying bird migration.

in Washington, D.C. Today, despite technological advances, bird banding is still one of the most important means of studying bird migration. About 5,000 federally licensed banders work in Canada and the United States, under joint supervision of the U.S. Bird Banding Lab and the Canadian Wildlife Service. Each year, about 1.2 million birds—mostly waterfowl—are banded and added to a database of more than 100 million records.

Each band, made of lightweight aluminum alloy, is stamped with a unique serial number. While banding was first devised to track the movements and migration of birds, by identifying each marked bird as an individual, it allows a researcher also to determine survival and mortality rates, longevity, mate selection, fidelity to breeding or wintering sites, and more.

Banders use a variety of means to catch birds, but the most common involves fine nylon mist nets. When strung in forests, they are almost invisible. When a flying bird hits the net, it drops into a long, horizontal pocket that holds it harmlessly until the bander extracts it. Researchers sometimes add one or more colored plastic bands to a bird's legs. The combination of colors allows the bird to be identified at a distance.

AUDUBON & THE PHOEBES

Not long after he came to America from France in 1803, Audubon became curious about the Eastern Phoebes (which he called pewee flycatchers) nesting in an old cave on the family estate at Mill Grove, Pennsylvania, not far from Philadelphia. Did the same phoebes return every year after their migration? Audubon decided to find out.

Reaching into the nest, he attached light threads to the legs of the chicks—threads they or their parents at first quickly removed. "I renewed them, however, until I found the little fellows habituated to them," Audubon wrote. Eventually, he replaced the cotton thread with fine silver wire, "loose enough not to hurt the part, but fastened so that no exertions of theirs could remove it." That autumn, his banded phoebes disappeared.

The next spring, when phoebes returned to Mill Grove, "I had the pleasure of finding that two of them had the little ring on the leg," Audubon said—the first case of a naturalist using banding to solve a mystery about bird migration.

EASTERN PHOEBE

Amur Falcon

HIGH-TECH QUESTS FOR MIGRATION MYSTERIES

Although bird banding is still the most widely used technique for tracking bird migration, advances in new technologies are allowing wildlife researchers to unlock secrets that would have been unthinkable a few years ago.

The first radar operators in World War II noticed "radar angels" on their screens—the ghostly images of bird flocks taking off at night. Scientists still use marine radar to track birds over the course of several miles, and they use the Doppler radar network to follow migration on a continental basis.

Radio transmitters—devices that have been used to study bird migration since the 1960s—have been miniaturized to the point that they can now be mounted on hummingbirds. But such transmitters have major drawbacks. A scientist with a receiver and antenna must follow the bird as it moves, staying close

A researcher on one of Hawaii's Leeward Islands holds a satellite transmitter used to study bird migration before fastening it painlessly to the back of an albatross, like the Laysan Albatross in the background.

The antenna of a transmitter can be seen behind a Black-tailed Godwit as it calls during flight. Solar-powered transmitters that communicate with satellites appeared in the 1990s, allowing scientists to follow bird migrations from anywhere.

enough by ground or air so that the signal isn't lost.

In the 1990s, a new generation of transmitters appeared, ones that communicated with satellites from anywhere in the world to determine a bird's location. Some transmitters are solar powered and can operate for years, allowing researchers to trace the movements of Amur Falcons migrating between Asia and Africa—or juvenile albatrosses wandering across more than 100,000 miles of the southern oceans—without ever leaving their labs. But besides costing thousands of dollars each (plus additional expense for the satellite time), such transmitters are still fairly bulky, restricting their use to larger species like raptors, seabirds, and waterfowl.

Newer versions have incorporated GPS technology to provide almost pinpoint accuracy, and some now communicate not through satellites, but by triangulating their position—and continually sending that information to researchers—through the ever-growing web of cell phone towers. Many transmitters do more than simply record location. With onboard sensors, they can track a bird's heart rate, respiration, wingbeat frequency, and body temperature. Wet-dry sensors record when a seabird is at rest on the ocean or in flight above it, while pressure sensors record altitude, or for diving birds the depths to which they plunge for food.

An Osprey grasps a trout in Finland. The "fish eagle" is one of the few bird species found worldwide except in Antarctica. Much studied because of a declining population, Osprey numbers have gained since the banning of DDT.

Light-sensitive geolocators, which record sunrise and sunset times for years at a stretch, allow scientists to roughly calculate a bird's daily position—it was this technique that allowed researchers to finally track Arctic Terns on their 49,000-mile-a-year odyssey. Genetic analysis allows ornithologists to tease out the relationships between migratory populations, reconstructing the evolution of migratory systems. And sophisticated new tests for chemical isotopes in a bird's very feathers—which vary by habitat, latitude, and other variables—permit researchers to determine, say, that an American Redstart caught in New England spent the winter in dry scrubby habitat in the Caribbean, rather than a moist mangrove swamp.

◆ WOOD STORK ◆

MYCTERIA AMERICANA: The Old English *storc* (later "stork") traces back to the similar *stearc,* meaning "stiff and strong," and is probably a reference to the bird's rigid posture. *Mycteria* derives from the Greek *mykter,* meaning "nose," and refers to the large bill; *americana* describes the bird's New World range.

All this has allowed a new discipline to emerge: the study of migratory connectivity, the ability for the first time to look at the complete, annual cycle of migratory birds, no matter how far they travel or where they roam—a chance to better understand and protect them.

Bird Brain

In 2009, choreographer Phillip Adams debuted his ballet *Aviary,* using live birdsongs recordings and the birdsong-inspired music of modern French composer/ornithologist Ulivier Messiaen. Male dancers adorned with feathers perform dances based on the elaborate courtship rituals and nest-building behaviors of birds of paradise and bowerbirds.

Scientists can study bird migration by examining isotopes found in the feathers of birds like this male American Redstart. The isotopes provide a chemical clue to where the bird was when it grew the feather.

POWER OF PEOPLE

Few areas of science have relied upon experienced, committed amateurs to the degree that ornithology does. That's especially true of migration science. Although many bird banders are federal or state agency personnel or academic researchers, for instance, many more are unpaid volunteers, who do the work out of curiosity and passion.

There are several areas of research, and particular projects, where birders can make tremendous contributions to our understanding of migration. Students across the United States and Canada participate in Journey North, tracking the seasonal movements of hummingbirds, swallows, loons, orioles, Red-winged Blackbirds, and other species while they learn about migration. Similar in its approach but on a much larger scale is eBird, a collaboration between the Cornell Lab of Ornithology and the National Audubon Society. Every month, birders enter roughly 1.6 million bird observations into eBird's electronic database, where they are automatically mapped—allowing everyone from backyard birders to migration scientists to track bird population movements across North America in extraordinary detail and something approaching real-time. Now eBird is expanding to Latin America, the Middle East, and elsewhere. Hawk-watching is another example. In 1934, a young conservationist named Maurice Broun began tabulating the migrating raptors passing Hawk Mountain Sanctuary, a promontory on the Kittatinny Ridge in eastern Pennsylvania, and the world's first refuge for birds of prey. It was also the first such migration count of its kind, and Broun's results—an average of about 18,000 hawks, eagles, and falcons passing each autumn—drew growing crowds of visitors.

Soon, many birders were watching for migrant raptors in their own areas, and hawk-watches—

Researchers Laurel Ferreira (top) and Aaron Viducich look for hawks migrating along Nevada's Goshute Mountains.

Bird Brain

Birds and brews seem to be a natural pairing, at least on beer labels. One online source lists more than 350 bottles worldwide with bird images. Ubiquitous Budweiser has flanking Bald Eagles. Lesser known U.S. brands include Golden Nectar Ale (Rufous Hummingbird), Quail Springs IPA (Gambel's Quail), and Bell's Best Brown Ale (Boreal Owl).

A bander with HawkWatch International prepares to release an American Kestrel from the group's migratory raptor research station in the Goshute Mountains. The mountains lie in one of the largest raptor migratory routes west of the Mississippi.

almost always manned by volunteers to provide daily, dawn-to-dusk coverage through the migration season—began popping up elsewhere along the Appalachians, around the Great Lakes, the Atlantic and Pacific coasts, in the inter-mountain West, and on the western Gulf of Mexico.

Today, the Hawk Migration Association of North America serves as an umbrella organization for more than 200 independent hawk sites, most of which are still mostly or entirely staffed by volunteers. And the movement has spread worldwide, with more than 500 count sites on every continent except Antarctica. At Veracruz, Mexico, an average of 4.5 million raptors is tallied each autumn, the largest such concentration known—but each site, however large or small, is a window into the global phenomenon of raptor migration.

◆ **WILLOW PTARMIGAN** ◆

LAGOPUS LAGOPUS: "Ptarmigan" comes from the Gaelic word *tarmachan.* The *pt* spelling is a mistaken Greek construction. This species frequents dwarf "willow" thickets in the Arctic tundra. *Lagopus* is a Greek construction meaning "hare-footed," a reference to the bird's heavily feathered feet and toes that resemble a rabbit's foot.

Blue-throated Barbet. Miniature painting by Ustad Mansur (painted 1615)

Bird on a branch and a butterfly. From a Persian manuscript of the Islamic period

BRINGING THE BIRDS BACK HOME

◇◇◇◇◇

Mark Catesby produced this hand-colored engraving of a Cedar Waxwing or "Chatterer of Carolina" in 1731.

FEEDING YOUR GUESTS

FOOD & FEEDER BASICS FOR YOUR BACKYARD

For many bird-watchers, their first experience with birds came at a bird feeder—perhaps outside their classroom window, while visiting a relative's home, or in their own backyard.

No other wild animal can be drawn so easily and harmlessly into viewing range for our pleasure and education. Yet birds remain independent—visiting but not becoming domesticated, migrating at the right time whether or not food is offered.

GIVE BIRDS SPACE

If you want to install multiple feeders, be sure to keep them a reasonable distance apart—at least 15 feet—so the birds don't feel crowded. Remember that birds feel safest away from bushes or other places where a predator may be hiding. Place feeders a good 10 to 12 feet from evergreen trees, brush piles, and the like.

Take into consideration that setting up and maintaining a bird feeder is not a one-time event. The structure requires cleaning and frequent refilling, and

This boy may become interested in his feathered neighbors by filling a backyard bird feeder. Birds feel safe when feeders are away from dense shrubbery where predators may be hiding.

A Coal Tit in England seems perturbed that a squirrel is muscling in on its food. Many commercial feeders claim they are squirrel-proof but few are. Hang feeders high if deer or bears are present.

you need to be vigilant about preventing the spread of disease among the birds that visit your feeders. Don't worry about filling the feeder when you go on vacation, however, as birds are resourceful and will find plenty to eat elsewhere.

PARTY CRASHERS

Even a kindhearted animal lover may fume with frustration when unwanted guests appear at a bird feeder. Raccoons, squirrels, and chipmunks are eager to help themselves, and birds such as crows and starlings can become a nuisance.

When buying your feeders, remember that many boast squirrel-resistant features, but none are truly squirrel-proof. Feeders with small openings, including tube and globe feeders, are the least likely to attract small mammals and larger birds.

Try to think like your foe when you're using your feeder. For example, are you planning to hang your hopper feeder from a tree branch? That will make it easier for animals—including deer and bears—to reach it. Planning to fill your feeder in the evening with enough seed to last a few days? Food left out overnight will attract prowlers.

HOSTING WITH STYLE

Feeding birds provides wonderful opportunities to view the avian creatures up close. Although one feeder will attract several species of birds, a variety of feeders and food will bring an even wider array of species to your yard.

TUBE FEEDER

The perches and holes in the sides of these clear plastic feeders are usually too small to attract squirrels. These feeders, which are typically 16 to 24 inches long, can vary in design, however. Some wider-diameter tubes with larger holes hold mixed seeds, which appeal to more species.

FINCH FEEDER

Very small holes in this specially designed tube feeder type dispense only tiny black "thistle" or nyjer seeds, which attract American Goldfinches, Pine Siskins, and Common Redpolls.

HOPPER FEEDER

These handsome feeders resemble pavilions with large feed compartments, known as hoppers. The feed spills gently onto the wide tray that makes up the floor of the pavilion, and birds eat while balancing on the tray's sides or on a perch, if one is provided. Hopper feeders can be found in many shapes, sizes, and materials.

TABLE FEEDER

Feeders of this design—a platform of fine wire mesh and edged with a low rim to deter spills—are an especially good choice for birders who are inclined to toss seeds out into the yard: When uneaten seeds spoil, they can host mold and bacteria, which can sicken ground-feeders such as Mourning Doves, Song Sparrows, and Dark-eyed Juncos.

GLOBE FEEDERS

Chickadees and other small birds are drawn to small, inexpensive globe feeders of clear plastic. The thin, closely placed perches discourage large birds such as jays, which would otherwise gulp down the sunflower or mixed seeds used with this feeder.

WINDOW FEEDERS

Apartment dwellers and others with no yard can still enjoy feeding birds. Their best choices are plastic feeders with suction cups for attaching to windowpanes or small covered trays for windowsills. Unfortunately, these feeders are often so small that they require frequent filling. They may also attract large birds such as jays.

HUMMINGBIRD FEEDER

Red plastic hummingbird feeders hold sugar water, offered to the birds through tiny tubes or holes. These feeders can be placed anywhere, even on porches a few feet from a window or door, helping to provide extra energy for hummingbirds' long migration.

SUET HOLDERS

Woodpeckers love square cakes of beef suet, often mixed with seeds, which can be hung in metal screen-type containers that are the same size as the cakes. An alternative to the cake is a log with plugs of suet or peanut butter inserted into drilled holes.

Menu Planning for Birds

A good host knows that when planning a menu for a group, a few well-chosen staples will satisfy a diverse clientele. This is true for feeding birds as well. To attract additional species, vary the menu of seeds with other foods such as nuts, fruits, and corn.

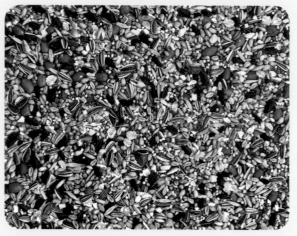

SUNFLOWER SEEDS

These familiar seeds come in two kinds. The smaller black-oil sunflower seeds will bring the greatest variety of species, from chickadees and titmice to jays. The larger, striped type is better for strong-billed birds such as Purple Finches and Evening Grosbeaks. Even woodpeckers will visit a hopper or tray feeder for sunflower seeds.

MIXED SEEDS

A birdseed mix is an important part of any backyard menu, but quality varies greatly. The best mixtures are combinations of black-oil sunflower seeds, white proso millet, bits of nuts and corn, and safflower seeds. Avoid the least expensive mixtures, which are filled with the small globes of red milo, which few birds except doves eat.

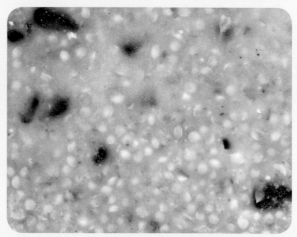

CORN

Larger birds including jays like cracked corn, which should be raked up if it gets wet. Scatter the corn on the ground or in a platform feeder and hope that the birds get their fair share before the squirrels arrive for breakfast.

SUET & PEANUT BUTTER

These high-energy winter foods are loved by many species. Suet is favored especially by woodpeckers. Peanut butter is a source of crucial energy for birds in winter, and it can be lifesaving for Carolina Wrens at the northern end of their range in a harsh season.

FRUITS

Oranges cut in half or apples and other fruits cut in pieces are favorites of orioles, especially when they return in the spring to breed. Berries are a favored winter food for thrushes, Cedar Waxwings, and Yellow-rumped Warblers, but these are best provided by landscaping with shrubs loaded with berries during fall and winter.

SPECIALTIES

Experiment with mealworms, a high-protein offering that parents feed to nestlings; crushed oyster and egg shells, a source of calcium; or stone grit, which various birds require to crush foods in their gizzard. Mealworms—a favorite food of bluebirds—and oyster shell can be found at pet food or wild bird shops.

NECTAR

To make nectar, nothing beats the classic recipe of one part white granulated sugar to four parts water. Bring the water to a boil, add the sugar, and stir. Do not use food coloring or artificial sweetener. Allow the mixture to cool before filling the feeder. A lightly more diluted mixture can be used for orioles—one part sugar to six parts water.

NUTS

Almost all seed-eating birds enjoy unsalted nuts broken into bits. This is easily accomplished by putting nuts in a sealed bag and crushing them with a rolling pin. You can scatter the broken nuts onto the ground or in a platform feeder. Watch to make sure squirrels and other critters don't abscond with most of them.

A woman thoroughly cleans a tube feeder, an important job to do once a month.
Birds can become sick from unclean feeders.

CLEANING UP AFTER YOUR GUESTS

It's important to clean all of your feeders at least once a month to attract more birds and minimize disease. Moldy mite- and bacteria-infested feeders threaten the health of backyard birds, and infected birds can spread illness to other backyards and wild populations.

Scrub and rinse plastic feeders in hot water with a dash of chlorine bleach. Use a weak disinfectant in hot water on wooden hoppers, scrubbing to remove dirt and seed remnants. Flush out hummingbird feeders with hot water (but no soap) once a week, especially around the holes. Replace suet (or peanut butter) logs regularly, and rake up hulls and uneaten seeds under feeders often. Seeds that have spoiled on the ground can make birds sick, too.

◆ CLARK'S NUTCRACKER ◆

NUCIFRAGA COLUMBIANA: A favorite food of this bird is pine nuts, and it is very adept at cracking open cones to get at them. William Clark of the Lewis and Clark expedition discovered this species in Idaho. *Nucifraga* is a combination of the Latin words *nucis* (nut) and *frango* (break).

BREAKING BREAD

Toddlers do it. Retirees do it. Filmmakers capture the sun setting as contemplative characters do it.
But we should think otherwise.

Many of us have enjoyed feeding ducks by casting pieces of old bread on a pond at the park or attracting legions of pigeons by scattering crumbs on a plaza.

But bread offers birds almost no nutritional value, and birds that grow satiated with bread may not seek out food with the necessary protein and fats they need to keep their bodies warm. Instead, they need high-energy foods like seeds and insects to stay warm, particularly during cold winter nights.

In addition, dry bread may swell once swallowed and cause serious digestion problems. Other complications include overcrowding in areas where feeding takes place, deformed and malnourished young, and the spread of disease. And rotting supplies of leftover crumbs can attract unwelcome pests such as rats and mice.

So save your stale bread for a meatloaf or batch of bread pudding.

Visitors to Rochester Castle in Kent, England, feed pigeons in 1909.

Kingfishers, Irises, and Pinks. Woodblock print by Katsushika Hokusai (published early 19th century)

Canary and peonies. Woodblock print by Katsushika Hokusai (published 1834)

HOME SWEET HOME

A PRIMER ON BIRDHOUSES IN YOUR BACKYARD

As your enthusiasm for watching birds grows, you may become eager to have them nest where you can observe them. By setting up a birdhouse, you are inviting birds to nest in your yard. Birdhouses are sold everywhere—resort boutique shops, cavernous home improvement stores, outdoors craft fairs—and they vary in design as widely as the places they are found.

All through the spring and summer, you can watch the passing parade. When a nesting pair chooses to settle in a birdhouse, they will haul nest material inside. They will make innumerable trips, flying back and forth, to carry food to their nestlings. Finally, the chicks will fledge and fly away.

But first you have to decide which birds you would like to attract; then buy—or build—the house appropriate to that species. You may find that the birds you were hoping to house are not likely to settle in a birdhouse. Birdhouses are suitable only for those species that naturally nest in holes or cavities. Many of our most beloved birds will use birdhouses, however, including chickadees, titmice, nuthatches, wrens, swallows, and bluebirds. To see what you might attract, check the range maps and nest types of the common species described here.

NEST BOXES & LEDGES

Nest boxes accommodate a pair of birds and their young. And a simple sheltered shelf is best for species that prefer to nest on a flat, open surface.

The nest box is the typical wooden birdhouse, available ready-made or in kits for home assembly. Building plans are also available in books, at your local Audubon chapter or bird club, and on the Internet. Nest boxes take many shapes and sizes, depending on the species they are meant to attract.

A nest box's length, width, and height are important. The diameter of the entrance hole is critical. Indeed, it often needs to be smaller than might seem appropriate: For example, it should be only one inch for a House Wren or a Black-capped Chickadee and one and a half inches for an Eastern Bluebird. If it's any larger, House Sparrows or European Starlings may usurp the box.

House Sparrows are an unwelcome, introduced species. Removing their nesting material will benefit native cavity-nesters.

BRINGING THE BLUEBIRDS BACK

EASTERN BLUEBIRD
ADULT AND HUNGRY YOUNG

One of the most gratifying conservation success stories is the comeback of the Eastern Bluebird, which was vanishing in recent decades as the availability of nest holes in old trees declined. But the bluebird population is now increasing because bird lovers are building special houses for them. Some people have even started "bluebird trails," installing dozens of boxes on fencerows along roads in parks and rural areas where volunteers monitor them. Western Bluebirds and Mountain Bluebirds have declined in parts of their ranges, too, and nest boxes can help them as well. The key online resource for information on bluebird conservation is the nonprofit organization Sialis, which is the scientific name for the Eastern Bluebird.

If you're building your own nest box, use untreated, unpainted wood such as cedar or pine. The birdhouse should have a sloped, overhanging roof, ventilation holes at the top of each side under the eaves, and small drainage holes in each corner of the floor. The roof should be hinged so you can clean out the inside easily. Don't add a perch—nesting birds don't need it, and predators such as jays might use it to poke into the hole.

Some species will nest on an open platform under a sheltering roof. With nothing more than a flat piece of plywood, six inches square, placed under an eave, you can attract Eastern Phoebes, Black Phoebes, Say's Phoebes, and Barn Swallows. Alternatively, buy a nesting shelf that resembles a nesting box without all of its sides. These species tolerate nearby humans, as long as the nest is not disturbed, so you can watch the parents feed newly hatched nestlings.

Barn Swallow

INVITING PURPLE MARTINS

More than a million North Americans put up the familiar "apartment-style" housing for Purple Martins. These familiar birdhouses can attract martins that chatter, swoop, and dart about, gulping down thousands of flying insects daily. Martins in the East nest only in human-made houses, while those west of the Rockies use natural cavities. Once martins nest at your location, they are likely to come back every year if you manage the site properly.

The requirements for a successful martin house are very specific. For instance, the amount of open space around the house is critical, and absolute precision is required in the dimensions of each nest compartment and its entrance hole. And unlike birdhouses that are mounted and essentially permanent, this house must be designed to be raised on its pole in the spring and lowered to the ground in fall. It is critical to raise the house during the particular week when the martins typically return to your locality from their spring migration.

Also, you must make a special effort to prevent European Starlings and House Sparrows from moving in and taking over a Purple Martin house. These and other details make being a martin landlord a challenging, yet rewarding, occupation.

A male Purple Martin prepares to enter a plastic gourd provided for its nest. North America's largest swallow, a voracious eater of winged insects, ranges across the continent but is almost totally dependent on artificial homes in the East.

Build a Purple Martin House

....

Purple Martins discover your location and nest there. They are apt to return
year after year if you maintain their house properly.

Providing housing for Purple Martins is a true hobby, and can bring great joy if you are so inclined. Keep in mind that expert advice may be needed to improve your chances of success.

The essential resource for well-researched information is the nonprofit organization Purple Martin Conservation Association, which offers extensive information online.

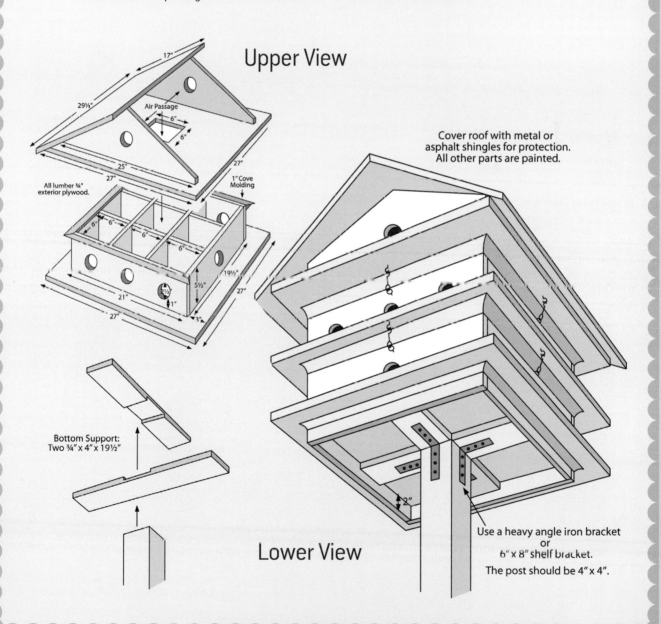

Upper View

17"

29½"

Air Passage

6"

6"

25"

27"

27"

1" Cove Molding

All lumber ¾" exterior plywood.

6" 6"

6"

6"

19½"

5½"

21"

2½"

1"

27"

3"

27"

Cover roof with metal or asphalt shingles for protection. All other parts are painted.

Bottom Support: Two ¾" x 4" x 19½"

3"

Lower View

Use a heavy angle iron bracket or 6" x 8" shelf bracket.

The post should be 4" x 4".

LOCATION, LOCATION

Situating and installing birdhouses—whether a Purple Martin–style house, a nest box, or a shelf or ledge— takes precision. Throughout their lives, birds are constantly avoiding dangerous predators, and poorly placed houses can offer them up as prey. Feral cats and house cats that spend time outside present challenges for which birds have never evolved defenses. And wild predators are always lurking about.

You need to check your yard and decide the best and safest location for your birdhouse. Three options offer important protection: on a pole, in a tree, or even on your porch.

The safest place for a nest box is atop an all-metal pole, and some birds such as House Wrens readily accept pole-mounted boxes. A wide, slippery, metal baffle surrounding the pole halfway up can help prevent egg-eating squirrels and raccoons from climb-

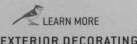

LEARN MORE
EXTERIOR DECORATING

Birdhouses can be functional and beautiful. But before you buy a decorated or themed birdhouse—or before you and your children paint your own—do some research into whether the birds you're hoping to attract will visit a colorful structure and whether the paints you're using are safe for the birds.

Also, never paint the inside of the house or the lip of the opening, where paint may chip away with use and get eaten by the birds. Remember that dark paint retains heat, and white and light colors reflect heat. Bright colors may attract unwelcome predators, whereas camouflaging may give extra protection.

The morning-song is the most cherished of the bird-lover's day.

OLIVE THORNE MILLER,
WITH THE BIRDS IN MAINE, 1904

---

ing to the top. Keep the box well away from hanging tree branches and tall shrubbery from which a squirrel could easily jump over to it. By wrapping the pole below the baffle with a sticky flypaper-type material, you prevent ants and other crawling insects from invading the birdhouse.

However, few bird species will nest in a box high out in the open. It is not their natural behavior. They prefer a nest box mounted on a tree trunk or a thick branch. Space nest boxes widely around the yard. Do not put more than one on a tree, and don't place them near feeders.

The nest entrance should face in a direction helpful to the birds inside. If your wind and rain come most often from the northwest, face the house opening to the east and south. If you live in a region where nights are cool, face the hole east, so the early

---

◆ FULMAR ◆

In Old English *ful* was the spelling of "foul" and refers to the fulmar's ability to spit smelly stomach oil at an intruder; these birds were once hunted for food. *Mar,* either derives from the Old French word for the sea, or perhaps is related to the Old English word *mew,* meaning "gull," which the fulmar resembles.

BIRDHOUSES ON POLES: HOW HIGH?

Different heights of birdhouses attract different birds. So, to encourage a variety of birds to visit your yard, hang houses on poles of assorted heights. Here are some examples.

Poles that are six to seven feet tall attract wrens, chickadees, and bluebirds. Poles eight to ten feet in height draw Downy Woodpeckers and Ash-Throated Flycatchers. Northern Flickers, Hairy Woodpeckers, White-breasted Nuthatches, and Great Crested Flycatchers like houses that range from 12 to 20 feet in height. And larger birds such as American Kestrels and Eastern Screech-Owls go for heights of 15 feet or more.

morning sun can shine into the birdhouse. Birds usually place their nests in a place sheltered from the midday sunshine, and you should do the same. If you're not sure about the best orientation, seek out an experienced backyard birder in a local birding organization and ask his or her opinion.

The porch of your house can also be a safe option for a birdhouse, particularly if the porch is covered. Not only does an enclosure there provide a nesting site, it also can offer protection from the elements and shelter in the winter—to help the birds survive the coldest days and nights.

Bird Brain

Cats Indoors is a program of the American Bird Conservancy (*www.abcbirds.org*) to educate cat owners and the general public that cats, wildlife, and people all benefit when cats are kept indoors. Nationwide, free-roaming cats kill hundreds of millions of birds every year—a staggering number. Belling a cat is not effective; in fact, one study found that cats wearing bells killed more birds.

ATTRACTING TWO FAVORITES

Perhaps your backyard is a small lot in a big city or a suburban lawn with flowerbeds and trees. No matter where it is, you are sharing it with birds. Two favorite birds that watchers like to attract are bluebirds and hummingbirds. Here are some basic tips to keep in mind to lure these favorites to your yard.

MOUNTAIN BLUEBIRD ON A FLOWERING LILAC

BLUEBIRDS

Bluebirds are cavity-nesting thrushes that greatly benefit when nest boxes are provided to them. None of the three species of bluebirds lives in cities or heavily wooded suburbs—they require fields, pastures, and open woodlands more typical of rural areas.

• Housing
Bluebird houses need to be the correct size. You can purchase them ready-made or construct your own. The basic house measures five inches long by five inches wide by ten inches high, and has a one-and-a-half-inch entrance hole without an exterior perch. Plans are available online. Mount your birdhouse on a predator-resistant metal pole about five feet above the ground. After the young have fledged, clean out the nest box. Where bluebirds are year-round residents, they may use the nest box for winter roosting. To find out more, visit the North American Bluebird Society's website at *www.nabluebirdsociety.org.*

• The Competition
Competition for scarce natural cavities and birdhouses can be intense. Bluebirds often lose out to starlings, Tree Sparrows, House Wrens, and House Sparrows. A bluebird house with the right size hole will exclude starlings. But if you see House Sparrows building a nest, remove their nesting material immediately.

• Mealworms
Live mealworms—a favorite food—can be purchased from many pet stores. Feed the birds in the morning and evening.

HUMMINGBIRDS

A combination of feeders and favorite flowers and plants is the best way to bring hummers to your yard. Many hummingbird feeder designs are available, from simple hanging bottles to large multiport models. Be sure to buy a feeder that is easy to take apart for cleaning—an essential feature. Basin-type feeders are easiest. Note that hummingbirds will not delay migration if you leave your feeder up in fall.

• Hummingbird Plants

A hummingbird garden is an excellent way to provide hummers with natural food. Some favorite plants are cardinal flower, scarlet sage, trumpet vine, and bee balm.

• Sugar-Water Mixture

Stick to this recipe: One part refined white sugar to four parts water. If you're mixing a small batch to use immediately, you can skip boiling it. Just use hot water. Do not use red food coloring or any sweetener other than refined white sugar.

• Maintenance

Replace the sugar solution every three to four days, or else it will ferment. Clean your feeder whenever you fill it. Use hot water (but no soap) and a bottle brush to clean the feeding ports.

• Placement

Hang your feeder from a window frame or overhanging eave, or under some sort of canopy that provides some protection for the hummingbirds. Also, consider placing the feeders in the shade of a tree. This allows the nectar you prepare to stay fresh longer.

A MALE RUBY-THROATED HUMMINGBIRD OVER A RED LANTANA

This "dummy nest" in a birdhouse was built by a House Wren, North and South America's most common wren species. Livable wren nests are neat cups, but the birds sometimes fill competitive birdhouses with wood to make them uninhabitable.

HOUSEKEEPING

Birdhouse cleanliness is crucial to birds' health and safety. Clean out the box or shelf in early spring when the house is not occupied. March is a good month, before the birds begin to breed. Use gloves to remove an old nest that may still be in the house. The nest is likely contaminated with bacteria and other germs, so dispose of it right away. As with feeders, clean the house inside and out with a weak chlorine bleach solution—one part bleach with nine parts water. Resist the temptation to line the inside of the nest box with a chemical coating to seal the wood or kill insects: Evaporating solvents—usually toxic—may linger inside the closed box for a long time, and birds are very sensitive to them. Allow the house to dry in the sun for a couple of hours.

◆ HARLEQUIN DUCK ◆

HISTRIONICUS HISTRIONICUS: "Duck" derives from the Old English *duce,* meaning "to dive." The Old French word *harlequin* referred to a troop of demons but later became associated with a stock character that dressed in outrageous multicolored costumes—not unlike the male Harlequin Duck's plumage.

TOP 10 BIRDS THAT LIVE IN BIRDHOUSES

Want to invite birds to move into your backyard? Here are the species most likely to accept the invitation and the sort of accommodations they will expect.

1 Eastern Bluebird An old favorite, very partial to birdhouses. These birds breed east of the Rockies. Wherever they are year-round residents, they will roost in birdhouses during cold winter nights.

2 Purple Martin Martins in the East nest only in housing provided by people. They live in colonies and find their way either to the familiar avian apartment buildings, set up on poles, or to hanging hollow gourds, a native American tradition.

3 House Wren To attract a wren, make sure the birdhouse entry hole is no more than an inch across. This feisty little species will push larger birds out and take over if it finds a birdhouse it wants to nest in.

4 Tree Swallow Our most common swallow and the one most likely to nest in a birdhouse, these birds line their nests with white feathers. Set out some old pillow feathers—even try coaxing a bird close enough to take them from your hand.

5 American Kestrel The smallest falcon in North America, this is the only one that will nest in a birdhouse. The house needs to stand on a pole 15 feet or taller to attract these colorful birds.

6 Screech-Owls Properly placed in a wooded neighborhood, a birdhouse on a pole 15 feet or taller can attract the Eastern or the Western Screech-Owl (depending on where you live).

7 Chickadees Familiar for their chirps and their presence at bird feeders, all of North America's species of chickadee will nest in birdhouses, particularly when they cannot find a natural tree cavity.

8 White-breasted Nuthatch A year-round resident across the continent and frequent visitor to bird feeders, this nuthatch will rub crushed insects around a birdhouse entrance, possibly to repel predators.

9 Titmice There is a Tufted Titmouse in the East and four other titmouse species from Texas to the west. All are cheeky, confident backyard visitors that will investigate and perhaps adopt a nest box.

10 Great Crested Flycatcher This bird would just as soon move into an old woodpecker hole for nesting, but it may be willing to use a birdhouse you put out instead, if the dimensions are right.

IF YOU PLANT IT, THEY WILL COME

A GUIDE TO LANDSCAPING BIRD-FRIENDLY YARDS

With feeders and nest boxes, we provide food, nesting opportunities, and shelter for birds. Your backyard is not only a home but also a neighborhood—a habitat. All birds require specifics in their habitats, and if you know how to fulfill those needs, you can make your backyard more bird friendly.

First, spend time observing the birds that already visit you, and begin improvements with them in mind. Then, consider the other regional species you'd like to see visit your yard. In the previous pages, we've addressed how to provide basic food and shelter, so now we can turn to offering water and plants for eating, courting, nesting, and cover.

DRAWING THEM IN

A yard with tall trees can attract tanagers or orioles. A yard with shrubs can attract Gray Catbirds and Song Sparrows. If your yard is nothing more than a wide open, manicured lawn, it may attract American Robins, European Starlings, and Common Grackles that poke around in the grass for worms and grubs, but that's about all. A smooth, closely mowed lawn is not a prime habitat for any bird.

Bird feeders hang over ornamental grasses in a courtyard. Studying bird activity can attract certain species by the kind of habitat provided. This one may draw birds that like low shrubs, but those that prefer tall trees will avoid it.

Three levels of plants—tall trees, shorter shrubs, and flowers—await bird residents in this backyard habitat. The flowers are purple coneflowers and taller black-eyed Susans. Assorted plants and different foods assure a greater variety of visiting birds.

Some species are remarkably adaptable: For example, House Finches live in cities, suburbs, and deserts. But most are very particular, and this gets to the essence of landscaping for birds. If you provide the largest possible diversity in habitat, you will attract the greatest variety of birds.

Assorted heights are one factor: trees, shrubs, and low understory plants. A range of food is another: Plants that provide different kinds of berries, fruits, and seeds as well as supporting caterpillars and insects. Seasonal diversity matters, too: Nectar-bearing flowers attract hummingbirds in summer, and berry-laden trees and shrubs attract Cedar Waxwings in winter. Landscapes designed for diversity not only offer food and shelter, but also provide varied locations, attracting different birds that stay to carve out or build a nest.

 LEARN MORE

LANDSCAPING DO'S AND DON'TS

Take these tips into consideration when you're working in your yard:

• Avoid clearing or disrupting existing plants during nesting season.

• Leave dead grass and fallen twigs so birds can use these materials for nesting.

• Provide plants at various heights and depths, since different species will be comfortable with different exposures.

• Study both non-native and invasive plants so you can make informed choices about what to remove and replace.

• Consult local birding groups and nurseries to find birders who have completed bird friendly landscaping projects and can offer advice.

Water Features—Irresistible!

Water is essential to every bird in every season. Birds both drink and bathe in water, and they will visit your yard more often and in larger numbers if you provide it.

Properly designed birdbaths are less than two inches deep and should be placed in an area clear of underbrush, where predators might lurk. Baths that rest directly on the ground and those that are elevated a few feet above are equally popular. The bath's surface should be slightly rough; slick metal, plastic, or ceramic make birds feel insecure. Place a few flat rocks or some gravel in the bottom of a bath that is too deep or slippery.

Movement and sound are key to drawing birds to water. A recirculating pump that creates a splash or trickle will multiply the bath's attractiveness tenfold. You can create a temporary moving-water feature by propping the nozzle of your lawn hose on a foot-long stick and letting it drip or spray onto the grass in an open area of the lawn.

People living in arid parts of the country know the power of water in attracting birds. But more importantly, birds' survival depends on finding good water—in the Southwest especially. In dry-air desert areas, a freshly filled birdbath appeals to visitors, even when it is not blazing outside.

Conversely, keeping the bath ice-free in winter with a small outdoor heater can be a lifesaving measure for species that overwinter. Add a de-icer to your existing birdbath or buy a model that has a built-in heater. Place sticks or other material that extends above the water level to give birds a perch without getting wet.

Cleanliness is essential, too. Flush out and scrub your birdbath every other day to remove debris, mosquito larvae, and droppings. A weak chlorine bleach solution will help control algae. Rinse the birdbath thoroughly after scrubbing.

Streams and ponds in larger backyards serve up a reliable banquet of minnows, crayfish, and frogs for wetlands migrants. If you have a backyard pond, keep it in balance with a healthy mix of filtering, free-floating plants, and root-anchored, surface-blooming specimens.

AN AMERICAN ROBIN STARES DOWN
A PLASTER PUPPY AT A BIRDBATH.

PLANTING FOR BIRDS

When preparing your yard for birds, keep in mind that each region has a different climate, different native plants, and different species to host. Furthermore, your position in your region—mountains versus seaside, fertile farmland versus arid plain—helps dictate the best landscaping choices.

Begin by creating a mix of evergreens and deciduous trees and shrubs. Next, add perennial and annual flowers. Consider growing vines over fences, up the sides of a house or garage, or on trellises out in the open. If you have any non-native flowering plants, consider removing them and replacing them with native varieties.

Understory plantings should include annual and perennial flowers that offer nectar for hummingbirds and seeds for finches and sparrows. Massed plants are more attractive to birds and people than single plants. Meadows using native prairie plants are attractive to insect- and seed-eating birds, lending a carefree charm that a mowed lawn lacks.

Brush piles, a by-product of any gardening endeavor, will beckon sparrows, cardinals, towhees, and other ground-dwelling birds, as they provide needed shelter from predators and weather. When raking your leaves in the autumn, don't remove every last one. Leave some piles here and there. Leaf litter, especially scattered under shrubs and spread across flowerbeds, is a good hunting ground for insect-eating birds.

Bird gardening enthusiasts recognize the value of dead or dying trees. Don't move them totally out of your yard. Cavity-nesting birds may find suitable nest

A luxuriant flower garden in California will probably attract birds to its great variety of flowers at different heights.

sites there, and insect-eaters treat them as favored larders packed with beetles. Smaller dead limbs, often called snags, are valuable, too. Some bird gardeners even go so far as to drag them out of the woods, dig holes, and "plant" them. Many birds appreciate tall, dead snags as survey, preening, and feeding perches. Hanging your feeders on snags can create a feeding station with great bird appeal.

Clearly, the use of pesticides is counterproductive when the aim is to attract lots of birds; insects, as a food source for birds, are a vital part of the backyard habitat.

LANDSCAPING FOR BIRDS IN THE NORTHEAST

The Northeast enjoys the presence of birds that nest and breed there in the warmer months. In spring and autumn, this region hosts temporary migrants, and it retains some species throughout the winter, depending on available food sources.

To attract more birds to your northeastern backyard, add plants that serve the needs of birds throughout the year. Evergreen trees such as pines and spruces provide year-round nesting, perching, and protection for birds, and the seeds within cones are a vital food source in the cold months. Birches produce seed clusters that several species favor. If possible, leave dead or dying trees, snags, and stumps on your property; they offer rich pickings in insect life to woodpeckers, chickadees, wrens, titmice, and others. Hedges offer shelter in winter and fine nest sites in summer.

Flowering annuals, perennials, and native grasses are sources of nectar, insect prey, and seeds. Many native shrubs have ripe berries in autumn, just when birds need extra-energy foods for migration. Berries that remain after the migrating flocks depart help resident birds survive through the cold weather. In spring, birds use native ornamental grasses for nest material, and some species use grasses as cover habitat.

A Northeast backyard should offer food sources useful to birds that frequent there.

LANDSCAPING FOR BIRDS
IN THE SOUTHEAST

Migrating species come through the Southeast in autumn on their way to the tropics and pass through again in the spring. Gardens that include berry-producing shrubs, open wet or boggy areas, late and early flowering perennials, and high-protein food sources like pines are welcoming to bird populations.

Evergreens such as hollies produce berries that attract birds. The cabbage palm and saw palmetto are important food sources for several kinds of birds. Persimmon, pawpaw, pecan, and other native trees provide bountiful fruit in the early autumn that sustains northern visitors flying south.

Look for southern varieties of bird-friendly trees usually identified with the North: birches, pines, and oaks. Some vines, shrubs, and perennials that shed their leaves in the North are evergreen in the South; these vines and shrubs add immensely to the shelter available year-round for resident birds.

Although numerous shrub varieties produce summer berries, the ilexes and viburnums are valuable for producing ripe fruit in autumn and holding it on the stems into winter. Insect-eating thrushes appreciate the soft soil of flowerbeds and the leaf-littered ground where frost is intermittent.

Migrating birds passing through the Southeast appreciate plants that produce food.

LANDSCAPING FOR BIRDS
IN THE NORTHWEST

The Northwest supports a wide range of plants with distinct growth habits that attract the birds of the region—it's almost impossible to generalize. That's why it is important to rely on plants suggested by local nurseries, other birders, or a nearby chapter of the Audubon Society.

Plant evergreens and conifers on the north side of your property; they'll shield you from north winds while they shelter the birds. Plant deciduous trees that flower and produce acorns or berries for birds to the south of your buildings, protected from the winds that strip early spring blooms.

Native grasses support songbirds, quail, and doves. You might also include a wildflower meadow. Many birds forage for insects among the flowers, and some strip seed heads after the insects are gone. Ground-nesting birds build nests in the cover that a dense meadow offers.

Where the soil is thin, rock gardens take advantage of natural conditions. Many rock garden plants produce nutritious seeds for birds. These are also places where they collect grit or forage for insects. Stone absorbs solar energy, creating winter shelter in the garden where birds can gather to warm up.

Plants in the Northwest should shield birds from the wind besides offering food. Stones create warmth.

LANDSCAPING FOR BIRDS IN THE SOUTHWEST

Because of the chronic dry conditions of the Southwest, backyards favored by both resident and migratory birds are those that offer water. Appropriate landscaping in the driest regions takes advantage of native plants that flourish without supplemental water. Sages, cacti, and desert grasses require less care here while appealing to the birds that naturally feed on and live among them. Cactus blooms and cactus fruits attract various insects that birds savor. Some birds eat the cactus fruits and peck through the stems for moisture. The large organ-pipe and saguaro cacti provide favored homes for many bird and animal species. Dryland pines, mesquite, Joshua trees, and Spanish dagger also serve as excellent shelter and nest sites. Try container plantings to conserve water. Opuntia, ocotillo, agaves, and small juniper species can be grown in containers.

Rock piles offer shelter, perching places, and prime hunting grounds for roadrunners that eat small reptiles and for owls that prey on rodents. Many desert-living birds eat more live food than seeds and berries. At high altitudes, a rock garden's warmth on a sunny day provides a welcome microclimate for both frost-tender plants and chilly birds.

Desert plants and water attract birds to a garden in the Southwest.

Blue Jay. Hand-colored print by Mark Catesby (published 1754)

Backyard Birding Basics

NEAR-HOME BUILDING

By watching birds we become intimately tied to the natural world through their life cycles, and the turn of seasons takes on new meaning. Many casual bird lovers eventually become birders—traveling to new places to see new species or planning vacations around bird migration times and routes.

Somewhere in between buying your first bird feeder and booking a birding trip to Africa is studying in detail the birds you see each day. While your backyard may not boast the most exotic species, it consistently brings you closer to wild birds than you can get in the field.

BIRDING NEAR HOME

Your feeders and birdbaths are installed, your birdhouses are in place, and you've invited the birds with attractive landscaping. With feeders placed close to windows, a house can become a big, comfortable blind. Even the most skittish birds soon learn

A Black-capped Chickadee is barely recognizable after bathing in a birdbath. Birds are drawn to moisture. Backyard birders derive enjoyment from putting up bird-friendly devices and watching different species come to their yards.

to ignore movement they detect through windows. Once birds feel comfortable being observed, you can study their interactions.

Watching birds from inside a window can be entertaining, but you're missing many other opportunities to find birds if you stop there. You're seeing only one small part of a larger bird community that is in and near the yard. These birds are in the air, high and often camouflaged in the trees, lurking in the shrubs, and feeding in the flowerbed around the corner of your house.

◆ Step Outside

To maximize awareness and recognition of what's there, go outside and watch carefully: Look at different times of the day. Begin by studying birds' daily patterns of activity. As you become aware of how they behave at various times, your enjoyment will be enhanced immeasurably.

Songbirds have a typical pattern of behavior within the 24-hour span of a day. They are most lively in the early morning, even before dawn in the spring and summer. Like us, birds wake up hungry after a long night of sleep and fasting. They spend the morning feeding, and then—in both midsummer heat and midwinter cold—many of them disappear from view, moving back into the bushes and trees to rest all afternoon. Finally, in the early evening until sunset, they come out and forage for the day's last meal before withdrawing out of sight again for the night.

During migration season, look intently into the trees. Right at eye level, you might see a well-camouflaged greenish-yellowish Orange-crowned Warbler passing

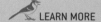 **LEARN MORE**

DISGRUNTLED AVIANS: THE ANGRY BIRD PHENOMENON

You won't find them in any standard field guide, but their features are universally known: a combined face and body of red, blue, white, yellow, or black, absence of both wings and legs, and thick black eyebrows knotted in a perpetual, menacing frown above a sharp, scowling bill. They rely on slingshot-assisted flight and have many specialized adaptations linked to extremely aggressive behavior toward egg-stealing green pigs. With a billion downloads in all versions to its credit, Angry Birds has gone extremely viral since its 2009 launch by Finnish computer game company Rovio Mobile, becoming a worldwide pop culture reference that loses nothing in translation. Angry Birds appears everywhere—from Israeli TV to 10 Downing Street to villages and cities in its fastest growing market in China—and the inevitable spin-offs include cartoons, a Christmas special, and feature-length films in development. The birds are here, there, and everywhere, like an invasive species that finds all habitats to its liking. And although Angry Birds does not advance knowledge of how real birds look and live, it keeps birds aloft in the conversation—and that's always good.

quietly through the yard. Look straight up, where a Broad-winged Hawk may be circling silently, during a migration that covers thousands of miles. Peek carefully down into shrubbery, and you could see a Gray Catbird or a Spotted Towhee creeping from low bush to low bush. The lesson here is to watch for movement. Even a brief flash of motion can call your attention to the fact that a bird is there.

Especially in the breeding season, be sure to look high into deciduous trees. You may spot a Bullock's Oriole or Baltimore Oriole hanging its pouchlike nest from a branch. If your yard borders a marsh, gaze out in the early morning for a burst of activity as male Red-winged Blackbirds vie for territory in the cattails. If you can see a lake or pond in the West, watch for Violet-green Swallows in search of insects, skimming over the water. Spring and summer—breeding season—represents the peak of watchable bird activities. Look around in winter, too. Besides the birds at your feeders, some may lurk in the shrubbery.

◆ Listen Carefully

Go outside just before sunrise in the spring and you may hear a disorganized symphony of birdsong that is called the dawn chorus. Males of dozens of species are singing all at once, trying their best to establish nesting territory and attract mates. When you hear a bird, try to figure out where the song is coming from. If you can find the bird, you can put song and species together. Above all, when you begin to learn songs, have patience. Watch one bird singing at a time. The more slowly you learn your yard's birdsongs, the longer will be your joy in day-to-day, year-to-year discoveries.

Three hungry mouths in a nest beg for food brought by an adult American Robin. Knowing the areas birds frequent increases bird-watching opportunities. Learning their songs can assure knowing the birds are there, even if they can't be seen.

Cozy Nests: Building Materials for the Birds

Birds make nests out of all sorts of materials they find in nature—
from twigs and grasses to feathers and horsehair.

A EURASIAN JACKDAW STEALS
HORSEHAIR FOR A NEST.

If you want to go all out for your avian guests, you can help by providing them with material for building their nests. Prepackaged material can be bought and set out in a holder. Common holders are ones that look like the cages that hold suet cakes.

You can also collect materials yourself. Tuck your collection into a hole in a tree, hang it in a mesh bag (like the ones onions are sold in), or pile it on the ground if it is unlikely to blow away. Avoid material like dryer lint, which often contains man-made fibers and chemicals. You can also collect paint-, dye-, and pesticide-free materials such as these:

- **Dead leaves**
- **Dead twigs**
- **Sheep's wool**
- **Pine needles**
- **String**
- **Pet hair (only if free of flea treatments)**
- **Human and horse hair (6 inches or shorter)**
- **Raw cotton bolls**

A Northern Cardinal male and female appear to kiss during breeding season in spring. The male of the species commonly feeds the female as part of a bonding process. Learning and observing such habits enriches backyard birding.

GETTING A GLIMPSE OF LIFE AS A BIRD

Seeing and hearing birds on a daily basis and coming to know their habits almost as well as we know our own, from courtship to defending territories and raising young—these are the rich rewards for the backyard birder.

◆ Feeding Time

A great deal can be learned about birds by observing them at your feeders. For example, watch the different ways birds shell seeds: Cardinals, finches, and grosbeaks nimbly handle the whole process with their bill and tongue; chickadees, titmice, and jays laboriously peck the hulls off while holding the seed in their feet; and nuthatches and woodpeckers lodge the seed in a crevice.

In spring, the nesting season, two cardinals may exchange a "kiss," as the male feeds his mate in early

◆ TURKEY ◆

The word "turkey" has a convoluted history. By 1500 African guineafowl were being imported to Europe via Turkey by traders known as turkey merchants. The American bird was originally considered a species of guineafowl and hence the "turkey" connection.

bonding. Later, young cardinals—their bills blackish, their plumage mottled with red—appear beneath the feeders. Male Mourning Doves guard their mates, following their every move, and stop to coo, inflating their throats with air. Young doves arrive, visibly smaller than their parents, their feathers scaled with white, pecking at anything that might be edible.

Woodpeckers depart with gullets stuffed with food as they ferry it to their young. In late summer, young woodpeckers peep, flutter, and cling near the feeders, begging for subsidy from their parents. We see their duller colors and dark eyes and begin to recognize individual birds, noting the age-related differences in their plumage.

Seeing birds forage for live food is rewarding, too. Robins cock their heads as they strut across your yard and then pounce in pursuit of hidden earthworms. Swallows dip in flight through a high swarm of insects. In the front yard, you may spot crows sorting through the pickings in a trash bag they've slashed open or doing their part to clean up roadkill.

◆ Group Dynamics

When a hawk swoops past, listen for other birds' high-

Feeding the inexperienced over Northern California, a White-tailed Kite parent passes a vole to its eight-week-old fledgling. Gull-colored but falcon-shaped, the raptors eat mostly rodents and ignore smaller birds.

Red-eyed Vireo

pitched alarm calls, and watch those birds flee or freeze in place, trying to avoid the hawk's detection. Listen for the scolding calls of a gang of chickadees or Blue Jays when they discover a resting owl or preening hawk. Mobbing—or attacking in a group— alerts other birds to the presence of a predator and tells the predator that it has been detected. Birds may also flock, or form groups, to decrease the chance that any one of them will be taken by a predator. Look for pigeons flying in a mass in one direction before wheeling to head the opposite way in precise maneuvers that may confuse a pursuer.

A Bald Eagle preens its tail feathers. Maintenance of feathers is important for flying and temperature control.

Blackbirds and sparrows fly in flocks to migrate. Watch for them gathering on power lines in the autumn. Notice how flocks of starlings or waxwings suddenly sweep through the yard, stripping ornamental trees and shrubs of their fruit. Mixed feeding flocks, with species as diverse as titmice, woodpeckers, kinglets, and warblers, range through the winter woods, searching for fruits, seeds, and dormant insects.

◆ **Preening & Hygiene**

A feeding station, a birdbath, and perches nearby help you observe feather maintenance behavior, such as preening and sunbathing. Preening is essential to bird survival: Clean, well-oiled, and groomed feathers offer better insulation against temperature extremes and dampness. Birds can be seen nibbling the oil gland at the base of the upper tail feathers; they spread that oil throughout the wing, tail, and body feathers with rapid movements and frequent fluffing.

A scuffed-up bit of bare ground serves as a dust bath where birds roll and flutter, spreading fine particles of soil through their feathers. This is thought to suffocate parasites such as feather lice and mites. On a sunny day, you may see a robin or cardinal lying on the lawn, seemingly stunned—its beak agape, its feathers fluffed, and its wings and tail spread—as it sunbathes.

◆ **Nesting & Raising Young**

Birds, untaught and unpracticed, form nests every year using beaks and the occasional assist from a claw. Bird species follow inborn instinct in the type of nest they build, whether woven fiber, basket-shape, or cavity.

But they can be inventive and innovative in choosing where to nest. House Wrens are famous for nesting in old gardening hats, clothespin bags hanging on the line, and the hollow crossbars along the tops of swing sets. In some species, the male flies off to find another female as soon as mating is over, leaving the mother to complete her nest, lay her eggs, and feed the baby birds all by herself. Well-filled backyard feeders are a great boon for these females, supplying nearby food so that they need be off their nest for only a few minutes.

In early spring you see birds collecting nesting material in your yard. With your binoculars, follow the flight path of a bird carrying something. If it is building a nest in or near the yard, you may be able to pinpoint the site for later observation. Do not approach the nest, though. Most birds are easily disturbed and will abandon a partly built nest.

A good rule for observing active nests is to stay 20 to 30 feet away. With binoculars, a field scope, or a high vantage point, you can see a lot from there. When eggs hatch, watch parent birds flying away with telltale eggshell to drop it far from the nest, putting predators off the track. Listen for cheeping as nestlings ask for food. Parent birds shuttle back and forth throughout the day, bringing food stuffed in their crops or dangling from their beaks. Birds you thought were exclusively seed eaters forage for insects, caterpillars, and fruit to give high-protein meals to their young.

The materials that a female Baltimore Oriole weaves into her hanging nest include string.

When the youngsters move out, watch as parents teach them foraging or bring them to the bird feeder. Note changes in plumage as the young birds mature: Pure russet feathers replace the black-spotted ones on robins' breasts; young male cardinals lose brown feathers and red ones grow in. Some fledglings stay close to their parents. If you see a group of three to six birds flying together, it may be a family with fledglings.

If your backyard is a good place for birds to raise their young, you'll be able to see the process every year.

BACKYARD BIRDING EMERGENCIES

Be sure to have gathered phone numbers for your wildlife rehabilitation facility, veterinarian, nature center, and other providers before you encounter a bird in need. Fellow birders in your area may have information to share.

◆ Fall From Nest

Sometimes a baby birds falls out of its nest to the ground. If you find a young bird on the ground and know for sure where its nest is, you can pick it up carefully and try to put it back when the parents are away. If you're not sure where the nest is, leave the baby alone and keep it under observation for a while. Parent birds may be caring for it on the ground.

If you don't see any signs of parenting, try to protect the baby from predators and weather, and get in touch with a local Audubon Society chapter or birding organization. Such a group can usually recommend a nearby wildlife rehabilitator licensed to deal with these situations. If necessary, a rehabilitator will hand-raise an orphan bird.

◆ Injured or Stunned Birds

As with young birds out of the nest, leave a stunned or injured bird alone unless you sense it is in danger from predators or cold weather. If you find it necessary to relocate or shelter the bird, place it gently inside a cardboard box with airholes and put it in a warm, quiet place. Resist the temptation to provide the bird

Looking angry at being rescued, a Common Swift in England sits quietly in its rescuer's hands before being released.

with food or water. When the bird awakens, you will hear some noise coming from the box.

Release a previously stunned bird outside, in an open area away from buildings. An injured bird is better released near shrubs or trees where it can rest safely while it recovers. If the bird is not responsive after an hour or if its injuries appear to be serious, seek treatment at a local wildlife rehabilitation facility.

◆ RUFFED GROUSE ◆

BONASA UMBELLUS: "Grouse" probably derives from the Old French word *griershe* or *greoche,* meaning "speckled"; "ruffed" refers to the neck feathers that can be displayed to resemble the ruffed (wrinkled) collars popular in the 16th century.

◆ Collision Trauma

The major cause of head trauma in birds is collision while in full flight. Migrating birds, or birds startled at feeders or birdbaths, may crash into windows, mirrors, or an overhead light. In the case of windows, the crash usually occurs because the glass is transparent and the birds can't see it. Or sometimes, they see a reflection of the outdoors and try to fly through what looks like unobstructed open space. In some cases, a bird is intentionally striking or pecking a window to attack an imagined rival—when in fact

A bird appears a thoughtless thing,
He's ever living on the wing,
And keeps up such a carolling,
That little else to do but sing
A man would guess had he.

CHARLES LAMB, "CRUMBS TO THE BIRDS," 1808

it's its reflection. This quixotic fellow will likely move from window to window, house to car, seeing its rival at every turn.

Serious head trauma can cause injury to the bird's beak as well as damage to its face; it can be fatal. If a bird flies full force into something, you should

Bird Brain

The male Indian Peafowl, aka peacock, doesn't in fact have a long tail. The five-foot-long, lacy green feathers ending in an iridescent "eye" are the upper tail coverts. The actual tail, hidden underneath, is short but serves a vital function: It elevates and supports the long lacy feathers during the male's courtship strut.

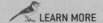 LEARN MORE

WINDOW TREATMENTS

It is hard to get a precise count of how many birds are injured or killed by striking reflective windows. The Audubon Society says that in North America, fatalities alone may claim as many as one million birds annually. The Fatal Light Awareness Program (FLAP) provides information for homeowners on its website *(www.flap.org)*, some of which we summarize here:

• **Window decals:** A single decal—no matter its shape—will not deter a bird, but a dense collection of decals will.

• **Noise or magnetic fields:** Some promote the use of high-frequency sounds, distress calls, or radiating magnetic fields to drive birds away from windows, but these have not been effective.

• **Plastic owls:** Birds are intelligent animals, and they figure out quickly that these decoys are unthreatening.

• **Window film:** Reducing the reflective properties of the window by applying a window film is the most effective treatment.

• **Exterior nets or screens:** This approach seeks to soften the impact more than prevent it: A tautly framed screen may minimize the injury.

• **Vertical string or ribbons:** By hanging evenly spaced ribbon on the exterior of your window, you draw the birds' attention to the presence of the glass.

• **Whitewashed windows:** If window strikes seem to occur only during migration season, you can employ this temporary method.

• **Move houseplants:** Houseplants next to the window add to the impression of foliage, so it's best if they are not placed where birds might mistake them for a place to rest.

quickly try to capture the bird, place it in a towel-lined box, and close the box to keep the inside dark. Take the bird to a nearby vet or rescue service. With proper treatment, it can recover from this potentially fatal damage.

To avoid incidents with windows, try keeping curtains or blinds partially closed to break up the reflection. Or you can hang something that moves in front of the window. To stop a bird from attacking its "rival," cover the outside of the window with newspaper or a semi-opaque painter's drop cloth. If the attacks persist, take comfort in knowing they will end once breeding season is over.

Bird Brain

It isn't certain which bird species is the heaviest one that flies: The Kori Bustard and Great Bustard are both in contention. Weights of 42 pounds for the Kori and 40 pounds for the Great Bustard have been reported. Both species can fly, but prefer to walk. Captive Mute Swans can weigh 50 pounds, but they may not be able to get airborne.

Stunned after colliding with a window, a male Scarlet Tanager rests. Birds crash into transparent glass at full flight because they don't see the glass, or they may interpret the glass's reflection of the surrounding landscape as an actual landscape.

THE TROUBLE WITH CATS

Many bird lovers are animal lovers—animal lovers who find themselves in a quandary when faced with cats stalking their bird feeders.

A significant threat to the wild bird population comes from cats. Not only hungry, feral, or stray cats hunt. Well-fed, cuddly indoor cats hunt, too. This behavior has little to do with hunger and much to do with instinct. The U.S. Fish and Wildlife Service reports that each year, hundreds of millions of songbirds and other species are killed by domestic and feral cats. The evidence of predation may be clear, with feathers or a carcass clearly visible. Or the signs may take some deciphering: scratch marks on a wooden pole under a nest box or feeder; crushed, matted grass at the base of a birdhouse; a nest emptied before the young had fledged.

What can you do? Be sure your bird feeders, houses, and baths are a good distance from low plants and shrubs where cats may hide. If cats are present, don't do anything to attract ground-feeding species. Some experts suggest setting chicken wire at the base of poles or trees that cats climb, since they won't step on the thin wire. You can also repel cats by installing a motion-activated water sprayer or by sprinkling dried predator urine on the ground or on plants to create a barrier. In a pinch, keep a super-size water soaker filled and ready, or make a noisemaker by filling a can with metallic bits such as coins or nuts and bolts.

In some cases, you may need to ask your neighbors to keep their pet cat indoors. If your neighbors insist that their cat must be let outside, ask that the cat be monitored or kept inside when birds are most active—in the early morning and evening—and request that they trim their cat's claws weekly to make it difficult for it to climb trees and wood poles. Discourage neighbors from feeding feral cats, because feeding them draws them into yards where birds are gathering. And, always set a good example by keeping any cats you own indoors at all times. Visit *www.abcbirds.org/cats* for more information.

CITIZEN SCIENCE

CONTRIBUTING TO OUR UNDERSTANDING OF BIRDS

As you gain experience in backyard bird-watching, your enthusiasm will continue to grow, and you will want to share it with others. Get your children involved at an early age. Share the pleasures with your spouse, friends, or neighbors. Then get to know the larger birding community—others in your area who are just as interested in birds as you are.

Some birders like to keep a journal of where and when they first saw a bird, with notes on its habitat, behavior, and other information. Add up all the species you have seen, and you have a "life list," a detailed chronicle of all the birds you have identified in your life. You may want to have a journal dedicated to the birds you see in your yard. Imagine charting the arrival and departure dates of migrants over the years or noting successful nesting of generations of birds on your property. Your anticipation will build each year as these dates approach.

Yellow-billed Cuckoo

Bird-watchers on a bridge focus glasses on a soaring bird, not visible in the picture. To join a group of birders, call the local Audubon Society or a nature center in your area and learn about activities.

URBAN BIRDING

Bird-watching in New York City? Paris? Rome? You bet. Birds live and thrive in urban environments. So you don't have to leave the city to get your fill of bird-watching. Whether on your lunch break, during a morning run, or while walking your dog, there are always opportunities to see birds. You just need to know how and where to look for them to find success.

Some obvious spots are in public parks, along water courses, or in green open spaces so prevalent in today's cities. For example, New York City's Central Park is home to more than 200 species of birds during the year. The experience is heightened during spring and fall migrations, when the park is a welcome island of green in the midst of a concrete jungle. On any given day, you might spot warblers, tanagers, falcons, robins—as well as the ubiquitous city dweller, the pigeon. If you live in a city, the Cornell Lab welcomes your help with Celebrate Urban Birds *(www.birds.cornell.edu/ celebration)*. This project provides volunteers with a packet with instructions, illustrations for easy bird identification, and forms for data collection.

A CROWD TAKES PICTURES OF DUCKS IN NEW YORK CITY'S CENTRAL PARK.

JOIN A BIRDING COMMUNITY

You may never have met them. You may not even know they exist. But in the area where you live, there may be dozens, even hundreds, who call themselves "birders"—people who go beyond their yards to make watching birds, traveling to see new birds, and studying birds a major passion in their lives.

Who are these birders? How can you get in touch with them? Start by calling the local Audubon Society chapter or another nature center in your area and asking for information on upcoming bird-oriented activities. Search the Internet for bird clubs in your state or local area. Look for publicized scheduled bird walks or bird counts led by experienced birders and join in on the fun.

Two of North America's most important birding organizations are the American Birding Association, or ABA *(www.aba.org)*, and the Cornell Lab of Ornithology *(www.birds.cornell.edu)*. The ABA publishes a magazine, *Birding,* for birders of all levels of experience. The Cornell Lab sponsors a host of citizen science projects, some of which are described in the following pages.

Ornithological organizations are often scientifically oriented, but all offer programs and welcome new members.

PARTICIPATING IN COUNTS & SURVEYS

Participating in counts and surveys is "citizen science" at its best: an opportunity to get outdoors and at the same time contribute important data that scientists can use to determine which species are increasing and which are declining. Although the Internet has recently popularized the idea of crowd-sourcing—that is, delegating tasks that had been assigned to a small number of centralized individuals to a dispersed, motivated group, often composed of volunteers—ornithologists have been collecting scientific data from bird-watchers for more than a century.

As you can imagine, observing hundreds of bird species over a significant portion of our continent is not only expensive, but also impossible for a single organization. Most projects that aim to study bird species over a large area or in migration would be cost-prohibitive if it weren't for the help of reliable volunteers in the field.

A selection of surveys and counts is noted here for birders with various levels of experience and interest:

Bobolink

Biologists at Delaware Bay in New Jersey carefully remove Red Knots from nets for scientific study. The sandpipers gather there in spring to eat horseshoe crab eggs, an important fuel for the remainder of their migration to the Arctic.

novices, those who wish to stay close to home, city dwellers, more experienced bird-watchers, and those open to traveling. In addition, the Cornell Lab of Ornithology maintains a list of national and local citizen science projects at *www.birds.cornell.edu/ citscitoolkit/projects.*

◆ Big Bird Counts

The National Audubon Society's Christmas Bird Count is the most famous and longest-lived birding activity for amateur and professional participants alike. In operation for more than 110 years, the Audubon CBC now boasts more than 60,000 volunteers throughout the country who go out on a scheduled day in late December or early January and count all the birds they can find. Visit the Audubon CBC website at *web4.audubon.org/bird/ cbc* for more information.

Another major bird count, the Great Backyard Bird Count—sponsored by the Cornell Lab, Bird Studies Canada, and the National Audubon Society—is an annual four-day event in February that captures an annual snapshot of birds across the continent. Anyone who is interested can participate: Just count birds in your yard, or anywhere you want to visit, for as long as you like each day of the count, even if you spend only 15 minutes doing so. Then send your checklist to the organizers, through their website *(www.birdsource.org/*

With colored leg bands, a Red Knot aids studies tracking its migration from the Arctic to South America.

gbbc), where you can also find more details on how to participate.

◆ Surveys

In partnership with the Smithsonian Migratory Bird Center and with funding from the National Science Foundation, the Cornell Lab developed NestWatch, a program that collects data gathered by thousands of birders who observe and take notes on North American breeding birds' nest sites, habitats, and species as well as the number of eggs, young, and fledglings in these nests—some of which may be in your yard. When compiled, information on birds' reproductive successes gives scientists a view of how their breeding habits adapt to environmental changes.

◆ OWL ◆

Ancient Sanskrit knew the owl as *uluka,* in Old Norse it was called *ugla,* and in Latin *ulula* (as in ululation). Many languages have similar-sounding names for this family of birds, and all the words are derived from the owl's hooting calls. The Modern English word descends directly from the Anglo Saxon *ule.*

Rock Pigeons of two different colors perch on an urban railing. In a program called PigeonWatch, the Cornell Lab of Ornithology in New York asks volunteers to learn the seven color groups of pigeons and observe their courting behavior.

Birders of all ages are invited to participate, and the NestWatch website *(www.nestwatch.org)* provides extensive material on finding and monitoring nests, understanding nesting cycles, and identifying the 24 focal species you're most likely to find during your observations.

PigeonWatch—yet another project developed by the Cornell Lab—asks participants to learn the seven color groups of the pigeon the project has defined and to observe courting behavior. Pigeons are especially interesting not only for their fantastic navigational skills, but also for the presence of several color morphs that have persisted in feral populations. No previous bird-watching experience is necessary; visit *www.birds.cornell.edu/pigeonwatch* for details.

Which species are reported most often at feeders in different regions? The Black-capped Chickadee in the North Atlantic, the Northern Cardinal in

---

◆ **COMMON EIDER** ◆

SOMATERIA MOLLISSIMA: These waterfowl are found mainly in Arctic countries, so it's not surprising that the English word comes from the Old Norse *aedr,* for "duck." Somateria is a composite of two Greek words: *soma* (body) and *erion* (wool, referring to the eider's thick down); *mollissima* is from the Latin for "softest."

the Southeast, the Dark-eyed Junco in the Central Midwest, and the House Finch in the Southwest. Without backyard armchair birders reporting their observations, no one could know those answers.

MORE OPPORTUNITIES TO VOLUNTEER

Other programs exist that continue to build the database on birds and their behavior. Volunteer participation is critical to these efforts as well.

Sponsored by the Cornell Lab and the National Audubon Society, eBird is a living encyclopedia of which species are being found where. It is an online checklist program that allows birders to enter their own bird lists online at *www.ebird.org*. Those individual bird lists are tallied—in January 2010, participants reported more than 1.5 million observations across

The red-breast whistles from a garden-croft;
And gathering swallows twitter in the skies.

JOHN KEATS, "TO AUTUMN," 1819

North America—becoming not just data for scientists, but also a treasure trove of information for average birders. For instance, let's say you plan to visit a certain town, park, or wildlife refuge next week. When you enter that location on eBird, you will find out which species have been seen there in recent days or recent weeks. Other website features include interesting articles about birds and birding.

My Yard eBird is an entry-level version of the wildly successful eBird project, described above.

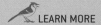 LEARN MORE
CHILD-FRIENDLY PROGRAMS

Did you know that many citizen science projects offer age-appropriate and educational materials for children? A teacher can plan a lesson in which students collect and share their data and observations. An adult could bring a child (or children) along on many projects, knowing each child can make genuine contributions. Scouting troops might take part and help the next generation develop a lifelong appreciation for wildlife and the outdoors.

Designed to appeal to casual and backyard birders, My Yard eBird gathers information on sightings in your yard, neighborhood, or local park. Participants can view the data they've submitted as well as that submitted for areas nearby online at *ebird.org/myyard*. A visit to the website also shows you all the information birders in your area have entered over time, giving you an idea of how scarce or abundant certain species are near you.

The North American Breeding Bird Survey (*www.pwrc.usgs.gov/bbs*) follows a rigorous protocol to collect data from predetermined but randomly placed roadside points across the United States and Canada. A collaboration of the U.S. Geological Survey's Patuxent Wildlife Research Center in Maryland and Environment Canada's Canadian Wildlife Service, this count generates population information on more than 400 bird species. This more committed project may require traveling a good distance from home.

The Cornell Lab has archived eight million high-definition photographs generated by its NestCams project, in which cameras are mounted in nests of more than 15 species breeding across the continent. The organizers are now asking citizen scientists for help sorting and categorizing these images online through the Cam-Clickr project. Once volunteers log on to the website at *watch.birds.cornell.edu/nestcams/clicker/clicker/index,* they view images, label (or "tag") them, and then classify the breeding behaviors evident in the photo.

About 20 years ago, the Cornell Lab launched Project Tanager, which focused on four tanager species in North American forests. The successful project led to the creation of Birds in Forested Landscapes, a study of forest-breeding birds—including hawks, thrushes, woodpeckers, and warblers—and their habitat needs. Volunteers can also be part of an acid rain study associated with the Birds in Forested Landscapes survey. More information is available online at *www.birds .cornell.edu/bfl.*

You can be part of other projects in your area sponsored by bird clubs, local Audubon chapters, state ornithological societies, and regional birding associations. These groups may need help with banding efforts or maintaining nest boxes, with trail maintenance or staffing tables at community events. Volunteering will give you an opportunity to promote birding and habitat preservation as well as a chance to meet other birders and learn new skills.

A Black-headed Gull presents a ghostly appearance as it lands at Lake Windermere in England. The ability to see and identify birds helps scientists understand their behavior and movements, as well as brings pleasure to the bird-watcher.

A Great Blue Heron stands in sunlit waters near Fort Myers beach in Florida. The large wading bird is common near the shores of North and Central America.

ARMCHAIR BIRDING

Backyard birders can also take delight in watching birds while sitting in the comfort of their homes. Put up your feeders, keeping in mind visibility from indoors, and get ready to enjoy. A variety of birds will perch on the feeders. Large windows help make observing aviary life more fun and interactive. And always have your binoculars at the ready to identify the latest arrival at your feeder.

Project Feeder Watch is a scientific project you can participate in simply by looking out your window from November through early April and counting the birds that visit your feeders. Submit your counts online to the Cornell Lab *(www.birds.cornell .edu/pfw)*, which sponsors the project along with Bird Studies Canada. Feeder Watch data help scientists track broad-scale movements of winter bird populations and long-term trends in bird distribution and abundance.

◆ **TRUMPETER SWAN** ◆

CYGNUS BUCCINATOR: "Swan" has ancient Indo-European roots in *swon* and *swen*, words that refer to making a sound or singing, and hence to the musical, buglelike calls of these birds. *Cygnus* is a Latin word for swan that derives from the Greek *kyknos*; and *buccinator* is Latin for trumpeter.

Wild Turkey with young. Hand-colored print by John James Audubon (published 1827–1838)

Heron.   Eagle.   Stor

Owl.   Raven   Ha

Swallow.   Sparrow.

BIRDOGRAPHIES

The World's Favorite Birds

Scott Weidensaul

ACORN WOODPECKER

Melanerpes formicivorus

Size: 9 inches
Range: Oregon and California, American Southwest to Central America
Habitat: Oak and pine woodlands

With their clown's-makeup plumage, raucous *waka-waka-waka* calls, and communal lifestyle, Acorn Woodpeckers are impossible to miss anywhere within their range. Highly social, they often live in colonies in which multiple males will compete to breed with several females, or vice versa. The colony also cooperates to create one or more "granaries"—trees, utility poles, or even wooden building exteriors in which they drill thousands of holes, filling them with acorns every autumn. A large granary may take generations to create and hold 50,000 nuts. Acorn Woodpeckers calling outside their honeymoon cabin in California inspired cartoonist Walter Lantz and his wife to create the character Woody Woodpecker in 1940.

ALBATROSSES

Family Diomedeidae

Size: Wingspan 6–11¾ feet; weight up to 26 lbs.
Range: Circumpolar in Southern Ocean; northern Pacific
Habitat: Open ocean; breeds on isolated islands

Albatrosses are the world's premiere oceanic aerialists, harnessing the ferocious winds of the high southern latitudes on wings longer and thinner than any other bird's—those of the Wandering Albatross, one of the largest flying birds on Earth, span almost 12 feet. The distances albatrosses travel, and the years they sometimes spend at sea, have defied many attempts to track them, but some species are now known to fly more than 100,000 miles annually across the gale-swept oceans. Many albatross species have declined dramatically from long-line fishing, which drowns them when they snatch the hooked bait, but new fishing techniques hold out the promise of a safer catch.

BALD EAGLE

Haliaeetus leucocephalus

Size: 31–37 inches; wingspan 6–7½ feet
Range: Most of North America
Habitat: Generally near rivers, lakes, and coastlines

The Bald Eagle, like the other seven sea-eagle species in the world, feeds heavily on fish, but it's far from fussy and will take a variety of food, including seabirds, waterfowl, and carrion. Most common near large bodies of water, the eagle's nest can be immense—some, used and tended to by generations of eagles, may eventually weigh a ton or more. The iconic white head and tail take up to five years to develop. As with several other species of raptors, bald eagles suffered tremendous declines in the mid-20th century from pesticide poisoning, but they have rebounded dramatically in recent decades thanks to chemical regulation and are again becoming a commonplace sight.

BALTIMORE ORIOLE

Icterus galbula

Size: 8¼ inches
Range: East, Great Plains, and Canadian parklands
Habitat: Open hardwood forests

The male's vivid orange-and-black plumage, early colonists thought, echoed the 17th-century coat of arms of Cecilius Calvert, Baron Baltimore and founder of Maryland—and so the Baltimore Oriole got its English name (and a baseball team later got its symbol). A common backyard bird in wooded neighborhoods, the oriole inhabits open deciduous woodlands west to the Rockies and across southwestern Canada's aspen parkland region. The female alone builds the pendulous, gourd-shaped nest, using horsehair, grasses, and tough fibers from plants like milkweed and grapevine; man-made materials like string, wool, and twine are eagerly added.

Barn Swallow

Hirundo rustica

Size: 6¾ inches
Range: Almost worldwide
Habitat: Open country and agricultural areas

One of the most familiar birds in the world, the Barn Swallow (known simply as the Swallow in Europe) has an enormous range, breeding across almost all of North America, Europe, Asia, and northern Africa, and migrating as far south as Argentina, southern Africa, and Australia. Fast and nimble in the air, it feeds almost exclusively on flying insects. The annual disappearance of swallows led some observers, beginning with Aristotle and lasting until the 18th century, to believe that the birds hibernated beneath lakes. Both sexes have long, forked tail feathers, more so in males—and females, studies show, prefer mates with longer, more symmetrical tail plumes.

Black-capped Chickadee

Poecile atricapillus

Size: 5¼ inches
Range: Northern North America
Habitat: Hardwood and coniferous forests; backyards

With its outsized personality, confiding nature, and appetite for sunflower seeds and suet cakes, the Black-capped Chickadee is one of the most beloved backyard feeder birds in North America. Although chickadee pairs defend breeding territories, by tearing out rotten wood fibers to excavate a nest cavity within a tree, in winter they gather in flocks, often rejoining their former flock mates from previous years. Although insects make up most of their summer diet, in winter it's a mix of arthropods, seeds, and berries—plus whatever's being served at the local feeder. The very similar and more southerly Carolina Chickadee (*P. carolinensis*) is moving north, hybridizing with Black-cappeds where they meet.

Blackburnian Warbler

Setophaga fusca

Size: 5 inches
Range: Appalachians to eastern and southern Canada; winters South America
Habitat: Mixed and coniferous forests

Birders often talk of their "spark bird," the one that hooked them on birding—and anyone seeing a Blackburnian Warbler for the first time is liable to be hooked for life. Among the most beautiful members of the colorful wood-warbler family, the male Blackburnian's tangerine-and-black plumage is stunning, while the female's is a subtler version of the same. Blackburnian Warblers sing high in both senses of the word—the males usually choose a lofty perch at the top of a hemlock, spruce, or oak tree, and their thin, buzzy song may climb well above the range that older human ears can easily hear. In winter, Blackburnian Warblers migrate to humid mountain forests in northern South America.

Blue Bird of Paradise

Paradisaea rudolphi

Size: 13 inches (26–28 inches including tail plumes)
Range: Papua New Guinea
Habitat: Humid montane forests

The 42 species of birds of paradise, found only in New Guinea, eastern Australia, and the Moluccas, comprise perhaps the strangest and most beautiful family of birds on the planet. Their colors are psychedelic, their plumage unearthly, their courtship rituals bizarre. The male Blue Bird of paradise, for instance, hangs upside down from a branch, his gauzy, sky blue flank feathers spilling out to create a triangular fan that quivers in time with the weird throbbing, humming sound he makes—all to impress a nearby female. As he displays, she closely inspects him—and as often as not, flies off to look for a better suitor.

Blue Jay
Cyanocitta cristata

Size: 11 inches
Range: North America east of the Rockies
Habitat: Deciduous and mixed forests, backyards

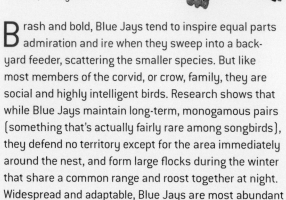

Brash and bold, Blue Jays tend to inspire equal parts admiration and ire when they sweep into a backyard feeder, scattering the smaller species. But like most members of the corvid, or crow, family, they are social and highly intelligent birds. Research shows that while Blue Jays maintain long-term, monogamous pairs (something that's actually fairly rare among songbirds), they defend no territory except for the area immediately around the nest, and form large flocks during the winter that share a common range and roost together at night. Widespread and adaptable, Blue Jays are most abundant where there are mature, nut-bearing trees like oaks.

Bowerbirds
Family Ptilonorhynchidae

Size: 9–15 inches
Range: Australia and New Guinea
Habitat: Primarily rain forest

Compared with their near-relatives, the birds of paradise, most of the bowerbirds are plain as mud, colored in drab greens, grays, or browns. They shine, however, as peerless architects and decorators—building elaborate courtship bowers from carefully assembled twigs, then garnishing them with flowers, fruit, shells, pebbles, and other colorful items; sometimes they even paint them using charcoal mixed with their own saliva. The Vogelkop Bowerbird creates an elaborate, cone-shaped hut, before which it assembles neat heaps of hundreds of blue, red, or equally bright objects. The Stain Bowerbird, on the other hand, makes a narrow, simple avenue of twigs, but scours its territory for any bright blue object—including man-made junk like plastic clothespins and baby pacifiers.

Canada Goose
Branta canadensis

Size: 30–45 inches; 5–9½ lbs.
Range: North America; introduced to Europe
Habitat: Freshwater; agricultural fields

"Sky carp" is one of the nicer names given to the flocks of Canada Geese that crowd urban parks, lakesides, and golf courses, leaving a carpet of gooey droppings behind. They are the descendents of largely sedentary birds from the Midwest, stocked across the country by well-meaning wildlife agencies, and show little appetite for migration. But plenty of Canada Geese still flow north and south with the seasons, following traditional migration routes to breeding grounds in the Arctic and sub-Arctic. Different populations also vary dramatically in size, although the tiny Cackling Goose of the Arctic, which weighs little more than three pounds, is now considered a separate species.

Cassowaries
Casuarius spp.

Size: 3⅓–5½ feet tall; weight up to 130 lbs.
Range: New Guinea, northeast Australia, and surrounding islands
Habitat: Rain forests

Second only to the ostrich as the heaviest living birds, the Southern Cassowary and its two relatives—the Northern and Dwarf Cassowaries of New Guinea—have a reputation for ferocity (though in fact, tales of them routinely disemboweling humans with a kick from their sharp-clawed legs are overblown, and the last human fatality occurred in 1926). Cassowaries forage through rain forests for fruit, and the curious, bony "casque" that rises like a fin from the top of the head may help them push through dense vegetation. But its true function, like much about these strange and little-studied birds, remains a mystery.

COMMON RAVEN
Corvus corax

Size: 24 inches
Range: North America, Europe, Asia, and northern Africa
Habitat: All terrestrial ecosystems except tropical rain forest

This largest member of the corvid clan is adaptable enough to thrive in Southwestern deserts and Arctic tundra, in remote Appalachian forests, or picking through dumpsters in urban alleys. The Common Raven is also among the most intelligent of all birds, as experiments to test its impressive reasoning power have shown. All of this, coupled with its hemispheric range, explains why the Common Raven has played a central role in the culture and mythology of societies from the Inuit to the ancient Celts, and the Vikings (who believed two ravens sat beside their god Odin) to the Indians of the Northwest, to whom Raven was a creator and trickster figure.

CONDORS
Gymnogyps and Vultur spp.

Size: Wingspan to 9 feet; 23 lbs. (California condor); to 10¾ feet, 33 lbs. (Andean condor)
Range: American West (California condor) and Andes (Andean condor)
Habitat: Mountains, usually in open country and scrubby forest

Although not closely related, these two immense vultures are among the largest flying birds in the world—though they pale in comparison with even larger scavengers known as teratorns, one of which (known from eight-million-year-old fossils in Argentina) had a wingspan of 26 feet. The Andean Condor has a wide range throughout the Andes, but the California Condor, once found from Baja to the Canadian border, was driven to the brink of extinction in the late 19th and 20th centuries. Captive breeding and reintroduction have brought small populations back in the United States and Mexico, but threats like lead poisoning remain a roadblock to recovery.

CUCKOOS
Family Cuculidae

Size: 6–28 inches
Range: Global
Habitat: Primarily forests

Although there are more than 130 kinds of cuckoos around the world, this family is known primarily for one species—the Common Cuckoo of Eurasia, enshrined in countless Teutonic clocks, which mimic its *cuck-oo, cuck-oo* song. The Common Cuckoo is also a highly evolved brood parasite, laying its eggs in the nests of other birds; the color and pattern of the shells vary regionally to match those of its most common hosts. Two North American species, the Yellow-billed and Black-billed Cuckoos, are not closely related to the Eurasian species, and while they sometimes lay their eggs in each other's nests, they typically raise their own chicks.

DODO
Raphus cucullatus

Size: 37–46 lbs.
Range: Mauritius (extinct)
Habitat: Forest (?)

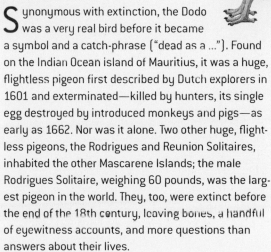

Synonymous with extinction, the Dodo was a very real bird before it became a symbol and a catch-phrase ("dead as a ..."). Found on the Indian Ocean island of Mauritius, it was a huge, flightless pigeon first described by Dutch explorers in 1601 and exterminated—killed by hunters, its single egg destroyed by introduced monkeys and pigs—as early as 1662. Nor was it alone. Two other huge, flightless pigeons, the Rodrigues and Reunion Solitaires, inhabited the other Mascarene Islands; the male Rodrigues Solitaire, weighing 60 pounds, was the largest pigeon in the world. They, too, were extinct before the end of the 18th century, leaving bones, a handful of eyewitness accounts, and more questions than answers about their lives.

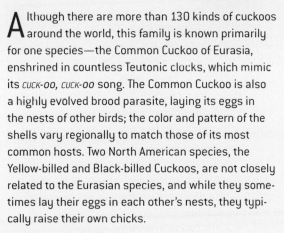

EASTERN BLUEBIRD

Sialia sialis

Size: 7 inches
Range: Eastern North America to Central America
Habitat: Orchards, field edges, open woodlands

Few birds are as universally loved as the three species of bluebirds, especially the widespread Eastern Bluebird—"the bluebird of happiness," a creature the great naturalist John Burroughs said carries the sky on its back and the Earth on its breast. The Eastern Bluebird is also emblematic of the impact simple actions can have on conservation. Abundant in the 19th century, it all but vanished from much of its range after House Sparrows and European Starlings—which compete with it for nest cavities—were introduced to North America. But starting in the 1960s, the widespread use of wooden nest boxes brought a renaissance for the bluebird, which is again a common sight in rural areas.

EMPEROR PENGUIN

Aptenodytes forsteri

Size: 38 inches tall; weight up to 100 lbs.
Range: Antarctica
Habitat: Feeds offshore; nests inland

The largest of the world's 17 species of penguins, the Emperor is restricted to Antarctica, where it hunts fish and krill in the frigid offshore waters. Its breeding behavior, however, is almost unfathomable. The penguins trek by foot as much as 125 miles inland to great colonies—the famous "March of the Penguins"—each pair laying a single egg that the male incubates on his feet for two months through the depths of the Antarctic winter, with temperatures reaching minus 60°F. All penguins are southern hemispheric, although several inhabit temperate waters in Australia and New Zealand, Africa and South America, while one almost reaches the Equator in the Galápagos Islands.

EUROPEAN STARLING

Sturnus vulgaris

Size: 8½ inches
Range: Europe to central Asia; introduced to North America
Habitat: Cities, residential areas, and farms

The story of the European Starling in America shows that even bad ideas must await the right moment. Through the late 1800s, groups known as acclimatization societies or songbird clubs tried to introduce dozens of species of Old World birds in North America. Repeated releases of European Starlings failed—until 1891, when a society dedicated to introducing every bird mentioned in Shakespeare's works released about one hundred in New York's Central Park. From that small flock, this aggressive, adaptable bird swamped the continent and now numbers about 200 million. Its success has come at a steep price for native species like bluebirds, flickers, and American Kestrels, which lose out to the starlings for scarce nest cavities.

FLAMINGOS

Family Phoenicopteridae

Size: 3–5 feet tall; weight up to 9 lbs.
Range: Caribbean and South America, Africa, southern Eurasia, and Middle East
Habitat: Lakes (usually highly alkaline), mudflats, and coasts

The world is upside down for a feeding flamingo, which tips its head so its peculiar, crooked bill lies perpendicular to the water and slightly gaped. Rows of fine, hairlike lamellae strain minute organisms and algae from the water, which are guided to the throat by backward-pointing spines on the tongue. The trademark pink coloration is something the flamingo metabolizes from its food; in captivity, flamingos must usually be given supplements or they look pale and bleached. A few Greater Flamingos sometimes wander from colonies in Mexico or the Caribbean to Florida or the Gulf Coast, but they are far outnumbered by their plastic brethren.

GREATER ROADRUNNER

Geococcyx californianus

Size: 23 inches
Range: California to Arkansas, south through Mexico
Habitat: Desert, scrub, and open woodlands

Roadrunners do not go "Beep-beep"—at least not the real ones, which are large, ground-dwelling cuckoos and which rattle their bills and give a descending *coo-coo-coooo* call instead. But they are fast and agile, running down lizards, mice, snakes, scorpions, smaller birds, and insects while avoiding predators—which, yes, occasionally include coyotes. In a sprint, its neck stretched low and its long tail streaming behind, a roadrunner is able to hit 20 miles an hour, but its flying abilities are far more limited. Most closely associated with the desert Southwest, roadrunners are actually found as far north and east as Oklahoma, Louisiana, and Arkansas.

HARLEQUIN DUCK

Histrionicus histrionicus

Size: 16½ inches
Range: Eastern Canada, and northern Rockies to Alaska, wintering along both coasts
Habitat: Fast rivers in summer; rocky coasts in winter

Few birds are as strangely beautiful as a male Harlequin Duck, named for the costumed character of Italian opera; even its Latin name means "a stage actor." But usually this uncommon duck stays far from sight, nesting in remote, fast-roaring rivers in the Canadian sub-Arctic, Alaska, and the northern Rockies and Cascades, where it feeds on aquatic insects and nests in tree cavities, rock crevices, or thickets. In winter, it migrates to the northern Pacific and Atlantic coasts, feeding in the violent surge of the tidal zone, where it dives for crabs and other marine invertebrates. Its squeaky, nasal call is one reason this bird was once called "the sea mouse."

HARPY EAGLE

Harpia harpyja

Size: 3½ feet long, wingspan 6½ feet, weight up to 20 lbs.
Range: Central and South America
Habitat: Tropical rain forest

Arguably the largest and most powerful raptor in the world (along with the Philippine Eagle and Steller's Sea-eagle), the Harpy Eagle symbolizes the rain forest wilderness of the neotropics, where it flies with surprising speed and agility through the canopy, hunting monkeys, sloths, anteaters, and other midsize mammals—challenging prey for any aerial hunter. But the Harpy Eagle is armed with eight massive talons backed by incredibly powerful feet and legs, and can kill sloths (a major portion of its diet) that weigh up to 20 pounds. Nowhere common, this magnificent predator is disappearing from many regions due to deforestation, but has been reintroduced to a few locations.

HELMET VANGA

Euryceros prevostii

Size: 12 inches
Range: Madagascar
Habitat: Humid forests

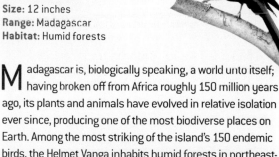

Madagascar is, biologically speaking, a world unto itself; having broken off from Africa roughly 150 million years ago, its plants and animals have evolved in relative isolation ever since, producing one of the most biodiverse places on Earth. Among the most striking of the island's 150 endemic birds, the Helmet Vanga inhabits humid forests in northeastern Madagascar, using its outsize bill to snatch insects, frogs, and lizards. Although Helmet Vangas are monogamous, other vangas are polyandrous (with more than one male mating with the nesting female); many also have "nest helpers," usually young males from previous broods that defend the territory or feed the chicks. Like many Madagascan species, the Helmet Vanga is threatened by habitat loss.

HIMALAYAN MONAL

Lophorphorus impejanus

Size: 28 inches
Range: Himalayan Mountains
Habitat: Conifer forests, alpine areas

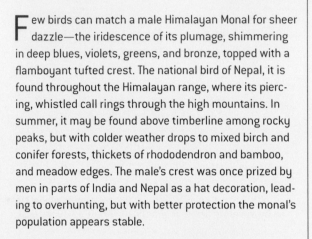

Few birds can match a male Himalayan Monal for sheer dazzle—the iridescence of its plumage, shimmering in deep blues, violets, greens, and bronze, topped with a flamboyant tufted crest. The national bird of Nepal, it is found throughout the Himalayan range, where its piercing, whistled call rings through the high mountains. In summer, it may be found above timberline among rocky peaks, but with colder weather drops to mixed birch and conifer forests, thickets of rhododendron and bamboo, and meadow edges. The male's crest was once prized by men in parts of India and Nepal as a hat decoration, leading to overhunting, but with better protection the monal's population appears stable.

HORNBILLS

Family Bucerotidae

Size: 12–48 inches; 3½ ounces to 13 lbs.
Range: Africa, southern and southeast Asia
Habitat: Primarily forest; some in savannas

Hornbills are a diverse and widespread family in the Old World tropics, ranging from tiny Dwarf-Hornbills little bigger than doves to Ground-Hornbills that may weigh 13 pounds and stand more than three feet high. Capping the huge bill is a casque—a hollow structure unique to this family, which may help their deep calls resonate. But the most unusual aspect of hornbill biology is the way the female, using mud, feces, or fruit, seals herself up within the nest cavity except for a small slit through which the male passes food. The females of some species break out of the nest once the chicks are partially grown, leaving them to reseal it; in others, she remains with the them until fledging. Regardless, the seal protects the eggs and nestlings from monkeys, a constant threat.

HOUSE SPARROW

Passer domesticus

Size: 6¼ inches
Range: Almost global
Habitat: Cities, residential areas, farms

Like the European Starling, the House Sparrow is another "What were they thinking?" bird introduction, and an astonishingly successful one. First brought to North America in the 1850s (ostensibly to control corn pests), it multiplied so rapidly that within half a century, it had overtaken the entire continent and become a pest itself, always living in close association with humans; other introductions have given it a nearly worldwide range. Like the starling, the House Sparrow's habit of usurping nest cavities has been a significant problem for bluebirds and other hole-nesting native birds. Ironically, House Sparrows have suffered a mysterious decline in the United Kingdom, where they are a beloved native.

IVORY-BILLED WOODPECKER

Campephilis principalis

Size: 19½ inches
Range: Originally southeastern U.S., Cuba
Habitat: Bottomland forests (U.S.), upland pine forests (Cuba)

The world was riveted in 2005 by the announcement that the Ivory-billed Woodpecker—assumed extinct for more than half a century—had been rediscovered in Arkansas. But that optimism soon degenerated into ornithological infighting, and a lack of further documentation has cast serious doubt on whether the sightings in Arkansas (and later in Florida) were a case of mistaken identity and wishful thinking. Once the king of the old-growth swamp forests of the Southeast, the Ivory-billed was decimated by a loss of habitat and by shooting, especially targeted collection for museums.

Lilac-breasted Roller

Coracias caudatus

Size: 14 inches
Range: Africa
Habitat: Acacia woodlands and savannas

One of the most conspicuous and beautiful of African birds, the Lilac-breasted Roller belongs to an Old World group whose name comes from their dramatic display flight, in which the bird swoops toward the ground, calling loudly while rotating its body and flapping its wings from side to side. Lilac-breasted Rollers, like most of their relatives, feed on arthropods, lizards, frogs, and even small birds, and are adept at using large mammals like elephants and antelopes to flush their prey. A wildfire will attract rollers from far and wide, snatching up animals that are too busy fleeing the flames to watch for danger.

Mallard

Anas platyrhynchos

Size: 23 inches
Range: Circumpolar north of tropics
Habitat: Wetlands and waterways of all kinds

The mallard is the prototypical duck—the ancestor of all domestic duck breeds except the Muscovy, and so adaptable that virtually no wetland, pond, marsh, lake, river, coastline, creek, slough, or trickle within its enormous worldwide range—which spans North America, Europe, and Asia—is without at least a few. Breeding males have the characteristic green head and rusty breast, while females are brown and streaked—as are males in midsummer through early autumn, when they enter "eclipse plumage" and are difficult to distinguish from the hens. Because most domestic breeds are derived from mallards, they hybridize easily, and urban lakes and parks often host a bewildering array of genetically shuffled ducks that resemble nothing in any field guide.

Marvelous Spatuletail

Loddigesia mirabilis

Size: Male 9½ inches including tail; female 5 inches
Range: One valley in Peru
Habitat: Forest edges

There are more than 320 species of hummingbirds, each one a marvel of aerodynamics and beauty—but none comes close to the Marvelous Spatuletail. The male's curved, six-inch-long outer tail feathers end in iridescent racquets which, during his courtship display, bob and weave on either side of him like backup dancers. Found only in a single valley in the northern Peruvian Andes, where deforestation has already destroyed much of its habitat, the spatuletail's population may be fewer than 1,000 and declining. Conservation groups are rallying to protect and restore its habitat, and visiting birders are providing a reason for local communities to join in the effort.

Northern Cardinal

Cardinalis cardinalis

Size: 8¾ inches
Range: Eastern and southwestern U.S., Mexico
Habitat: Thickets, woodland edges, backyards

Seven states—Illinois, Indiana, Kentucky, North Carolina, Virginia, and West Virginia—have chosen the Northern Cardinal as their state bird, more than any other species. (The Western Meadowlark, picked by six states, is second.) And why not? The male cardinal is radiantly colorful and the female subtly so, they brighten backyard feeders, and their whistled *to-wit, to-wit, wha-cheeer!* song is a signature sound from Maine and Nova Scotia to Arizona. (Both male and female cardinals sing, something unusual among songbirds.) Once primarily a southern species, cardinals have expanded their range far to the north and west since the 19th century.

NORTHERN MOCKINGBIRD

Mimus polyglottos

Size: 10 inches
Range: Southern half of U.S., Mexico
Habitat: Field edges, yards, thickets

"The many-tongued mimic" is the translation of the Northern Mockingbird's Latin name—an apt one indeed for this storied singer, though the habit of unpaired males to sing right through the night has irritated more than one insomniac. Thomas Jefferson called the mockingbird "a superior being in the form of a bird," and kept many as pets, including during his presidency. Mockingbirds are renowned as mimics and learn a vocal repertoire of hundreds of song fragments, adding more throughout their lives. A mockingbird repeats each song three or more times, while the closely related Brown Thrasher, which sings its notes in pairs, is even more accomplished and may acquire several thousand song fragments.

OSTRICH

Struthio camelus

Size: 7–9 feet tall;
weight 220–290 lbs.
Range: Africa
Habitat: Deserts and savannas

Towering over a human, and able to race along at more than 40 miles an hour, the Ostrich is the largest living bird, and the most instantly recognizable member of the ratites—the order of flightless birds that includes the Rheas, Emu, Cassowaries, and Kiwis. Once hunted extensively, Ostriches began to be farmed in the 1830s for their feathers, meat, and eggs, but wild populations continue to decline in many areas; the Middle Eastern subspecies is probably extinct. Also gone are the elephant birds, a number of flightless ratites found only on Madagascar. One species, Aepyornis, was a 10-foot-tall behemoth weighing more than 800 pounds—and like all the elephant birds, it had disappeared by at least the 17th century.

PAINTED BUNTING

Passerina ciris

Size: 5½ inches
Range: Southern Plains, lower Mississippi, and Southeast coast
Habitat: Thickets and forest edges

The French settlers in Louisiana called the Painted Bunting *nonpareil*—"without equal"—and it's hard to fault their judgment. One of the most colorful of North American birds, the male is a gaudy patchwork of red, green, and blue, while the female has a delicate greenish tone, with a hint of blue at the shoulders. In the 1830s, John James Audubon recounted how thousands were trapped each spring for the caged bird trade, and Painted Buntings are still caught (mostly illegally) on their wintering grounds in Mexico and Central America for the same reason—perhaps one reason why this species is in decline, especially the small Southeast population.

PARROTS

Family Psittacidae

Size: 3½–40 inches
Range: Worldwide in tropical, subtropical, and austral regions
Habitat: Primarily forest; some species in open country

The parrots comprise a huge family with more than 330 species, from pygmy-parrots little bigger than warblers to macaws that are more than three and a half feet long. (Parakeets are merely small parrots, but the distinctive cockatoos belong to their own, closely related family.) Their complex social structure and extraordinary intelligence may be tightly linked, and these attributes, along with their bright colors, have made parrots popular cage birds for centuries. Scientists are just beginning to plumb the dimensions of parrot intelligence, however, and research with individuals like the late African Gray Parrot Alex are generating an ever-greater appreciation for what it means to be a "bird brain."

PELICANS
Family Pelecanidae

Size: 4–6 feet; wingspan to 11½ feet
Range: Worldwide in temperate and tropical regions
Habitat: Coastlines, lakes, and rivers

Pelicans have held a cherished place in human culture, from pious religious imagery to irreverent limericks ("A wonderful bird is the pelican/his bill will hold more than his belican"). A medieval belief—inaccurate, as it turns out—that the female pelican would feed her chicks from her own blood made the bird a symbol of sacrifice. There are seven species, including the Dalmatian Pelican of Eurasia, which at almost 30 pounds and with an 11½-foot wingspan is one of the largest flying birds in the world. The fabled pouch serves as a fish scoop, and because it is rich in blood vessels, it also helps to cool the pelican in hot weather.

PUFFINS
Fratercula spp.

Size: 11–16 inches
Range: North Atlantic and North Pacific
Habitat: Rocky cliffs, open oceans

Puffins may look vaguely like penguins, but these Northern Hemisphere seabirds are members of the Auk family and can do something that penguins can't—fly. In fact, the three species (the Atlantic, Tufted, and Horned Puffins) are living examples of evolutionary tradeoffs: in this case, the need for wings that are just big enough to support them in the air, yet reduced enough to allow them to "fly" in the much more viscous medium of water. One relative, the now-extinct Great Auk of the North Atlantic, took the final evolutionary step, becoming large and flightless—in fact, it was to the Great Auk that the name "penguin"—possibly from the Welsh meaning "white head"—was first applied, and only later given to true penguins.

RESPLENDENT QUETZAL
Phuromachrus mocinno

Size: 14 inches (plus 24 inches for male's plumes)
Range: Southern Mexico, Central America
Habitat: Montane cloud forests

Arguably the most beautiful bird in the Western Hemisphere, it comes as little surprise that the Resplendent Quetzal (pronounced ket-ZAHL) was revered by the Maya and Aztec who shared its world. The male's electric, green-blue plumage and scarlet belly are startling enough, but the long, snaking plumes that trail and twist behind him in flight appear almost otherworldly. (The plumes are not the tail, per se, but four highly modified rump feathers, which the somewhat drabber female lacks.) Pre-Columbian cultures reserved quetzal plumes for nobility, and killing one was a capital crime.

ROBINS
Turdus migratorius (American Robin)
and Erithacus rubecula (European Robin)

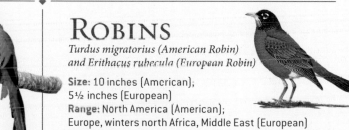

Size: 10 inches (American); 5½ inches (European)
Range: North America (American); Europe, winters north Africa, Middle East (European)
Habitat: Widespread in diverse habitats (American) Woodlands, parks, and yards (European)

What's in a name? European colonists, nostalgic for home, took one look at the largish, orange-breasted thrush they found in the New World and named it "robin," after the small, plump, orange-breasted bird they remembered, even though the European Robin is actually an Old World flycatcher. Yet distant relationships aside, both are the most familiar of backyard birds in their respective ranges. American Robins inhabit one of the widest arrays of elevation, habitat, and climate in North America, from Arctic tundra to desert scrub and southern swamp forests. European Robins prefer woodlands, parks, and yards.

ROCK PIGEON

Columba livia

Size: 12½ inches
Range: Global
Habitat: Urban, residential, and agricultural areas

Rock Pigeons—the common city pigeon, beloved by few, despised by multitudes—is in truth a feral form of the oldest domesticated bird in the world, dating back as many as 10,000 years to the eastern Mediterranean. Whether people first captured wild Rock Pigeons and raised them, or the pigeons underwent "self-domestication" as they began nesting in villages, no one knows—but the result has been the development of hundreds of named breeds for show, food, and racing. Today wild Rock Pigeons still live in much of Eurasia and Africa, and their feral descendants have been introduced around the world, where bridges and skyscrapers stand in for cliffs.

SACRED IBIS

Threskiornis aethiopicus

Size: 33 inches tall, wingspan 4 feet
Range: Africa
Habitat: Waterways and wetlands, fields and villages

To the ancient Egyptians, the annual life-giving floods of the Nile River—which replenished farmland and made civilization there possible—were inextricably entwined with the flocks of Sacred Ibis, wading birds that followed the floods north out of Africa each year. Considered an embodiment of the god Thoth, symbol of wisdom, the ibises were often mummified as sacrifices; 1.5 million ibis mummies are known from a single location, and recent CT scans show that many had their stomachs packed with grain—a final "meal" to carry them into the afterlife. Ironically, this species disappeared from Egypt in the mid-19th century.

SHOEBILL

Balaeniceps rex

Size: 4 feet tall
Range: Africa
Habitat: Swamps and papyrus marshes

The Shoebill—a bizarre African wading bird also called the whalehead—looks like a stork, and has sometimes been classified as one, though it shares some attributes with herons, while its DNA suggests it could be nearer to pelicans; for now, it occupies its own family. Hunting through the papyrus marshes of eastern and central Africa, the Shoebill catches fish, lizards, and other prey with a technique called "collapsing," in which the bird lunges forward, wings flailing, plowing its massive bill through vegetation and water to clamp the razor-sharp beak on its prey. Because of its weird appearance and remote habitat, the Shoebill is prized by birders.

SNOWY OWL

Bubo scandiacus

Size: 23 inches, wingspan 51 inches; weight 4–5 lbs.
Range: Circumpolar
Habitat: Tundra, sea ice, open country

The ghost hunter of the North, the Snowy Owl sometimes appears, unpredictably but always dramatically, far south of its usual haunts in the Arctic, exciting birders and non-birders alike with its huge, white presence along coastlines, airports, and in open country. Heavy and powerful, Snowy Owls feed primarily on small mammals, but they are surprisingly agile aerial hunters, and thanks to satellite tracking, it's now known that a few spend much of the winter entirely at sea, roaming the pack ice in perpetual darkness, feeding on sea ducks like eiders that crowd patches of open water. For young readers, though, the Snowy Owl has a magical side as well—immortalized as Hedwig, Harry Potter's messenger owl.

Spoon·billed Sandpiper

Eurynorhynchus pygmeus

Size: 6 inches
Range: Breeds northeast Russia, winters southeast Asia
Habitat; Coastal tundra in summer; tidal mudflats in winter

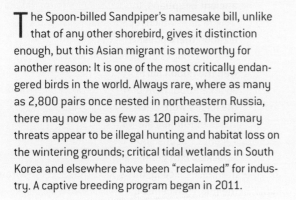

The Spoon-billed Sandpiper's namesake bill, unlike that of any other shorebird, gives it distinction enough, but this Asian migrant is noteworthy for another reason: It is one of the most critically endangered birds in the world. Always rare, where as many as 2,800 pairs once nested in northeastern Russia, there may now be as few as 120 pairs. The primary threats appear to be illegal hunting and habitat loss on the wintering grounds; critical tidal wetlands in South Korea and elsewhere have been "reclaimed" for industry. A captive breeding program began in 2011.

Storks

Family Ciconiidae

Size: 3–5 feet
Range: Worldwide, except for most of North America
Habitat: Wetlands, savannas, towns

Each spring, flocks of thousands upon thousands of European White Storks return from Africa, pouring through migratory choke points like the eastern Mediterranean, Gibraltar, and the Bosporus, returning to their colonies across Eurasia. Each pair settles back into its bulky stick nest, which may occupy the rooftops of castles, churches, and houses where storks have nested for centuries. Not all of the world's 19 species of storks show this affinity for people; some, like the Jabiru in the neotropics, tend to nest in remote tropical wetlands. Although storks have a worldwide distribution, only one member of the family makes it into North America—the Wood Stork of Mexico and the Southeast.

Toucans

Family Ramphastidae

Size: 12–25 inches
Range: Neotropics
Habitat: Tropical forests

A specialty of the New World tropics, toucans are instantly recognizable thanks to their outsize bills—which may look heavy and awkward, but which are really hollow and light, braced inside with thin struts for rigidity. The bill—as with all birds—is covered with a living layer of keratin called the rhamphotheca, which among toucans is a dazzling paintbox of colors and designs. The long bill of species like the Keel-billed Toucan of Mexico and Central America allows it to reach fruit near the ends of branches too slender for its considerable bulk, and to poke inside tree cavities for lizards, frogs, and the eggs or chicks of other birds.

Wild Turkey

Meleagris gallopavo

Size: 37–46 inches; weight 9–16 lbs.
Range: North America
Habitat: Forest, field edges

At daybreak on a spring morning, the woodlands ring with the explosive gobbling of strutting male turkeys—a sound now commonplace from Maine and Washington State to Florida and the mountains of Mexico, but which was rare as recently as the early 20th century, when turkey populations were at a pre-conservation nadir. Domesticated by Mesoamericans and taken back to Europe by early explorers, farm-reared turkeys are a far cry from their cagey, lean wild cousins. Benjamin Franklin famously favored the Wild Turkey as a national symbol for the United States instead of the Bald Eagle. U.S. turkey consumption peaks at Thanksgiving but cannot hold a candle to Israel, the world leader, where each person consumes an average of 28 pounds per year.

FURTHER READING

Alderfer, Jonathan, and Jon L. Dunn. *Birding Essentials*. National Geographic, 2007.

Alderfer, Jonathan, and Paul Hess. *Backyard Guide to the Birds of North America*. National Geographic, 2011.

Baicich, Paul, and Colin J. O. Harrison. *Nests, Eggs, and Nestlings of North American Birds*, 2nd ed. Princeton University Press, 2005.

Beletsky, Les. Global Birding: *Traveling the World in Search of Birds.* National Geographic, 2010.

Collias, Nicholas E., and Elsie C. Collias. *Nest Building and Bird Behavior.* Princeton University Press, 1984.

Dunn, Jon L., and Jonathan Alderfer. *National Geographic Field Guide to the Birds of North America,* 6th ed. National Geographic, 2011.

Elbroch, Mark, and Eleanor Marks. *Bird Tracks and Sign: A Guide to North American Species.* Stackpole Books, 2001.

Elphick, Chris, John B. Dunning, and David Allen Sibley, eds. T*he Sibley Guide to Bird Life and Behavior.* Knopf, 2001, 2009.

Feduccia, Alan, ed. *Catesby's Birds of Colonial America.* University of North Carolina Press, 1985.

Feduccia, Alan. *The Origin and Evolution of Birds.* Yale University Press, 1996.

Gill, Frank B. *Ornithology,* 3rd ed. W. H. Freeman and Co., 2006.

Hanson, Thor. *Feathers: The Evolution of a Natural Miracle.* Basic Books, 2011.

Heinrich, Bernd. *The Mind of the Raven.* New York: HarperCollins, 1999.

Hill, Geoffrey E. *Bird Coloration.* National Geographic, 2010.

Johnsgard, Paul A. *Arena Birds: Sexual Selection and Behavior.* Smithsonian Institution Press, 1994.

Kastner, Joseph. *The Bird Illustrated: 1550–1900.* H. N. Abrams, 1988.

Kaufman, Kenn. *Lives of North American Birds.* Houghton Mifflin, 1996.

Kroodsma, Donald E. *The Singing Life of Birds.* Houghton Mifflin, 2005.

Leahy, Christopher W. *The Birdwatcher's Companion to North American Birdlife.* Princeton University Press, 2004.

Lebbin, Daniel J., Michael J. Parr, and George H. Fenwick. *The American Bird Conservancy Guide to Bird Conservation.* University of Chicago Press, 2010.

Pasquier, Roger F., and John Farrand, Jr. *Masterpieces of Bird Art: 700 Years of Ornithological Illustration.* Abbeville Press, 1991.

Podulka, Sandy, Ronald W. Rohrbauch, Jr., and Rick Bonney, eds. *Handbook of Bird Biology.* Cornell Laboratory of Ornithology in association with Princeton University Press, 2004.

Proctor, Noble S., and Patrick J. Lynch. *Manual of Ornithology: Avian Structure and Function.* Yale University Press, 1993.

Roth, Sally. *Bird-by-Bird Gardening.* Rodale, 2006.

Tudge, Colin. *The Bird: A Natural History of Who Birds Are, Where They Came From, and How They Live. Crown, 2008.*

Weidensaul, Scott. *Of a Feather: A Brief History of American Birding.* Harcourt, 2007.

Welty, Joel Carl, and Luis F. Baptista. *The Life of Birds,* 4th ed. Saunders College Publishing, 1988.

Zickefoose, Julie. *The Bluebird Effect: Uncommon Bonds With Common Birds.* Houghton Mifflin Harcourt, 2012.

Zickefoose, Julie. *Letters from Eden: A Year at Home, in the Woods.* Houghton Mifflin, 2006.

CONTRIBUTORS

◇◇◇◇◇

JONATHAN ALDERFER, artist and author, is the birding consultant for National Geographic Books. He contributed illustrations to four editions of the *National Geographic Field Guide to the Birds of North America* and with Jon Dunn co-authored the recently published sixth edition. He has co-authored or edited other National Geographic books, including *Backyard Guide to the Birds of North America* (2011), *Field Guide to the Birds of Eastern North America* (2008), *Field Guide to the Birds of Western North America* (2008), and *Birding Essentials* (2007). His paintings and drawings of birds were exhibited at the National Geographic Museum in Washington, D.C., in 2009. He lives in Washington, D.C.

KIMBALL L. GARRETT has managed the ornithology collections at the Natural History Museum of Los Angeles County since 1982. With Jon Dunn, he co-authored *A Field Guide to Warblers of North America* (1997)—a Peterson guide—and *Birds of Southern California: Status and Distribution* (2012). He is director and past president of Western Field Ornithologists and is a member of the American Birding Association Checklist Committee and the California Bird Records Committee. Since 2000 he has served as Southern California regional coeditor for the journal *North American Birds*. An active birder in southern California and beyond for more than 40 years, he currently lives with his wife, Kathy Molina, in Tujunga, California.

A former National Geographic staff member, CATHERINE HERBERT HOWELL served as an editor and writer for the first three editions of the *National Geographic Field Guide to the Birds of North America*. She has written extensively on natural history for both adults and children, authoring four volumes in the National Geographic Nature Library and three in the My First Pocket Guide series. She recently explored the myriad relationships between people and plants in *Flora Mirabilis: How Plants Have Shaped World Knowledge, Health, Wealth, and Beauty* (2009). Howell shares her fascination with urban wildlife as a master naturalist volunteer in Arlington, Virginia.

SCOTT WEIDENSAUL is the author of more than two dozen books on natural history, including *Living on the Wind: Across the Hemisphere With Migratory Birds* (2000), a Pulitzer Prize finalist, and *Of a Feather: A Brief History of American Birding* (2007), a history of American ornithology. His most recent book, *The First Frontier: The Forgotten History of Struggle, Savagery, and Endurance in Early America*, was published in 2012. A contributing editor for Audubon magazine, Weidensaul lives in the mountains of eastern Pennsylvania, where he studies the migration of hawks, owls, and hummingbirds.

(LO), John C. Pitcher; 197, AP Images/Matt Dunham; 198, University Library System, University of Pittsburgh; 199, The Pierpont Morgan Library/Art Resource, NY; 200, Academy of Natural Sciences of Philadelphia/Corbis; 201, "There was an old man with a beard, who said, 'It is just as I feared!' ", from A Book of Nonsense, published by Frederick Warne and Co., London, c. 1875 (color litho), Lear, Edward (1812-88)/Private Collection/© Look and Learn/The Bridgeman Art Library; 202, Smithsonian Institution/Corbis; 203, Louis Agassiz Fuertes/National Geographic Stock; 204 (UP), Jonathan Alderfer; 204 (LO), Fuegian oystercatchers, Falkland Sound, c.1935 (oil on canvas), Jacques, Francis Lee (1887-1969)/Peabody Museum of Natural History, Yale Uni., Connecticut/Photo © Boltin Picture Library/The Bridgeman Art Library; 205, Alfred Eisenstaedt/Time & Life Pictures/Getty Images; 206, Roger Tory Peterson/National Geographic Stock; 207, Roger Tory Peterson/National Geographic Stock; 208, Library of Congress Prints & Photographs Division, LC-USZ62-74343; 209 (LE), David Quinn; 209 (RT), Walter A. Weber/National Geographic Stock; 210, Frans Lanting/ Frans Lanting Stock; 211 (UP), Joel Sartore/joelsartore. com; 211 (LO), Jonathan Alderfer; 212 (UP), David Quinn; 212 (LO), Lincoln Karim; 214, Joe McDonald/Visuals Unlimited; 215 (UP), Greg Marshall, NGS; 215 (LO), Thomas R. Schultz; 216, Gouichi Wada/Nature Production/Minden Pictures; 217, Duncan Usher/Foto Natura/Minden Pictures; 218, Mike Lovett/Brandeis University; 219 (UP), David Quinn; 219 (LO), Jean-Paul Ferrero/Auscape/ Minden Pictures; 221, Donald M. Jones/Minden Pictures; 222-3, BHL/MBOT (Catesby, Natural History); 224, BHL/ SIL (Gould, A Monograph of the Trochilidae); 226, Steve Young/FLPA/Minden Pictures; 227, Markus Varesvuo/ NPL/Minden Pictures; 228, Allan Brooks/National Geographic Stock; 229, Courtesy of Zeiss; 230-1, Spread from the National Geographic Field Guide to the Birds of North America, Sixth Edition. Photograph by Rebecca T. Hale. Bird art by Jonathan Alderfer; 232, Steve Byland/ Shutterstock; 233, Brian E. Small; 234, Jose B. Ruiz/NPL/ Minden Pictures; 236, Louis Agassiz Fuertes/National Geographic Stock; 237, Louis Agassiz Fuertes/National Geographic Stock; 238, Louis Agassiz Fuertes/National Geographic Stock; 239 (LE), Richard Day/Daybreak Imagery; 239 (CTR), David Hosking/FLPA/Minden Pictures; 239 (RT), Art Wolfe/Art Wolfe Stock; 240, Daniel Prudek/Shutterstock; 241 (UP), Jonathan Alderfer; 241 (LO), Catcher of Light, Inc./Shutterstock; 242, Johann Schumacher; 243, pandapaw/Shutterstock; 244, Hennie van Heerden/hvhe1/Flickr; 245, Greg Lavaty; 246, Jonathan Alderfer; 248, Bill Houghton/National Geographic My Shot; 249 (UP), Mark Lewer/National Geographic My Shot; 249 (LO), frantisekhojdysz/ Shutterstock; 250, Tom Mangelsen/NPL/Minden Pictures; 251, Paul Sawer/FLPA/Minden Pictures; 252, University Library System, University of Pittsburgh; 253, University Library System, University of Pittsburgh; 254, Duncan Usher/Foto Natura/Minden Pictures; 255, S & D & K Maslowski/FLPA/Minden Pictures; 256, Marc Shandro/ Getty Images; 257 (ALL), Jonathan Alderfer; 258 (UP), Hugh Robateau/National Geographic My Shot; 258 (LO), Jonathan Alderfer; 259, David E. Seibel; 260 (UP), Jonathan Alderfer; 260 (LO), Larry Ditto; 262, Bob Gibbons/FLPA/Minden Pictures; 264, Arthur Morris/ BIRDS AS ART; 265, Maresa Pryor-Luzier/Lightwave Photography; 266, David Schultz/National Geographic My Shot; 267, Stephen Dalton/Minden Pictures; 268-9, DEA / A. DE GREGORIO/Getty Images; 270, Allan Brooks/ National Geographic Stock; 272, Jurgen & Christine Sohns/FLPA/Minden Pictures; 273 (UP), University Library System, University of Pittsburgh; 273 (LO), H. Douglas Pratt; 274, Greg Lavaty; 275, Bence Mate/NPL/Minden Pictures; 276, Gary Crabbe/Enlightened Images Photography; 277 (UP), Michael Durham/FLPA/Minden Pictures; 277 (LO), Cynthia J. House; 278, Ingo Arndt/ Minden Pictures; 280 (UP), Jonathan Alderfer; 280 (LO), Judd Patterson; 281 (LE), Tom Vezo/Minden Pictures; 281 (RT), S & D & K Maslowski/FLPA/Minden Pictures; 282 (UP), John Eastcott and Yva Momatiuk/National Geographic Stock; 282 (LO), N. John Schmitt; 284, Tom Marshall/NPL/Minden Pictures; 285, Jonathan Alderfer; 286, BHL/SIL (Martinet, Planches enluminées d'histoire naturelle); 287, BHL/SIL (Martinet, Planches enluminées d'histoire naturelle); 288, Jari Peltomäki; 289 (UP), Ralph Eldridge; 289 (LO), N. John Schmitt; 290 (UP), Mark F. Wallner; 290 (LO), Thomas R. Schultz; 291, Allan Brooks/ National Geographic Stock; 292, Grzegorz Lesniewski/ Foto Natura/Minden Pictures; 293 (UP), Ron Niebrugge/ WildNatureImages.com; 293 (LO), Thomas R. Schultz; 294, Gerrit Vyn/NPL/Minden Pictures; 295, David Tipling/ FLPA/Minden Pictures; 296, Donald L. Malick; 297, John Downer/NPL/Minden Pictures; 298 (UP), Jonathan Alderfer; 298 (LO), Winfried Wisniewski/Foto Natura/ Minden Pictures; 300 (UP), Kirsten Phelps/National Geographic My Shot; 300 (LO), Jonathan Alderfer; 301, Jim Ridley/National Geographic My Shot; 302, Michael Quinton/Minden Pictures; 303, Asturianu/Shutterstock; 304, University Library System, University of Pittsburgh; 305, University Library System, University of Pittsburgh; 306, Johann Schumacher; 307 (UP), Duncan Usher/Foto Natura/Minden Pictures; 307 (LO), N. John Schmitt; 308, Susan Cole Kelly; 309 (UP), Shattil & Rozinski/NPL/ Minden Pictures; 309 (LO), Thomas R. Schultz; 310, SuperStock/Getty Images; 311, Danita Delimont/Gallo Images/Getty Images; 312, David Tipling/FLPA/Minden Pictures; 313, Visuals Unlimited, Inc./Joe McDonald/Getty Images; 314 (UP), David Quinn; 314 (LO), Frans Lanting/ Frans Lanting Stock; 315, Krijn Trimbos/Foto Natura/ Minden Pictures; 316 (UP), Scott Linstead/Foto Natura/ Minden Pictures; 316 (LO), Diane Pierce; 317, Rolf Nussbaumer/NPL/Minden Pictures; 318, Scott Sady/ TahoeLight.com; 319 (UP), Scott Sady/TahoeLight.com; 319 (LO), Kent Pendleton; 320, Erich Lessing Culture and Fine Arts Archives; 321, Scala/Art Resource, NY; 322, BHL/ MBOT (Catesby, Natural History); 324, Jean Michel Labat/ardea.com; 325, Chris Knights/ardea.com; 326 (UPLE), Bill Leaman; 326 (UPRT), Scott Leslie/Minden Pictures; 326 (LOLE), Elliotte Rusty Harold/Shutterstock; 326 (LORT), Elaine Davis/Shutterstock; 327 (UPLE), Eirik Johan Solheim/Shutterstock; 327 (UPRT), Steve Maslowski/Visuals Unlimited/Getty Images; 327 (LOLE), Tami Freed/Shutterstock; 327 (LORT), Michael Rubin/ Shutterstock; 328 (UPLE), Anna Kucherova/Shutterstock; 328 (UPRT), Meirion Matthias/Shutterstock; 328 (LOLE), FLariviere/Shutterstock; 328 (LORT), BW Folsom/ Shutterstock; 329 (UPLE), Kazyavka/Shutterstock; 329 (UPRT), EW CHEE GUAN/Shutterstock; 329 (LOLE), Richard Day/Daybreak Imagery; 329 (LORT), FLariviere/ Shutterstock; 330 (UP), Gary K. Smith/FLPA/Minden Pictures; 330 (LO), H. Douglas Pratt; 331, Topical Press Agency/Hulton Archive/Getty Images; 332, V&A Images, London/Art Resource, NY; 333, Réunion des Musées Nationaux/Art Resource, NY; 334, Erkovich/Shutterstock; 335, Maslowski Productions; 336 (UP), David Quinn; 336 (LO), S & D & K Maslowski/FLPA/Minden Pictures; 337, Andrew Knauss; 338, Jonathan Alderfer; 339, Frances A. Miller/Shutterstock; 340, S & D & K Maslowski/FLPA/ Minden Pictures; 341, Richard Day/Daybreak Imagery; 342 (UP), John B./Dendroica cerulea/Flickr; 342 (LO), John C.

Pitcher; 343 (LE A), Bryan Eastham/Shutterstock; 343 (LE B), Pictureguy/Shutterstock; 343 (LE C), David Kay/ Shutterstock; 343 (LE D), Jim David/Shutterstock; 343 (LE E), Richard Day/Daybreak Imagery; 343 (RT A), Rick & Nora Bowers/Alamy; 343 (RT B), S & D & K Maslowski/ FLPA/Minden Pictures; 343 (RT C), Douglas Graham; 343 (RT D), Clive Varlack; 343 (RT E), Animals Animals/ SuperStock; 344, Kate Gadsby/Garden Picture Library/ Getty Images; 345, Richard Day/Daybreak Imagery; 346, Hamiza Bakirci/Shutterstock; 347, David Liebman; 348, Richard Day/Daybreak Imagery; 349, Kathleen Houlihan/ velokitty/Flickr; 350, Allan Mandell/Garden Picture Library/Getty Images; 351, iShootPhotos, LLC/ iStockphoto; 352-3, BHL/MBOT (Catesby, Natural History); 354, Linda Freshwaters Arndt; 356, Montell Hall/ National Geographic My Shot; 357, Jan Smit/Foto Natura/Minden Pictures; 358 (UP), Rolf Nussbaumer/ NPL/Minden Pictures; 358 (LO), Kent Pendleton; 359, Phil Seu; 360 (UP), Jonathan Alderfer; 360 (LO), Critterbiz/Shutterstock; 361, Jeff Milton/Daybreak Imagery; 362 (UP), Nailia Schwarz/Shutterstock; 362 (LO), Kent Pendleton; 364, Basheer Tome/basheertome/Flickr; 365, Dmitri Izosimov–izosimov.tyumen.ru/Flickr/Getty Images; 366 (UP), Jonathan Alderfer; 366 (LO), Rob Jordan/2020VISION/NPL/Minden Pictures; 367, Patti McConville/Alamy; 368 (UP), Jonathan Alderfer; 368 (LO), Steve Greer Photography; 369 (UP), Joel Sartore; 369 (LO), Donald L. Malick; 370 (UP), Andrew Booley/ Shutterstock; 370 (LO), Jonathan Alderfer; 372, Christopher Hoyle/National Geographic My Shot; 373 (UP), Arthur Morris/BIRDS AS ART; 373 (LO), Cynthia J. House; 374-5, University Library System, University of Pittsburgh; 376, Bible Natural History, English School, (19th century)/Private Collection/© Look and Learn/The Bridgeman Art Library; 377, Donald L. Malick; 378 (UPLE), Donald L. Malick; 378 (UPRT), David Quinn; 378 (LOLE), Jonathan Alderfer; 378 (LORT), Jonathan Alderfer; 379 (UPLE), David Quinn; 379 (UPRT), Michael O'Brien; 379 (LOLE), Jonathan Alderfer; 379 (LORT), Tim Laman/ National Geographic Stock; 380 (UPLE), H. Douglas Pratt; 380 (UPRT), David Tipling/FLPA/Minden Pictures; 380 (LOLE), Cynthia J. House; 380 (LORT), Richard Gore/ wildlifeartcompany.com; 381 (UPLE), Jonathan Alderfer; 381 (UPRT), Donald L. Malick; 381 (LOLE), David Quinn; 381 (LORT), Martin Camm/wildlifeartcompany.com; 382 (UPLE), H. Douglas Pratt; 382 (UPRT), Jamie Watts/ wildlifeartcompany.com; 382 (LOLE), H. Douglas Pratt; 382 (LORT), Jonathan Alderfer; 383 (UPLE), H. Douglas Pratt; 383 (UPRT), Jonathan Alderfer; 383 (LOLE), Jamie Watts/wildlifeartcompany.com; 383 (LORT), Nick Garbutt/NPL/Minden Pictures; 384 (UPLE), Norman Arlott/Wildlife Art Co/Minden Pictures; 384 (UPRT), Norman Arlott/Wildlife Art Co/Minden Pictures; 384 (LOLE), N. John Schmitt; 384 (LORT), Donald L. Malick; 385 (UPLE), Norman Arlott/Wildlife Art Co/Minden Pictures; 385 (UPRT), Cynthia J. House; 385 (LOLE), Murray Cooper/Minden Pictures; 385 (LORT), David Beadle; 386 (UPLE), N. John Schmitt; 386 (UPRT), Richard Gore/Wildlife Art Co/Minden Pictures; 386 (LOLE), N. John Schmitt; 386 (LORT), Jonathan Alderfer; 387 (UPLE), Jonathan Alderfer; 387 (UPRT), Thomas R. Schultz; 387 (LOLE), Thomas Marent/Minden Pictures; 387 (LORT), H. Douglas Pratt; 388 (UPLE), H. Douglas Pratt; 388 (UPRT), Donald L. Malick; 388 (LOLE), Christophe Courteau/NPL/Minden Pictures; 388 (LORT), Norman Arlott/Wildlife Art Co/Minden Pictures; 389 (UPLE), David Quinn; 389 (UPRT), Norman Arlott/Wildlife Art Co./Minden Pictures; 389 (LOLE), Chris Shields/ wildlifeartcompany.com; 389 (LORT), Kent Pendleton.

National Geographic Bird-watcher's Bible

Published by the National Geographic Society
John M. Fahey, Jr., Chairman of the Board and
    Chief Executive Officer
Timothy T. Kelly, President
Declan Moore, Executive Vice President;
    President, Publishing and Digital Media
Melina Gerosa Bellows, Executive Vice President; Chief Creative
    Officer, Books, Kids, and Family

Prepared by the Book Division
Hector Sierra, Senior Vice President and General Manager
Anne Alexander, Senior Vice President and Editorial Director
Jonathan Halling, Design Director, Books and Children's
    Publishing
Marianne R. Koszorus, Design Director, Books
Susan Tyler Hitchcock, Senior Editor
R. Gary Colbert, Production Director
Jennifer A. Thornton, Director of Managing Editorial
Susan S. Blair, Director of Photography
Meredith C. Wilcox, Director, Administration and Rights
    Clearance

Staff for This Book
Barbara Payne, Text Editor
Sanaa Akkach, Art Director
Miriam Stein, Illustrations Editor
Elisa Gibson, Designer
Carl Mehler, Director of Maps
Noel Grove, Picture Legends Writer
Jennifer Conrad Seidel, Contributing Editor
Judith Klein, Production Editor
Mike Horenstein, Production Manager
Galen Young, Rights Clearance Specialist
Katie Olsen, Design Assistant

Manufacturing and Quality Management
Phillip L. Schlosser, Senior Vice President
Chris Brown, Vice President, NG Book Manufacturing
George Bounelis, Vice President, Production Services
Nicole Elliott, Manager
Rachel Faulise, Manager
Robert L. Barr, Manager

The National Geographic Society is one of the world's largest
nonprofit scientific and educational organizations. Founded
in 1888 to "increase and diffuse geographic knowledge,"
the Society's mission is to inspire people to care about the
planet. It reaches more than 400 million people worldwide
each month through its official journal, *National Geographic,*
and other magazines; National Geographic Channel; television
documentaries; music; radio; films; books; DVDs; maps; exhibi-
tions; live events; school publishing programs; interactive
media; and merchandise. National Geographic has funded
more than 10,000 scientific research, conservation and
exploration projects and supports an education program promoting geographic literacy. For more information, visit www
.nationalgeographic.com.

For more information, please call 1-800-NGS LINE
(647-5463) or write to the following address:

National Geographic Society
1145 17th Street N.W.
Washington, D.C. 20036-4688 U.S.A.

For information about special discounts for bulk purchases,
please contact National Geographic Books Special Sales:
ngspecsales@ngs.org

For rights or permissions inquiries, please contact
National Geographic Books Subsidiary Rights: ngbookrights@
ngs.org

ISBN: 978-1-4262-0964-2

Printed in U.S.A.

12/QGT-LPH/1

Acknowledgments
The National Geographic Society wishes to thank the University Library System,
University of Pittsburgh for the use of the Audubon images in this book. Their
magnificent first edition of John James Audubon's *Bird of America* is one of only
120 complete sets known to exist. It is available for viewing online at: *http://
audubon.pitt.edu.* The Biodiversity Heritage Library is a consortium of natural
history and botanical libraries that cooperate to digitize and make accessible the
legacy literature of biodiversity held in their collections and to make that literature
available for open access and responsible use as a part of a global biodiversity
commons—we thank them for access to their remarkable collection at: *http://
biodiversitylibrary.org.* The text of chapters five and seven was assembled from a
variety of National Geographic sources, including *Birding Essentials,* by Jonathan
Alderfer and Jon L. Dunn, and the direct-mail edition of *Complete Birds of North
America.* And thanks to author and blogger Laura Erickson for supplying the White-
throated Sparrow musical notation reproduced on page 54.